Jesse James

Soul Liberty

Jesse James

Soul Liberty

Volume I

Behind the Family Wall
of Stigma & Silence

ERIC F. JAMES

Cashel Cadence House
Danville, Ky. 2012

Published by CASHEL CADENCE HOUSE

James, Eric F. (Eric James), 1943 –
  Jesse James' Soul Liberty: Vol. I, Behind the Family Wall of Stigma & Silence / Eric F. James
Authorized historical biography of the family of Frank & Jesse James, 1776-2012, drawn from primary family sources. Includes family photos, letters, documents, memoirs, interviews, genealogy, source citations, notes, bibliography, and index
1. James, Jesse, 1847-1882 2. United States - History - 1776-2012 - Biography 3. Outlaws - West (U.S.) - Biography 4. Kentucky - Biography 5. Missouri - Biography 6. United States - History - 1776-2012 7. Frontier and Pioneer Life - West (U.S.) 8. West (U.S.) - Biography 9. Southwest, Old - Biography 10. Women - United States - Biography I. Title

  ISBN 978-0-9857469-0-2
Manufactured in the United States of America
First Edition

Dedication

For all who asked, but received no reply,
I dedeciate this book to my Uncle Dick,

RICHARD DONALD JAMES 1926 - 2009

A private man, who when asked,
Told all he knew, little as it was,
Leaving the next generation a path of discovery
To the knowledge of self and one's own

Remember the days of old,
Consider the years of many generations:
Ask thy father, and he will show thee;
Thy elders and they will tell thee.

Deuteronomy 32.7

Contents

Volume I

Behind the Family Wall of Stigma & Silence

James Character & Soul - Self-Defined

Jesse James

Soul Liberty

Edward II

A Heritage of Silence

Neither Frank nor Jesse James had yet appeared on the world stage when King Edward of England, a progenitor of the James brothers, ascended to the tower with his son for a fatherly lesson in leadership, politics, and warfare. On each subject Edward posed a question of his son. The first response Edward deemed to be incorrect. His son's second response was incompetently rendered. Edward fell into a fury. The third worthless response caused Edward to grab his son by the collar and thrust the boy out the turret to his death.

Peppered throughout the royal houses of Europe, antecedents of the James family defined the family's character, personality, and behavior. An abundance of genetic hallmarks passed through each generation to James descendants in America. Aside the mythology attached to them, no hallmark proved more harmful to the family of Frank and Jesse James than did the violence of the James family's silence.

The James were formed from an emboldened family dynasty, only to shred, disintegrate, and to become entombed of their own volition in the Victorian era. Across centuries, the James ancestral roots spanned broadly across the European continent, passing through the Plantagenet and royal lineages of Wales, England, Scotland

Europe, and further into the Romanov families of Russia. Its enduring seed had been deeply planted in the ancient world of the Middle East and its biblical kings of Judah and Solomon of Israel.

In the emerging democracy of colonial Virginia, the early Kentucky frontier, and throughout the American heartland, the James were renowned as community builders, public office holders, ministers of faith, financiers, educators, writers, and poets. From these roots shot Frank and Jesse James.

Following the Civil War, Frank and Jesse James eclipsed the family's destiny. War may have splintered the family ideologically, but Frank and Jesse James disjoined the family's compass and direction, casting a longer and darker shadow on the James family, like no other.

Like their royal ancestors of old when beset by crisis, the James family turned suspicious and distrustful of its own. The larger James family kept apart from one another, holding in muted reverence what relic of itself that it could. The line of Frank and Jesse James was left isolated, unsupported, and abandoned. Goaded by family in-laws, the Jesse James family withdrew into a citadel of its own. Their ostracism was enforced by every other family line of the James.

By the dawn of the 20st century, the *noblesse* of the James family was seized with fatalism. By the sunset of the century, the family was partitioned, fragmented, and surrendered to their individual survival. Each family imprisoned itself in cells of isolation and anonymity. One James family line could not recognize the other. Penitence for the outlaws among them was paid with silence. The cost has endured since.

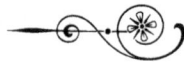

Mary Joan Malley-Beamis,
the author Joan Beamis

Chapter One

Some Kind of Outsider

"Since the publication of the genealogy of the ancestry of Jesse James, sponsored and distributed by The Kentucky Historical Society...some members of the younger generations consider the connection something to be proud of."

                    - Joan Beamis, Unto the Third Generation [1]

B y 1971, almost a gneration had passed since Joan Beamis began to research and compile the first genealogical sketch of the Jesse James family - *Background of a Bandit*. The anticipation of Joan's book set off alarms within the James family. Joan was oblivious to the simmering brouhaha that was about to boil over and scald her.

Following publication of her book of genealogy, Joan wanted to write an autobiography of the James family, documenting the family's treasure of untold stories. Joan wanted to ply the memory of living family members, first for her personal knowledge, and secondly for history. She imagined the historical record would prove invaluable to the family who had yet to grasp its own history as she had. A published record would be valuable equally to a public that chronically pricked the James family with fabricated claims of unsubstantiated relationships and misinformation about itself.

The family alarms warned that Joan and the progeny of her era, whom Joan self-described as "the third generation," held a far different view of the long established relationship between the James family and its outlaws. The third generation disregarded the family's long maintained silence, and its traditional outright moral dismissal of the miscreants. The great grandchildren in "the third generation" were breaking the James family code.

No response came to Joan from her inquiries to family members requesting information about their long hidden and storied past. Her very own relatives turned a deaf ear to her.

The irony was not lost on Joan. She was accustomed to silence, and to defeating it. Since childhood, Joan had been growing clinically deaf. Each day Joan read lips. Each day Joan defeated every silence that confronted her. As she had dealt with the physical silence given to her by God, Joan came to deal with the silence of the James. Joan already had given the James a genealogy none of them had known previously. Now she would transfigure their silence into another family gift in writing. They could accept it, or cling to the disease of their silence and leave it.

In writing *Unto the Third Generation*, Joan Beamis made no apology for acquiring as much knowledge as possible about her family. Its character and history were invaluable, no matter its implicit nature or its consequences. Joan did not require any protection from the James family. Joan needed instead to be informed, so she could be empowered to resolve her family's history and its meaning for herself.

In *Unto the Third Generation*, Joan Beamis cited who within the family was responsible for its destructive silence. Afterward, Joan sequestered her essay. She left her assessment of the James family and its culture of secrecy like a worn out diary, confined to the darkness of abandoned artifacts claiming dust. Perhaps a future generation would discover her essay, and appreciate it for what Joan intended it to be.

MARY JOAN MALLEY-BEAMIS RESIDED IN NEW ENGLAND, WHERE SHE WAS BORN. Unlike the Jesse James family which still lived in Kearney and Kansas City, Missouri, Joan was a great granddaughter of Drury Woodson James, an uncle of the outlaws and son of the family patriarch John M. James. Drury's daughter Mary Louisa James married Edward Frederick Burns. Joan's mother, Marguerite Hazel Burns, was born

Drury Woodson James

Grandfather of Joan Beamis
Uncle of Frank & Jesse James

Mary Louise James-Burns
"Nanna"

Daughter of Drury Woodson James
Grandmother of Joan Beamis

Marguerite Hazel Burns-Malley

Granddaughter of D. W. James
Mother of Joan Beamis

to them in California at Drury's home at Paso Robles. Like her cousins in Kansas City, Marguerite was sent east for her education.

When Marguerite Burns married James Frances Malley in New Haven, Connecticut, the couple established their residence in Massachusetts in the town of Beverly. Their first-born child was Joan's oldest brother James Burns Malley. Jim entered the law profession but later became a Jesuit priest. Joan's next oldest sibling, John Crohan Malley, practiced farming. Joan herself, a teacher, was the next born; followed by her younger sister, Janice Ann Malley, also a teacher.

Naming Joan and her siblings became a family amusement. "We were four: Jimmie, Joan, Jack, and Janice, born in that order and all named by Nanna because Mom and Dad could never agree on a name. He was adamant against a 'junior,' and Nanna finally solved the dilemma with James Burns Malley. With me," Joan continued, "every girl's name seemed to remind Dad of some peculiar character, and when Mom threatened to name me 'California'...he quickly acquiesced to Mary Joan. When Jack came along, it was decided to name him after Daddy's father, Crohan Malley, but Dad thought that was unusual and would lead to unpleasant nicknames; but Nanna's suggestion of 'John Crohan' met with instant approval. By the time Janice arrived, we already had three 'J's, so Nanna thought it would be nice to continue the alliteration, and named the beautiful, blue-eyed baby after her favorite book *Janice Meredith, a Story of the American Revolution*."[2] The book contained sixty-five chapters. Nanna was well armed with many more name recommendations from *Janice Meredith*, should her daughter bear any more children.

"Actually, there were three parental figures in the family," admitted Joan's eldest brother, Jim. "My father was the child of Irish immigrants. He worked as a boy in the local factories and went on to become a shoe manufacturer. He was born and brought up in Randolph, Massachusetts. My mother came from Paso Robles, California, where my maternal grandmother [Nanna] was also born. She [Nanna] had been educated in the East and lived for long periods in Boston after her father lost everything in the San Francisco Fire. Mother and Dad met through mutual friends...on a visit to Boston. My maternal grandmother lived with us as a *de facto* member of our immediate family until I was thirty. She [Nanna] was a very important member of our family."[3]

Drury Woodson James named his daughter after her mother, Mary Louisa Dunn, nicknaming her Mamie, sometimes spelled as Mamye. When Mamie lived among her daughter and grandchildren, Mary Louise was revered by the Malley clan most affectionately as their Nanna.

For twenty years, Nanna was married to Edward Frederick Burns. A native of Boston, Burns worked for Drury Woodson James as manager of his El Paso Robles Hotel. Burns and Nanna were married in the old San Miguel Mission, north of Paso Robles, where Drury's wife practiced her Catholic faith. The Franciscan missionary Fr. Mutt, who baptized Nanna and became friends of the James family, married the couple.

In 1895, Drury Woodson James relocated his family to San Francisco. He had lost his fortune, his hotel, and also his town of Paso Robles to financiers in the economic recession that started two years earlier. In San Francisco, Drury and his wife owned and operated the Lennox Hotel at 628 Sutter Street. Burns owned and operated the very profitable Hamman Turkish Baths at 11 Grant Street, an ornate private club and spa celebrated for its elaborate oriental decoration. The San Francisco earthquake of 1906 wiped out Drury's remaining fortune a second time. The Lennox Hotel was lost. Drury died four years later, after having been rescued by a young boy from a disastrous apartment fire in which Drury nearly burned to death. Drury's widow, Mary Louisa Dunn-James proceeded to work during the next twenty years for the Bishop of the Catholic Archdiocese of San Francisco. Mary Louisa distributed food and clothing in the streets on a daily basis, until she finally succumbed to hypertension, arteriosclerosis, and senility in St. Joseph's Hospital on April 8, 1930.

The fortune of Nanna and her husband was equally destroyed. Preceding the ruinous earthquake, Burns had begun to construct a new Hamman Baths. But the old baths and the new construction next door were all reduced to rubble in the quake and its resulting fire.[4] As proprietor of the baths, Burns was widely known to many of San Francisco's old timers.[5] When Burns died at the Adler Sanatorium in 1918, Nanna moved to Boston to be close to her children and her son Walter Irvin Burns. Nanna lived with Joan's mother, Marguerite, and her Malley grandchildren.

Fr. Jim assessed Nanna's unique influence on the Malley children. "In a way, she was a unique kind of person. Her father was Protestant; her mother was Catholic. She was brought up in Paso Robles, California, conscious of being Catholic. She and her mother used to drive in the wagon to the old San Miguel Mission every Sunday. But when she came home, they'd have breakfast and then hitch up the horses and she would drive down to Atascadero to go to the Baptist Church with her father. She also used to sing in their choir. So she had a very profound ecumenical experience as a child. She was way ahead of her time."[6]

Nanna gave Joan and her siblings a moral grounding in tolerance when the Malleys were confronted by New England's religious bigotry. "The 'Revised Klan' was everywhere in those days," recalled Fr. Jim. "We Catholics were a small minority. I don't mean that we were hated by most people, but we were certainly suspect. I always felt myself to be some kind of 'outsider.' That's why I've always tried to gravitate toward people who feel like they're outsiders."

Almost fifty years following Emancipation, the Ku Klux Klan in its "revised" stage often targeted immigrant families with bigotry, a xenophobic practice endemic to America, especially promoted among those seeking to carve political constituencies for election purposes.

Joan's beloved father, James Francis Malley, was born in Randolph, Massachusetts, but her grandparents Croghan Malley and Mary Ellen O'Donoghue came from Timons, Ireland. They brought their Catholic faith with them. Fr. Jim said about Nanna, "She was very important in my life. She once said to me when I was being teased about being a Catholic, 'Jimmy, Jesus said that when two or three gather in my name, I'm with them.' And she added, 'Jesus didn't say anything about Protestants and Catholics. We all just try to serve the Lord.' That was very important to me. Also very important to me throughout my whole life was her compassion for losers."

Nanna's sensitivity for the underclass was endemic to her James ancestry. "I remember one time we were walking down the street in Boston around 1930 in the bottom of the Depression." Fr. Jim recounted their encounter. "We saw a drunk lying on the sidewalk. She looked at him and gave him some money. Then she said: 'Just imagine how that poor fellow feels.' I've never forgotten it," said Fr. Jim. "It made such an impression on me that it influenced my whole life. It gave me a vision of Christianity has led me to try and reach out to losers and the marginalized. I figure that if I do that for them, the Lord may be moved to take care of me."

Joan's parents were subject to Nanna's ecumenism, as Fr. Jim pointed out. "I remember my mother saying, 'If a person is sincere in their belief,

God loves them.' My family operated in this way, quite independently of church statements. Our friendship circle included many Protestant friends... As I said, my Dad was in the shoe business, and he had loads of Jewish friends. Good friends. Our friendship circle embraced everybody. And I've often felt a bit 'strange' as a priest, because I've never felt much of an urge to convert anybody. I try to understand people and talk to them. When I go to a Jewish family for Friday evening services, which includes dinner and candle lighting, I know God is with us. The changes in the Church and the growth of dialog are, for me, a great liberation."

Joan's father, James Francis Malley, agreed with Nanna on the value of a solid education as a tool for overcoming barriers. His Irish immigrant parents had provided him a costly and sacrificial education that was excellent. Malley graduated Thayer Academy in 1906. The founder of the military school, Gen. Sylvanus Thayer, became known as the Father of the American Military Academy, despite some early disagreements with President Andrew Jackson that caused Thayer to resign as superintendent of the school. The academy's motto was "Duty, Honor, Country." Thayer afterward graduated Dartmouth College, valedictorian of his class. Malley graduated Dartmouth in the Class of 1911.

When Malley entered the U.S. Army in 1917, he first was made a sergeant major in a signal battalion. Malley's innate talent and character, supported by his fine education, soon trumped ordinary military duty. Malley advanced to the office of the Secretary of War and was charged with solving labor problems. James Francis Malley became chairman of the Arbitration Board that made the "Buffalo Award," which eventually gave machinists of the Industrial Revolution era the eight hour workday.

Later, he arbitrated labor disputes at the Panama Canal. Malley was discharged from the Army as a first lieutenant.

Returning to the shoe business in New England, Malley traveled among the towns of Randolph, Massachusetts; Rochester, New York; Salem, Massachusetts; and Dover, New Hampshire, selling shoes much as did Frank James in his retirement. By 1922, Malley ran the Farmington Shoe Manufacturing Company as its president and treasurer.

Malley retired from the shoe business twenty-five years later to enter politics. The year following his resignation, Malley was elected a delegate to the New Hampshire State Constitutional Convention, representing the 5th

Jim, Janice, & Jack Malley
Siblings of Joan Bemai

Ward of Somersworth. He soon was elected to serve in the New Hampshire legislature, a position he held for almost twenty years until the age of seventy.

At his 50th class reunion, Dartmouth College bestowed an honorary Master of Arts degree upon Rep. James Francis Malley. At the time of his death in 1974, Malley was still serving faithfully as secretary for his Dartmouth class.[7]

ALL THROUGHOUT HER YOUTH, JOAN ENDEARED HERSELF TO HER SIBLINGS. Her brothers were most vocal in their respect of Joan. Brother Jack recalled her. "She had a happy childhood in Newton, Massachusetts, Summered with the family at York Beach, Maine thru 1939, and that same year moved with us all to Somersworth. New Hampshire. Took piano lessons as a child in Newton. Was always a great reader."[8]

Jack was the first to reveal Joan's lifelong physical affliction. "At an early age Joan was stricken with a severe ear infection, and was left with significant hearing loss." Fr. Jim elaborated; "It was only when she was about 4 or 5 years old that our Aunt Molly was visiting. She was a nurse, and she told my parents that she thought that Joan was reading lips rather than hearing conversations at the dinner table. They tested Joan's hearing then and, sure enough, she was notably hard of hearing. Like so many New Englanders, she contracted ear infections in both ears as a baby - before her first birthday, I believe. There were no antibiotics then and the treatment was to lance the ear drums, which they did on Joan on successive days. Then they drained the ears and hoped for the best. Joan 'recovered,' but her hearing was permanently and seriously impaired. She WAS lip-reading with a talent she had developed on her own. Joan began immediately to work with the Boston Guild for the Hard of Hearing and with a private teacher, Miss McNutt, with whom Joan worked all her life. She had lip reading lessons all during her school and college years."[9]

Fr. Jim accounted the valuable education Rep. Malley had provided Joan, despite her physical impairment. "Our own mother had spent part of her high school years at Elmhurst, but I believe that Joan did not. I believe that she began her grammar school in the Newton, Massachusetts public schools at the Angier School in Waban. In what would have been either her 4th or 5th grade, perhaps in 1933 or 1934, she transferred to the Newton Country Day School of the Sacred Heart, run by the Religious of the Sacred Heart in Newton, Massachusetts. She commuted to the school from our home in Waban. Our family moved from Waban to Somersworth, New Hampshire in 1939, so Joan and her younger sister, Janice, became 'weekly boarders' at the Newton Country Day School, boarding there from Sunday nights through Friday afternoons, but spending the weekends at Somersworth with the family. I believe this arrangement continued until Joan graduated from the Newton Country Day School in May or June of 1941. From the Newton Country Day School, she enrolled, by her own choice, at the Manhattanville College of the Sacred Heart, then in New York City and also run in those years by the Religious of the Sacred Heart...

"Joan was highly intelligent," Fr. Jim continued, "and she was encouraged by our parents to look over several women's colleges, at any one of which I am confident she would have been accepted. She told me years later that she had a great deal of love and respect for the Religious of the Sacred Heart and on her visits, she felt immediately 'at home' when she visited Manhattanville. The alumnae of the Religious of the Sacred Heart were, and still are a close-knit group with strong bonds to one another, to the Religious of the Sacred Heart, and to their respective schools and colleges run by the same Religious. Manhattanville was a topflight college in every sense of the word and the Religious of the Sacred Heart were an order of highly educated, deeply spiritual, and thoroughly 'modern' body of women, remarkably tolerant and ecumenical for their time. They were topflight educators."

Manhattanville had built a reputation for addressing social problems. From the Depression through World War II, students were encouraged to spend one day per week working with disadvantaged children in New York's Bowery district at the Barat Settlement, and in East Harlem at Casita Maria.

"Manhattanville answered Joan's desire for an excellent education … where she felt both challenged and at home," Fr. Jim observed. "Joan was always a quietly and deeply spiritual and religious person in a way that was tolerant of others while being comfortably Catholic in her personal piety and beliefs. The Catholic intellectual and spiritual dimension of Manhattanville was important to Joan and was a good 'fit' for her then and in her later life. She was happy there and popular among her classmates among whom she formed lifelong friendships.

"After she graduated from Manhattanville," Fr. Jim continued, "I believe she returned to live at our family home in Somersworth, New Hampshire. I don't believe she ever lived in Boston though she may have commuted there from Somersworth to take courses, or be in contact with her old teacher at the Boston Guild for the Hard of Hearing. I know she was living in Somersworth when I got back from the Navy in July of 1946. I have the impression that she must have studied in some sort of formal program(s) to become a professional teacher of lip-reading for the hard-of-hearing and that she also she took training in the theory and then prevailing technology of audiology. This may have begun in her last year(s) at Manhattanville and I am sure that she had already chosen her life work with the hard-of-hearing (especially children) by the time I came back to the family home in July of 1946. It was her lifelong vocation. She certainly had the credentials as a professional audiologist and lip-reading teacher, actually designing and running the testing program for primary school children for the State of New Hampshire.

"At least when Joan moved into her 30s, her hearing began to deteriorate further and reached a point in the last 15 or so years of her life she had moved from being 'hard of hearing' to being 'deaf.' However, she had become truly expert in lip-reading (one of the best), but I remember her telling me that, as good as she was, she would miss words and have to fill in the gaps…She had hearing aids, but they became less and less useful. Her lip-reading and close captioned programming let her catch speech, but she lost the ability to hear music, which was a terrible deprivation for her.

"She gave her life to helping little children who would otherwise have been dismissed as 'stupid' when their impairment was deafness. She was grateful that our parents (thanks to Aunt Molly) had spotted her problem for what it was and were able to embark on topflight training in lip-reading. If Joan could see your face, you would not suspect she had a hearing loss. She could even read lips in profile. But that accomplishment carries with it a lot of fatigue because of the heightened concentration that a deaf person needs. In social settings the concentration and effort required is very high, which is why deaf people will sometimes avoid situations (restaurants, social gatherings, etc.) where their hearing is severely challenged. I know because I do it now myself because my own hearing is getting very impaired from age. But Joanie hung in there and made the effort. She probably encouraged hundreds of little kids in the New Hampshire public and parochial schools to believe in themselves and build normal lives despite their handicap. She gave her own life to help them and shared with them (and their families) the courage and hope she had. She was the one who spotted my own hearing loss when I came back from a mission trip and she hustled me right into the Boston Guild and a hearing aid. In her dedication to the deaf and hard of hearing, she was a gifted and generous saint."

Brother Jack in his terse way summarized his sister, "she devoted a lot of time to her James and Malley family research. Also, loved stamp collecting. Was always an avid reader. Loved the daily *New York Times* crossword puzzle. A great cook. Some of my favorite dishes are her recipes. Above all she was a great mother. She helped me during my farming years sketching all the new born dairy calves so we could register them with the Guernsey Cattle Club. A very special sister who was always there to help [my wife] Irene with our new babies. Took Irene to the hospital for our first born as I was out straight haying and had cows to milk too." Fr. Jim concurred. "Let me close just by seconding my brother's observation of Joan's generosity. She was the one who jumped in and handled all the details of inviting people and making the arrangements for the celebration of my first high mass. A LOT OF WORK. Believe me. I love her and still miss her and pray for the help of her prayers now in Heaven."

Much love bound the Malley children together. If only her James cousins accepted Joan's assistance, they might have found the same affection. The history of the James might have been recognized less for the stigma it bore or for the obfuscation it rendered. The James might have found like the Malleys a binding identity, cohesion, and joyful intimacy, quite different than the glue of the outlaw brothers that bound the James to silence, inhibition, and suppression.

THWARTED IN WRITING ABOUT THE JAMES FAMILY SHE DIDN'T KNOW, JOAN TRIED WRITING ABOUT THE MALLEY FAMILY SHE DID KNOW. Joan knew much more about her Irish Malley family than she knew about her James family. However, what Joan wrote in only two chapters revealed unconsciously how much her Malley side was dominated by the James side of her mother's ancestry.

Joan's briefly written history revealed a harmonious New England household, living under an Irish brooding specter of doom, which forecasted an early demise within her family. Yet this immigrant Irish family which Joan wrote about was entirely dominated by a Welsh character who spoke fluent Spanish directly out of the rough and tumble, old West. Joan's short history revealed the polyglot influences that made her family so uniquely American. Joan's first chapter began,

"First of all, our maternal grandmother, Nanna Burns, lived with us all our lives… Nanna loved to talk…and she was inclined to 'snort' at social taboos." Joan quoted Nanna as saying, *"why we were smoking in California when no lady in Boston would dream of doing so!!!"* Nanna referenced a type of Spanish cigar. *"Nanna rolled her own cigarettes and smoked Bull Durham until the day she died at eighty-two."*

Joan's Nanna brought to life the distant history of the old West Joan herself could only imagine.

"We were constantly in Nanna's company. At her knees, we were enthralled with the stories of her childhood. Her mother went (from Australia) as a bride to the

La Panza Rancho in 1866, and lived there for two years...She was unhappy there because she was afraid of Indians, and she lived a good two days drive from the nearest settlement. She moved into Paso Robles in 1868, in time to have her first child, our Nanna, on August 15, 1868. It was a thrilling, though vicarious experience, to be actually talking to someone who knew someone who was actually afraid of Indians!"

With that emotion lodged in her genes, Joan vividly imagined herself living in her great grandmother's shoes in that distant time.

"Nanna told tales of the ranch, her Negro Mammy, her first donkey, her first horse, the cowboys, the vaquero, the round-ups, etc...The story of the spring rodeo was a never ending fascinating tale...The vaquero and cowboys would ride into Paso Robles days in advance, warning all the residents of the hotel and the town that the steers were coming, and to be out of the way. These were the wild, Texas longhorn cattle who roamed the country free and unhampered since the spring before. One year, Nanna and several of her brothers and sisters climbed a huge oak and decided to get a real, close-up view of the round-up. As the steers came roaring into town, one of the children in the tree began to cry with fright. The head-tossing wild animals looked up and saw the children, and without further ado stampeded through town - thousands of head of Texas longhorns gone wild. Nanna said it took days to round up the stock, and the hotel grounds were ruined. Sixty years later, she would tell us in grateful reminiscence. "Thank God, my mother never found us out!'...

"The only thing Nanna never discussed," Joan wrote further, *"was her relationship to the famous James brothers. All of us Malleys were almost twenty when Dad, driving us home from college one day, inadvertently let the cat out of the bag. Nanna would 'clam' up at the mention of their name."*

Nanna's daughter Marguerite inherited Nanna's embarrassment and silence. Fr. Jim confessed, "Our Mother was somewhat ashamed of her James cousins and did not care to discuss the subject with anyone, [not] even family!!! My Mother was the only one who would not talk about the James brothers. She was somewhat of a Boston socialite in her premarital years. We, her children, thought it was terrific, and our grandmother...was 'pumped dry' for stories."

Pump as the Malley children did, Nanna's well of stories about Frank and Jesse James did not flow effortlessly. Eventually, Nanna acknowledged that the boys had visited Nanna's father about the time Nanna was born, and that her father never told her mother that the visiting brothers were family. That was all Nanna would tell about her cousins Frank and Jesse James. All of Nanna's other endless stories depicted her life in the far West in dramatic, colorful, and attention grabbing detail. As Joan would conclude, *"She made them live for us."*

Nanna adored her father, Drury Woodson James, the gentle, kindly, Southern gentleman, as she depicted him. The uncle of Frank and Jesse James was a stern disciplinarian. How he came to be known throughout San Luis Obispo County principally as Don Diego, and escaped being known as the uncle of notorious outlaws, was a story left unexplained. *"I was to rue the day she went to the grave with her stories of them untold,"* wrote Joan.

In a curiously self-disconnected way, that evidenced Joan had not fully accepted Nanna's family history as her own, Joan added, *"I did a genealogical study of her ancestry, or rather the ancestry of Jesse James, and I would often think of how much she could have helped me, but like all the rest of her family, any discussion of her notorious cousins were taboo."*

SILENTLY, NANNA DREW JOAN TOWARD HER HERITAGE IN THE JAMES FAMILY. When Joan began to write her second chapter, she no longer could avoid writing about her James family. *"But I seem to have started this story without a beginning,"* she began again. Joan fnally crossed her self-imposed barrier to write about her mother, Marguerite, Nanna's daughter and the granddaughter of Drury Woodson James.

"Mother was thirty when she was married, and Dad was going on thirty one. The hilarious tales of their courtship and marriage enriched many a Sunday dinner table. Dad said, 'the fourteenth time I laid eyes on your mother, I was kneeled down getting married to her!' The attraction was instant, the courtship swift, and the marriage a good one.

"Mother was convent bred, gently and strictly reared in the fashion of the early twenties. She was utterly ignorant of anything pertaining to money or finances. And my father, to protect his children and family, set about to teach her how to run the house. All his life, he <u>knew</u> he was going to die young…Since he <u>was</u> going to die young and leave a widow and small family; he wanted to make sure they were left in capable hands. He was a good tutor, for I often heard him pay Mom the compliment that he wished she worked for him in the factory! But once a month came the day of crisis - Mother had to balance the checkbook! Everyone waited

with bated breath until the great moment of success arrived and we could relax again until the following month.

"Mother was an extremely devout and religious person, and she had certain prayers that <u>had</u> to be said every day. She had a long list of people that she felt she must pray for, and her days ground to a standstill and no one spoke to her unless it was absolutely necessary until my prayers are said. This list was to grow year by year until her old age, when her whole day was spent in prayer for people and for things...Each friend, or relative of a friend, was added to her 'list.' Included in the 'list' was many a soul that she feared had no one to pray for them. Carole Lombard, the movie actress, was one example. A notorious criminal, sentenced to die in the electric chair for murdering a policeman, was another on her list."

For her own children, Joan noted, *"Discipline was strict, fair, and instant. Her favorite weapon was a switch cut from the lilac bush, stripped of its leaves, and used to flick the back of the legs and behinds, as we charged up the stairs in banishment to our rooms. The four of us were constantly arguing and fighting. Mother's cardinal rule was that it made no difference whose fault it was, or who started the fight - we all got sent to our room, or punished in some other appropriate manner.*

"Jack, the second boy and third child, was the tease, the imp, the bane of mother's existence. His discipline was reserved for Dad, while she prayed nightly that she might live to see her children grown. She felt no step-mother would ever put up with Jack. And yet Jack was the one most beloved by all family. Friends and help in the house always favored the lovable imp. He could, and often did, reduce the Sunday dinner table to utter diatribe and chaos. No one would be on speaking terms. And Jack, who had so innocently precipitated the whole crisis, would push back his chair from the table and announce, 'Boy! That was a wonderful meal!'

"But overshadowing us all was the unusual character of Dad...By any standard he was a moderately well-to-do man, but we children were not aware of this. Mother held the purse strings tight...He was extravagant in only one field - the field of education. He gave us the finest education money could buy, trained us in any profession we chose, and then turned us out to earn a living."

Briefly referencing her wealthy Kansas City cousin Thomas Martin James, an elder brother of Drury Woodson James, Joan stated, *"we were not children of a rich man, reared to go through life living graciously. And I was the only one living at home. Having chosen teaching as my career, I paid my mother board and room until the day I married at the age of thirty."*

Then, curiously, Joan wrote of the silence within her father's own family, a silence that her father once broke with a slip of his tongue. *"Dad was pure Irish in every respect. He had a remarkable father, and he was a remarkable son. No unnecessary words were spoken in that house, and mealtimes were occasions of strict silence, where one only spoke when spoken to. Because of this upbringing, Dad always encouraged free discussions around our table."* Joan knew firsthand the value of communication that was open and free. That quality which Joan treasured and esteemed highly, she perceived to be missing among the James.

Before concluding her short memoir of Malley family life by delving deeply into her father's Gaelic heritage, Joan concluded about her father, *"Dad emerged as the best educated man I have ever known. No question ever stumped him. No fact ever escaped his attention, or his memory. He carried around in his head a 'department of useless information.' And from this storehouse would come answers that would stymie many an expert. How many people of today know that the Balearic Islands lie east of Spain in the Mediterranean, and were famous for supplying the ancient Roman army with sling shot shooters? Dad threw a history class at Dartmouth into an uproar with such an answer - the only one who could give it...To us he was not a frightening figure, rather a worshiped one. The worse punishment mother could inflict on us was to say: 'and now you will have to tell your father!'."*

Four years after Nanna died, Joan wrote on May 14, 1954 to Gilbert A. Cam, the Executive Assistant at the New York City Library. *"No information can be had from any member of the family for, almost without exception, they are reluctant to admit their relationship with 'those boys.' I was specifically warned not to try any correspondence at all with any relatives in Missouri...I am trying to gather material about all the brothers and sisters of my great grandfather* [Drury Woodson James]. *This too is proving difficult without family co-operation. But I am digging."* [10]

Joan was first sent digging by Nanna. Sensing the approach of her demise, Nanna had summoned Joan to memorialize her beloved father, Drury Woodson James. Nanna plainly did not want his kindness and generosity shrouded for eternity by the disrepute and loss that befell her father's fortunes in his tragic final years. With notes prepared in hand, Nanna read to Joan from her script what Nanna wanted Joan to write. Her final dictation of memories fanned Joan's desire to embark upon a journey of discovery of what else had been left unsaid. Beyond Nanna's passing, Joan tried to find any nugget of history still unknown to her that might yet exist.

When Joan began to write *A History of Drury Woodson James, as Told by his Daughter*, Joan specifically stated, *"The above history is exactly as Nanna dictated it to me in 1949, at the age of 81. I remember she had a lot of notes in her hands, but she evidently destroyed them before she died, probably because they were all included in the above."*

Crossing the threshold of Nanna's death, Joan suspected Nanna had thwarted any further historical legacy. But very soon, Joan was astounded by a discovery among Nanna's relicts.

In the confines of Nanna's room, Joan found a family tree inside Nanna's travelling case. While living, Nanna never had mentioned the tree, nor alluded to its existence. Evident for the first time in the document Joan held, Joan plainly saw her relationship to Nanna's family and to the notorious outlaws, all of whom were long since departed

Joan also found Nanna's letters. Joan began her research by writing her own letters of inquiry to those with whom Nanna had corresponded. Joan wrote to Othor MacLean. She found him still living, and received his response.[11] MacLean was a local historian in Paso Robles. His family had known Drury's La Panza Ranch. MacLean was personally acquainted with some of those who worked Drury's ranch. Joan corresponded further with Mrs. R. C. Heaton, a widow whose husband had acquired subsequent ownership of Drury's foreclosed El Paso Robles Hotel. Both contacts confirmed information that Joan first learned from Nanna.

From their collective recall, Joan learned that Nanna's colorful stories - told as if they were fanciful fiction of the old West - were in fact true. *"I find that my old Nanna's memory was amazingly accurate,"* Joan recorded. *"She made only two errors which I have taken the liberty of correcting in the original text. She said her father was born in Louisville Kentucky, but he was actually born in Logan County, Kentucky, on the banks of the Whippoorwill River, near Adairville in the southern part of the county."* Nanna more aptly meant that Drury Woodson James was raised, rather than born, in Jefferson County. The Mimms family store and plantation, where Drury Woodson James was adopted by his eldest sister Nancy and her husband Rev. John Wilson Mimms and where he grew up after being orphaned by the death of his father John M. James, was located in Jefferson County at Westport, east of Louisville. Nanna also stated that her father died in 1909. But Joan obtained his death certificate from the Bureau of Vital Statistics in San Francisco that stated he died in 1910.[12]

From information found among Nanna's effects regarding the Poor family of Mary "Polly" Poor, the late life consort of the family patriarch John M. James, Joan learned, *"It has definitely been established on the mother's side, that Drury's grandfather, Robert Poor, served as a cornet with Lee's Partisan Legion of the Virginia Continental troops in the Revolutionary War. His great, grandfather, Abraham Poor, too old to fight, furnished supplies to the Army for which he was suitably reimbursed by the Commissioner of Public Service Claims of the state of Virginia on September 10th, 1785. His grandfather, Shadrack Mimms and two of his three brothers were awarded land grants in the Georgia Colony in recognition of their service in the Revolutionary War. The information pertaining to the James side of the family is still being searched."*

Living in New England, where so many take prides in their historic family connections to the American Revolution, Joan quickly grasped from the discovery of her ancestry among the Poor family that she herself might be eligible for official membership as a Daughter of the American Revolution. Quickly adopting the additional objective to become a D.A.R. member, Joan became even more passionate about researching her James family's lost past, and specifically the ties of her James ancestors to the War of the American Revolution.

Seven years had passed since Joan first wrote to Gilbert Cam at the New York Historical Society. In all that time, Joan learned little more about the James. Meanwhile, Joan hired independent researchers to find any documents that evidenced the James family's past.

FINALLY, JOAN BEAMIS RECEIVED THE COMMUNICATION SHE LONG HAD BEEN SEEKING. Nanna had been dead eleven years when Joan received a letter from Stella James, the wife of Jesse Edwards James Jr., the outlaw's son. Writing on personalized stationary from her Los Angeles home at 4124 Slauson Avenue, Stella McGowan James wrote to Joan on December 6, 1961:

My Dear Mrs. Beamis,

It was nice hearing from you and I hope I can be of some help in giving you the information you need. Yes, my daughter did write to your Grandmother [Nanna] some time ago. But she did not receive an answer. Jo Frances did want

Jesse Edwards James Jr. & Stella Frances McGowan
Wedding Photo, January 24, 1900

to locate the old James family bible or tree. It seemed the bible was destroyed in a fire some years ago. Since you seem to have about all the information I would be able to give you about the James family and the Mimms family...I have asked Lutie Mimms Gray who is a devoted family historian to fill you in on the D. W. James and other facts about the Daughters of the American Revolutionary War, and she can tell you of her visit to and with the Drury W. family in 1903 - were [sic] she met and enjoyed all of his daughters. Lutie was also state president of the D.A.R. and is yet very active in their work. Lutie is a retired school teacher and a wonderful person. Her father was Robert Mimms, the brother of Zee James, who was the wife of Jesse James. Her mother was a sister of Zerelda James-Samuel. Jesse and Zee were first cousins. Lutie is very close to both the James and Mimms familys [sic] and a dyed in the wool D.A.R.

Stella's letter concluded, *"...I am eighty years old on next February 27 - Lutie I think is a little older..."* For Joan, Stella's statement of age was a clear signal that time was of the essence. Stella signed her letter first as *"Stella James,"* then she pointedly clarified in parenthesis in case Joan did not know or was unaware of who was writing to her, *"Mrs. Jesse James Jr."* Stella also added a postscript, characteristic of the James family's native suspiciousness. *"How did you get my address?"*

Jessie Estell, Jo Frances, Lucille Martha & young Ethel Rose James

Daughters of Jesse Edwards & Stella McGowan James

Granddaughters of Jesse Woodson James & Zerelda Amanda Mimms

Stella confirmed what Joan already factually knew. Indeed, Jo Frances James had written to Nanna. Jo's letter of October 30, 1939 was written on personalized stationary of her own, in the exact style of her mother's stationary. Joan found the letter among Nanna's effects, with other letters written to Nanna by other James family relatives whom Joan never had heard about or knew. Like Joan, the granddaughter of the notorious outlaw herself had a desire to know her James family's past. At the age of thirty-six, just two years younger than Joan herself, Jesse James' own granddaughter Jo Frances James previously wrote to Nanna:

Dear Mamie:

...If you can find that family tree you have I would certainly appreciate it. I do so badly want to trace the James family back as far as I possibly can; and if you do not have it all the way back to the first James in America or rather to the first one of our ancestors who came over, you might have enough that would help me definitely establish it by what you have. I could then go further by having someone in Virginia trace it. I will take good care of it and will return it to you...

Your cousin,

Jo James

Jo Frances James-Ross

Lucy Ethel "Lutie" Mimms

Great Granddaughter of John M. James & Mary "Polly" Poor

Granddaughter of Mary James & Rev. John Wilson Mimms

Jo's letter informed Joan that the grandchildren of the outlaw Jesse James also knew very little, if nothing at all, about their James family ancestry or their history.

Stella's stated intention to write to Lutie Mimms Gray on Joan's behalf produced an immediate response from Lutie. On December 20, 1961, Lutie wrote formally to Joan:

Dear Mary Joan Beamis:

Mrs. Stella James asked me to write you in answer to your letter. I am Lutie Mimms Gray, the young woman who brought my great aunt Elizabeth James West to San Francisco in 1903. I came on a Shriner's excursion, and we visited your grandfather Drury Woodson James and Aunt Louise.

Now he was raised by my grandmother Mary James Mimms, and was about the same age as my father R. H. Mimms. Uncle Woodson and my father came to California with a wagon train before the War Between the States, and my father stayed out there twenty years, and came back to Kansas City, Mo. and married my mother at age 41.

I understand that the James family bible was burned in a storage house in Kansas City; so those records were lost.

I have the Mimms family history and I hope the following information will be of help to you...

Lutie directed Joan to the Library of Congress, where Joan could find *The Douglas Register, as Kept by Rev. William Douglas from 1730 to 1797*. Therein, Lutie stated, Joan would find Lutie's Mimms and Woodson ancestries as well as Joan's own. With that information, Joan then could make application for membership in the Daughters of the American Revolution. As if to emphasize the distance that formerly separated the two newly found cousins, Lutie wryly signed her letter *"sincerely, your 'remote cousin'."*

In a postscript Lutie added, *"Great Aunt Elizabeth West* [i.e. Elizabeth James, wife of Tillman Howard West in Kansas City, and daughter of John M. James and Mary "Polly" Poor.] *knew more about our ancestors than anybody. She told me that the first Jameses* [sic] *to migrate to America was a younger brother of James VI of Scotland and James I of England. The king gave him a large tract along or near the James River in Virginia, also near Jamestown."* Lutie added, *"She could not verify it, however."*

Unknown to Lutie and Joan, precisely the same family lore was handed down to the descendants of John M. James of Pulaski County in Kentucky. His grandson, John James of Alvarado, Texas, wrote on February 1, 1921 to Mrs. M. A. Romjue on official letterhead stationary for the City of Alvarado, Texas, that identified him as the town's mayor,

My Dear Lady Relative:

On Aug 7, 1914, you wrote me asking about the James Family, and if I was of the branch of said family, that emigrated from Va. to Ky. in an early day; and also stating that you had heard that I was gathering data of that family, for the purpose of writing a history of them...

I have also traced the James family from James 1st, King of Scotland, born in 1394, and on down the line of the 6 Kings of Scotland when the crown of Scotland and England were united, and the VI King of Scotland, became the 1st King James of England...

So here I have, what seem to be the two ends of a broken rope, and so far I have not been able to draw them together sufficiently close to unite them...

Here I am reminded of the James boys, Frank and Jesse, whose cousin William Wythe James came to see me 4 years ago, having heard of me at Fort Worth Texas, and brought me a sword, that they captured in the last raid they made on the 'Jay Hawkers' [sic] as they called them, just before abandonment of the Quantrells [sic].[13] Also stated that Frank had been trying to meet me for several years before he died...I shall be very thankful for all the information you are able to give me.[14]

Mrs. M. A. Romjue is Mary Ann Thompson, wife of Judge and U. S. Congressman Milton Andrew Romjue of Macon County, Missouri. Maude, as Mary Ann was called, is a third great granddaughter of John M. James of Pulaski County. Maude Romjue was not only seeking to establish her own lost James family ancestry; Maude also was seeking like Joan her own membership in the Daughters of the American Revolution. Maude's own James family lore had repeated stories of her family's relationship to Frank and Jesse James.

Joan Beamis continued her correspondence with Lutie Mimms. Due to progressing age, unreliable financial circumstances, and advancing illness, Lutie courteously directed Joan more and more to external sources for Joan to research. In her letter of January 19, 1962, Lutie directed Joan to the State Historical Society of Missouri for additional Mimms information, and also to Sam Mims, author of *Leaves from the Mims Family Tree*. Lutie additionally stated to Joan's distress her bottom line about the James own knowledge of their ancestry. *"I'm very sorry to have to tell you that neither Stella, her daughter Jo, nor myself have documentary evidence to prove that D. W. James was the son of his father* [John M. James]. *With the family bible of the James family destroyed by fire, the main source of the information is gone…"*

To simplify her inquiries and more easily acquire responses, Joan resorted to sending Lutie question lists, with space available beneath each question for Lutie to enter her responses. On April 12, 1962, Lutie replied with two pages of copious answers to Joan's list of interrogatories. Her letter concluded, *"I find that I am eligible to belong to the D.A.R., Colonial Dames, and Daughters of 1812, as my grandfather on my mother's side was Robert Thomason. Through that line I belong to the United Daughters of the Confederacy (UDC). I'm a delegate to their state convention in May."* Joan understood her own candidacy for D.A.R. membership now was supported by both her Mimms and Thomason ancestral lines, but still not through her James line. Joan began to pursue other resources of information.

In April, Joan received a letter from Carl Breihan, author of *The Complete and Authentic Life of Jesse James*, published almost a decade earlier. Breihan offered Joan a skeletal explanation for the lack of progress Joan experienced in learning about her James family. *"Most of the relation(s) will clam up when the boys are mentioned, the Barr boys moreso* [sic] *than most. Don't know why."* Breihan's reference was to the brothers Lawrence Henry Barr and Forster Ray Barr, grandsons of Jesse James. Each of the Barr brothers had experienced employment problems, Breihan added. *"You'd be surprised that some employees still would resent it, and you could not tell what might happen. Not too long ago such an incident did happen."*

With only Nanna's recollection, Nanna's archive of hidden letters, and Nanna's long sequestered family tree of Drury Woodson James' descendants, now combined with Lutie's corresponding Mimms ancestry that linked her Mimms to the James family, Joan wrote one final time almost a decade later to Gilbert A. Cam at the New York Public Library. Cam's response to Joan of October 21, 1963, must have disappointed her deeply. *"There is so much more information about Jesse James' family in your letter than we have been able to find in our collection. The James genealogies we have do not include him, and the biographies of Jesse James contain very little genealogical information."*

Cam presented Joan with an additional obstruction she had not expected. *"Some of the latter books tend to confuse the issue due to the fact that several people have claimed to be Jesse James and have shown documents to prove it. We would be delighted to have any information that you have uncovered about his ancestry. There are very few clues we can offer about this particular James Family..."* The perversity of fake claimants to the Jesse James family threatened Joan's own discovery of her factual ancestry. Cam's letter also appeared to indicate that a pall had been cast over Joan's own statement of relationship to Frank and Jesse James.

Perhaps overwhelmed by the disappointment of Cam's letter, and his inadvertent cast of suspicion, Joan ignored Cam's closing comments. She should not have.

In closing his letter, Gilbert Cam noted John James of Pulaski County, Kentucky, citing specifically the appearance of John James in the 1790 Kentucky census with his brother Daniel James, identified formerly of James City in Virginia, then residing in Fayette County, Kentucky. Cam had provided to Joan a relevant and most important investigative lead about the identity of the James family's patriarch John M. James. Joan should have followed Cam's lead. Disappointed by Cam's response, and never having heard anything before about Pulaski County, Joan mistakenly ignored Cam's information.

JOAN'S TIME WAS RUNNING OUT FOR COMING TOGETHER WITH HER COUSINS IN THE JAMES FAMILY. Shortly after March 31, 1964, Joan received a letter from Lutie about the death Jesse Jr.'s daughter, Jo Frances James.

My very dear Cousin Joan!

Joe's passing was a great shock to us all! She had just had a good breakfast, dressed, and started for the door, when she fell to the floor and was gone. Her heart just gave out, I suppose. Now don't mention this, but she was a heavy smoker! She was the only one in the family, with the exception of Estelle's husband Mervyn Baumel who smoked and died at the age of 52, with lung cancer.

At the time of her death, Jo was working as an escrow officer at Bank of America in Culver City, California.

A year and a half after January 12, 1966, Joan received a letter from

Stella James that seemed occasionally rambling, sometime incoherent, and difficult to read.

My Dear Joan:

Your very interesting and most welcome letter came yesterday and I was happy to receive it - I am not going to answer that letter just now and I will explain after I ask you this question.

Are you writing a book - or something to be published about the James family?

I have turned my records and family history into a script - that - I had intended to have as a record for my daughters, grandchildren, and great grandchildren when a very good friend and author of several Jesse James books advised me to have a reading of my script by a publishers or agent - But - knowing my incapability as a writer, I consulted a Literary Consultant, who read and studied my script - advised that with a little help my manuscript would be publishable and interesting, and advised that I put the script in the hands of a good agent. Now it was a while I had this in mind I first heard from you, and before I had decided to have my script read by a publisher. I am telling you this because I want you to know why I have been slow in sending you pictures or fact of the James family before I had reason to believe my script would not be published. Now that I have had an example of your knowledge of the James history and your interest in it - and your capability - I want to talk with you and see if you agree that with your research and my close personal contact with and knowledge of the life they lived and my husband's family that we may be putting my script and your interest and ability together we may come up with an interesting historical book. I would want you to read my script before giving this idea consideration. I think you may be able to tell me, as in other words I would like your advice before paying a consultant a thousand dollars for his advice. Please Joan think this one well and let me hear from you real soon - for at my age I must get some kind of action started or just forget it...

Stella

P.S. I will get a letter to Lawrence Barr in the mail at once - and tell him I have ask[ed] you to write to him. I did not get to visit Lawrence and Thelma last summer, but they came to visit me with the daughter Bettie. Bettie visited with Estelle last summer, a very sweet girl of seventy four years.

Time was closing in. Strongly sensing Stella's advancing frailty; Joan resorted to sending Stella the simple and direct question lists she had used so effectively with Lutie Mimms. Joan also had begun to experience medical issues of her own that would begin to hinder her further research. To Joan's relief, Stella's following response was saturated with the intimate personal history Joan had been seeking for so long.

Dear Joan:

I was glad to get your nice long letter. Sorry to hear of so much sickness. It does seem that you have had more than your share. I do hope that you come back from your vacation a brand new Joan. This has been our rainy season. It has been raining for four days now. We will be glad to see it shine. No, Dear, our Christmas party was not held in my apt. It was at Jim Ross', Jo's son. They had enlarged their home last summer by adding a very large den, game room, bar, two new baths, two outside dressing rooms near the swimming pool. They have a nicer large yard - inclined play yard. Our dinner was served in the den as it is much larger than the dining room. I am a lady of leisure at the family partys [sic]. There are five of the younger girls, as may I say women. All try to outdo the other in fancy salads and goodies of all kinds. This year all four of my great grandchildren were with us. Lucille's son Jim came home from England with his wife and small son. He did miss Jo. She was the lively one. His two grandchildren called her Joie.

Question 1. *Yes, it was Jesse Jr.'s mother with whom I lived just after we were married. But Jesse Sr.'s mother Zerelda spent a part of two winters in our home after her colored boy Perry was married. Grandma could not keep help on the farm in the winter. Jesse would send one couple after another one to the farm from the city. They would not stay long. Grandma would not understand why she should feed and pay two people to do the work Perry had done. Perry was born in to the family. His name was Perry Samuel. He was cook, maid, and side man - and driver for Grandma. Her would just fell apart when Perry married at the age of 45 years. Grandma decided to close her house and go to a hotel in Kearney. There was two hotels. She tried both. Then a private family. When a letter came asking Jesse Jr. to send another couple one, and she would go back home. Jesse and I had a large house, a good cook - Jesse Jr.'s mother's sister,* [i.e. Zerelda's half-sister Martha Ann "Mattie" Thomason-Mimms] *a widow would spend months at a time with us. She was wonderful with children. I told her we may be able to make her comfortable for the winter in our home. Well, Grandma came the last of November, bag and baggage. Our cook left in two weeks. Grandma would plan the meals. Sometimes changed the order shortly before meal time. Our next cook, a big Irish woman, became boss of the kitchen, and Grandma was tamed for the very first time in her life. Aunt Sallie took over the children. I would dress Grandma twice a day. You may know that she had only one hand and arm. She had never bothered to learn how to use it to help herself. Grandma had many visitors come to the farm. She would change into her black alpaca dress, big with bow tie, and be ready for her visitors at home. She felt should be ready and dressed at our home. Sometimes the tie would be too stiff, other times, not stiff enough. About the big* breast piece, *with Jesse and Frank's picture. That was to be in the center of the bow tie - one day Jesse's picture turned out, the next day Frank's. I had to help remember whose turn it was each day. By this time, you may has guessed that Zerelda Samuel was a woman who ruled. Grandma enjoyed her stay with us. The second time she came several weeks early. By this time Aunt Sallie and I had grown a little stronger. The Irish cook had left, and Grandma went home a little early. Aunt Sally went with her, and Perry and his wife came home for the summer.*

No, I do not have the James family tree. I did have the Mimms tree, but I gave it to Lutie. It was by Sam Mimms, same family, but the Northern branch spelled with two m's.

Dear Joan, if I have not sent you my family pictures it may be that I want all family picture copy rite [sic], *as I did not want them published. I will send some that you may keep. Others that I have only one copy, you may send back after having a copy made for your own.*

No, I have never heard of Johnnie James of San Luis Obispo County or Paso Robles.[15] *Yes, I have heard a great deal about Jesse and Frank's visit to their Uncle Drury Woodson's farm from Grandma Samuel, Uncle John Samuel, Fannie, and Sallie, half-sisters of Jesse and Frank, I may have told you that.*

Aunt Elizabeth was a guest at my wedding. I can understand Mae [Mrs. Robert James, daughter-in-law of Frank James] *not answering your questions. Mae never does answer questions. Robert had told Jo and I that he would give us some pictures and some letters that Frank and Jesse had written, if he ever got control of his mother's trunk after her death. But we did get them. May gave Ethelrose one of Uncle Frank's letters to his wife Anne, written just after he surrendered to Governor Crittenden. Mae told Ethelrose she would give me several of Jesse's letters. She had changed her mind when I asked for them last summer while I was visiting the old home and Maw, who now lives in Excelsior Springs. Mo.*

No, I do not have a picture of D. W. James or his family. Thanks for the picture you sent to me. Ethelrose was to type this letter for me, but she came down with the flu and a kidney infection. So I will send it as is. I hope you will be able to read it.

When I started out to write my memor [sic–i.e. memoir] *of the James family and the close association with them, it was to be for the girls. I may now get some help to put it into a book. If I do not, I will send you a copy to read.*[16]

If I have not answered all of your questions, I will go over your letter again before mailing this and try to do so. I may have to send this partial part, if it gets much longer. By [sic] *for tonight. More tomorrow, Sunday.*

Stella continued with her long letter the following day.

Joan, I do not like to send this to you marked up as it is. Please bear with me this time. I feel that you will. You are a wonderful and understanding person, one that I have loved from the very start. I will enclose a clipping from the Independence, Mo. paper and some pictures under separate cover.[17]

Love,

Stella James

P.S. Jesse Jr.'s mother Zerelda Mimms James died in November 14th, 1900, just ten months after Jesse Jr. and I were married.

The absence of Jesse Jr.'s mother was noticed in the newspaper reporting of Stella's wedding. Zerelda's non-attendance long since fired rumors and speculation about the James family. Stella continued...

Our plan was to be married in June, owing to Jesse's mother's illness becoming more serious, we moved the time forward to January 24. Jesse's sister Mary moved to a rented apt., and brought her mother home from the hospital and nursed her mother with help of her mother's sister Sallie. Mrs. James had improved at home. And when spring weather arrived she wanted to come back to her cottage. From May to November the four of us were together, Mary, Zerelda, Jesse, and I. Zerelda was able to be up in her chair and I would visit with her. I did not want to ask her questions about Jesse Sr., her husband. She would at times talk to me about him.

This is in my manuscript, which I hope you will be able to read sometime.

I have heard the story of Jesse and Frank's visit to Uncle Drury many times from grandma Samuel, Uncle John Samuel, my Jesse, and Fannie Hall. [Also] Sallie Nicholson, half-sister of Jesse and Frank who I love to visit in their farm home near the old James home. Mary James was married at Aunt Sallie's home in March, after her mother died in November 1900. Jesse and I attended Mary's wedding. After the guests had all left, Jesse, Aunt Sallie, and I sat up and talked until the break of day. Jesse wanted Aunt Sallie to tell him all she could remember about his father's last visit at her home, just a week before he was killed. This all in detail in my manuscript...

I have a very large picture of Sally Nicholson. None of Susan James Parmer. Several of Mary James Barr. I think I will send you one of Mary and Jesse taken together the day we left Kansas City to come to California for the winter that was Sept. 26, 1926. We never did go back to K. C. to live. Jesse was recovering from a brain operation. At that time, Lucille was spending her vacation with Uncle John Samuel in Long Beach City at the time. Ethelrose, our youngest daughter, came with us. She was 18 years old at the time. Jo was married; her little son was three months old. Estelle was working and was with Jo until we were to come home in the spring. When we did not go back in the spring, Estelle joined us in Long Beach, Calif.

Questions 5-6-7-8 and nine, the answer is no. I wish I did have more pictures but all of the pictures of older members of the family that Jesse's mother had, Mary keep [sic]. Jesse [Jr.] got the trunk, with his father's guns, boots, [illegible] long, wallet, and other relicts [sic], and I still have them here in my home. I have had many offers of big money for them. But I know Jesse would not want me to sell them. I will divide them with Mary's three boys and Jesse's girls.

Yes, I do have a copy of the family tree. Thank you for sending it to me.

No, I did not know Aunt Elizabeth West very well, or have contact with her family. Joan, your letters will never tire me. I am sorry to have to send this scratch up disconnected mess to you. I will do better next - and have my letter type written.

Loads of Love,

Stella

I will tell you much more of Grandma Samuel in next letter.

Joan received no further letters from Stella McGowan James.

THE FAMILY HISTORY JOAN WANTED TO GATHER WAS FAST ESCAPING HER. Four years had passed before Joan received a response to the letters she wrote to Jesse James' grandson Lawrence Henry Barr. When finally the letter came, the response was not from Lawrence himself, but rather from his wife, Thelma Duncan Barr. On October 26, 1970, Thelma wrote to Joan:

Lawrence Henry Barr
Son of Mary Susan James & Henry Lafayette Barr

Mary Susan James

Daughter of Jesse Woodson James & Zerelda Amanda Mimms
Mother of Lawrence Henry Barr

Dear Mrs. Beamis,

My name is Thelma Duncan Barr. My husband is Lawrence Barr.
We were in Los Angeles, Calif. in Oct. on our way home from Hawaii. We visited several days with our cousins, the daughters of Aunt Stella James. Ethel Rose James Owens gave me your letter Sept. 1970 to read. I wanted to write you and offer an explanation for my husband's not answering your letter of several years ago.

I am sorry he did not see fit to answer your letter. You have no idea how many inquiries he gets through the mails. He simply didn't want to be bothered. I told him at the time he should have answered your letter. However, he does not know very much about the historical facts of the family. Mother Barr would not let it be 'talked about' in her home. Now Forster [Lawrence's brother] *has always been interested in the 'James Stories' and got into his possession all he could find about Jesse James. He has all the keepsakes, historical data, pictures (what there are) etc. Lawrence has very, very little about his grandfather! Only in the past few years has he become interested. If I recall you were asking for a picture of Drury Woodson James.*

He did not have it and has only very few pictures of his mother. What we do have is in books we have had to buy and newspaper clippings. Forster was always the one who answered people's letters. Now that is the best excuse I can give him, believe me...

A long time ago, when on a trip to Calif., we went to see Aunt Lutie Mimms. She gave me, to bring home with me, a Genealogy of the Mimms family. She & Mother Barr were double cousins. At that time it was all a gig-saw[sic] *puzzle to me. I read, read, and read it before I could begin to understand it. When I finished copying it, I found a 'gap' in it that directly linked the Mimms and the James families together. She* [Lutie] *said her niece had it. I never did get it from Lutie, her niece, or Aunt Stella.*

We went to the nursing home to see Aunt Stella & she did know us!

I am interested in where you get your information on the exact connection of Mimms or (Mims) & James line. I 'think' I have it figured out, but I am not sure I am correct!

The only data we have on Drury Woodson James was that he was the youngest of 8 children [of John M. James who married Mary Polly Poor]. *He was born Nov. 17, 1825...*

If you are going to give our copies of your "James Family" I'd love to have one...

It has been nice visiting with you. Please don't think too harshly about my husband. He just doesn't see the importance of our work. He thinks I'm wasting my time!

Most sincerely,

Thelma Duncan Barr

On April 2, 1971, the following year, Thelma wrote to Joan again. Though the news was distressfully sad, Joan must have felt very fortunate to receive this letter.

Dear Mrs. Beamis – Joan,

Just a note to let your know that Aunt Stella James passed away last night, April 1, 1971 about 9:00 p.m.

We got a "special deliver" letter from Estelle last night about 9:30 p.m. giving us the details of her illness. Then today 'our' Betty called out to L.A. & talked to the girls & she had passed away last night.

On March 24th Aunt Stella fell and broke her hip & dislocated it. She had fallen many times but this was "the one." They had to operate the next day. Then she had a massive stroke on Friday. She never regained consciousness after that. Had she lived she would have been paralyzed and perhaps would not have been able to even talk. She never even moved after the stroke. The girls gave her "every care that was possible;" but it was not possible. Poor dear, had been so ill and mixed up for some time.

How are you coming with your book? I have been looking for it. Did you ever get it printed? …Let me know about your book…

Flat Lick Baptist Church

Chapter Two

Talented, but Erratic

In Kentucky, Joseph McAlister James perceived recklessness as a James family trait. To deliver himself from the branding of public embarrassment or social impairment, he created an altered identity for himself. He intended his new identity to represent propriety, and not impropriety. He endured under his shroud for a lifetime until his death in 1905, a decade before Frank James died.

Arriving in Danville, an upset and disturbed Joseph McAlister James assumed the lead of a noteworthy Scotsman, who made his life there, succeeding with a near perfect reputation. Dr. Ephraim McDowell distinguished himself when he performed the first hysterectomy on Christmas day of 1809 with no benefit of anesthesia for his patient. McDowell's reputation spread quickly far outside Kentucky. President James Knox Polk employed McDowell as his personal surgeon. McDowell further enhanced his reputation when he married Sarah Simpson Shelby, daughter of Gov. Isaac Shelby. At his core, however, the Scotsman was a modest man. He preferred to be addressed simply as Mack.

Arriving in Danville from his birthplace in Pulaski County, Joseph McAlister James introduced himself as Mack James. He wrote his signature as Joseph McJames. The tartan bow tie Mack proudly sported rooted him to the Scottish clan McAlister of his mother Martha McAlister. Although called Patsy inside the family, for propriety's sake Mack's mother always insisted she be called Betsy in public.

Mack's grandfather, Rev. Joseph McAlister, was a patriot of the American Revolution, who became a tailor, farmer, minister, and a judge. He first enlisted in Capt. Thomas Posey's company in February, 1776, under Col. Alexander McClanahan's 7th Virginia Regiment. He attended the capture of Gentleman Johnny Burgoyne on October 17, 1777, after Burgoyne had invaded New York from Canada to seize Fort Ticonderoga. Two tours in the Gilmore's Rifles Militia followed under Mack's future father-in-law, Capt. James Gilmore.[1] In December of 1780, Gen. Nathaniel Green assigned Mack's grandfather to Lt. Col. William Washington under Col. Daniel Morgan, a future namesake in the James family. At the Battle of Cowpens on January 17, 1781 in South Carolina, Joseph McAlister was one of an army of backwoodsmen lead to victory by Col. Morgan over Banastre Tarlton's battle hardened British Regulars.[2]

Following military service, Joseph McAlister married Capt. James Gilmore's daughter, Nancy Agnes Gilmore, in October of 1781.[3] With the Gilmore clan, Joseph McAlister migrated from Virginia to Lincoln County, Kentucky where Mack's grandfather John M. James also had settled, following his own service in the Revolution. Mack's grandfather McAlister engaged in some Indian fighting. Mostly, he plowed his fields in summer, and in winter he stitched buckskin clothing for arriving settlers. His daughter Patsy married Mack's father, Rev. Joseph Martin James.[4] When John M. James formed Pulaski County in 1798 out of Lincoln County, Gov. James Garrard appointed the first Court of Quarter Sessions to be held on July 23, 1799, *"the worshipful James Gilmore, Joseph McAlister"* sat as the first Justices of John M. James' emerging new county.[5]

Mack believed his plaid bravura cleverly distracted attention from his troublesome Welsh background on his father's side of his James family. Mack's grandfather, John M. James, also was a patriot who had served in the Revolution in Virginia's Culpeper Militia.[6] Later, he too became a judge. But it was Mack's own father, Rev. Joseph Martin James, a Baptist minister, who had become Mack's intolerable embarrassment. Rev. Joe evidenced a flaw of moral character, more unbearable than any among his family, even more than his cousins, Frank and Jesse James.

REV. JOSEPH MARTIN JAMES WAS A BRILLIANT BAPTIST MINISTER, BUT HE WAS FLAWED. Despite every capability and probability, Joe squandered becoming a Baptist Divine. The illiteracy of Joe's youth was inherited benignly from his ambitious father and seven siblings. John M. James was too obsessed with politics to provide Joe a formal education. The family was settling a frontier. They were securing an emerging nation militarily. Also, they were advancing the kingdom of Christ. All of these objectives were pursued vigorously at once, if not vaingloriously at times. Joe's schooling was the kind learned by example, observation, and imitation. Energetically gifted with a tireless mind, young Joe was instructed daily in the practicality of applying his common thinking to greater goals, a family principle each James has been expected to pursue.[7]

John M. James held great expectations when his wife Clara Nall presented John with Joe's birth. The infant was the couple's third son, born to their family of seven children. Clara requested of John, "What shall our son be named, Mr. James?"

John thought of the old Indian agent Joseph Martin. John first met Martin during the war when they both fought in North Carolina. There, Martin played a pivotal role in the Battle of King's Mountain. The astute Martin held the Cherokee in check, using no physical force whatsoever. Instead, Martin's shrewd intelligence, wit, and cunning negotiation insured the Patriots' important victory for the Colonies, one that left the Crown demoralized with neither the support of the Native American people nor the colonists. Later, Martin fortified an outpost twenty miles at the entry to the Cumberland Gap. There Gen. Joseph Martin facilitated passage and settlement for pioneers entering into Virginia's District of Kentucky.

John inquired of his wife Clara, "Mrs. James, do you recall Joseph Martin?" John and Clara had encamped at Martin's Station when John brought Clara into the Kentucky with their Traveling Church. Born outside Charlottesville in Jeffersonian Albemarle County to Capt. Joseph Martin Sr. and his wife Susannah Chiles, both immigrants from Bristol, England, Joseph Martin Jr. was disinherited by his father. At age sixteen, young Martin ran away from home to join the army and spend his life on the frontier. Like Joseph Martin, John M. James himself had been outcast. He, too, ran away from the home of his father Joseph James the Elder. Martin's father was the perfect Englishman, as was his grandfather, who was described as, "Large and athletic, bold, daring, selfly willed and supercilious, with the highest

Gen. Joseph Martin 1740-1808

sense of honor." But the young Joseph Martin was born on American soil. He grew totally unconstrained. He matured among social structures that were yet to be fully formed. Martin's own immediate family bore evidence of it. While fighting the Shawnasee, as Martin called them, Martin fathered seventeen children among five wives and partners, one of them a Cherokee he favored. Another wife came from the stately family of Thomas Graves, with whom the James would marry later and form financial partnerships.[8] Martin advanced to become Brigadier General of the 12th Virginia Militia. After the Revolution, he served in the Virginia Legislature.[9] Educated in the life of a planter, Martin's eccentricity came of his own design. A trait of self-purpose John M. James himself highly esteemed. Martin had prospered greatly in his self-defined willfulness. Where opportunity abounded, Martin amassed large land holdings. Later Martin bought Belmont Plantation on Leatherwood Creek near Martinsville in Virginia from Benjamin Harrison, the James family's neighbor.[10] John M. James himself had served under Harrison in the War of the Revolution. Martin earned respect from both white and Indian alike. For all bestowed upon Joseph Martin, he never felt comfortable in the old Virginia caste of his British aristocratic ancestry.

John M. James wished every power of self-directed character and self-learned ability that was evident in Gen. Joseph Martin be endowed in John's newborn son. The boy should grow to be an independent individualist, self-reliant, and naturally influential as any foreign born aristocrat.

Under the old English naming pattern for children, the newborn boy, being the couple's third son, should have been named after John's father, Joseph James the Elder. Having abandoned the Virginian mold as antiquated, John and Clara did not adhere to the old naming format with their previous children. Instead, John adapted the pattern cleverly, molding a new naming pattern of his own. "Mrs. James," John replied to Clara, "our son will be named Joseph Martin James."

COMING TARDY TO CHRIST WHEN HE WAS ALMOST THIRTY YEARS OLD, JOSEPH MARTIN JAMES WAS BAPTIZED BY BROTHER ELIJAH BARNES, a colleague of Joe's father. The guidance of Joe that followed directed Joe toward Baptist ministry.[11] John M. James was an occasional preacher himself, in the manner of his own contemporary and mentor, Rev. Elijah Craig. Another colleague, Brother John Taylor who pastored at Clear Creek Church in Kentucky's Woodford County, had baptized Craig. Taylor well assessed the preaching style of Elijah Craig that John M. James envisioned for his son:

"His preaching was of the most solemn style - his appearance as a man who had just come from the dead, of a delicate habit, a thin visage, large eyes and mouth, of great readiness of speech, the sweet melody of his voice, both to preach and sing bore all down before it; and when his voice was extended, it was like the loud sound of a sweet trumpet."[12]

John M. James was no mentor of ministry to his son. When John had the casual opportunity to preach, John's preaching was diffused by his preferences for plantations and politics. Joe would have to find a preaching model of his own. There were ample preachers, among the James family's religious community, whom young Joe could call upon.

Joe preferred the confrontational technique of exhortation he observed in the compelling preaching style of his own brother-in-law, Rev. Jeremiah Vardeman. The *Christian Repository* in 1854 reported of Vardeman,

"His manner of preaching was ready, and always without notes before him, and apparently extempore. His style was fervent and cleat, yet simple; and always directed toward the heart, rather than the mere intellect. His sermons were

calculated to leave the impression upon an unprejudiced mind, that he was anxious to do good than to be thought a great preacher."

Brother Jerry was fifteen years Joe's senior. Jerry's tall, physical presence towered over Joe's stocky frame by nine inches, maybe more. Over his lifetime, Brother Jerry would stand more than six feet and would bloat well beyond three hundred pounds.[13] His physical mass required him eventually to remain seated while preaching. Even when seated, Rev. Jeremiah Vardeman still exhilarated a draft of energy that impressed the faithful toward surrender and conversion.

Joe's stocky muscularity embodied a physical presence and voice well formed to create his own preaching style. Typical of his family, Joe broadcast an effortless voice that is natural and God given to the James – booming, surprising, deep and resonant. With energy of solicitation, if not outright seduction, Rev. Joe could withdraw the timbre of his voice to a crisp whisper, cleanly heard. Intently supplicating the men seated on the right in his church, the women seated on the left, and the enslaved standing in the gallery, Rev. Joe suffused them all with his imperceptible power, lofting the unchurched before him to Christ.

As a boy, Joe observed Brother Vardeman in the old Cedar Creek Church in Crab Orchard. Vardeman was young and inexperienced himself at preaching. Over time, Joe witnessed Jerry mature into his preaching style to become pastor at Boone's Creek Church in Fayette County. He heard about other churches Vardeman formed in Bardstown and distant Nashville that also resulted in his founding and pastoring the First Baptist Church of Lexington, all testaments to Vardeman's unequaled powers of presentation, solicitation, exhortation, and conversion.[14] With no formal education, Jerry never bothered to persuade minds. He admitted, *"I aim more for the heart than the head."*[15]

About 1810, Vardeman pastored at David's Fork Church outside Lexington. While remaining pastor full time at David's Fork, he split his remaining time ambitiously among the churches called Lilbegrud, Grassy Lick, and Bryan's Station. As the migrant population entering Kentucky grew, so also grew Brother Jerry's power to draw the unsettled migrants to Christ.[16] Having firmly established a generation of churches, Jerry and Rev. Joe's sister Betsy were properly dismissed from David's Fork in September of 1830. Missions in the Missouri Territory waited.

Rev. Jeremiah Vardeman 1775 – 1842

Husband of Elizabeth "Betsy" James abt 1778 – 1822
Founder of Schools of Theology at Georgetown College in Kentucky
& William Jewell College in Missouri

Following Jeremiah and Betsy's departure, Rev. Joe continued to pastor at Sinking Creek. Assignments soon drew him to Rock Lick, then New Hope and Mount Olivet Churches, all of which became names Vardeman gave to new churches on the Missouri frontier, where Brother Jerry Vardeman convened them in an association, later known as the Missouri Baptist Convention.[17] By the grace of his mentor, Rev. Joe soon earned a valued reputation himself among Baptists, as the *"ablest preacher in the Cumberland Association."*

Joe inherited Flat Lick Baptist Church, founded by his father on the fourth Saturday of January in 1799 with other preachers.[18] Blind Brother Thomas Hansford, esteemed for his plainness, illiteracy, and age preached previously at the Cedar Creek Church in Crab Orchard in Lincoln County where Jerry Vardeman first learned to preach. Joe's father urged Hansford to bring Jerry Vardeman into ministry.[19] Within months of the founding of Flat Lick Church, Hansford left to reform the old Sinking Creek Church as the First Baptist Church of Somerset. In 1816, Hansford then brought Rev. Joe from Flat Lick to Somerset, to replace himself as pastor of First Baptist. Family friend Rev. John M. Sallee also followed from Flat Lick to pastor the First Baptist Church in the years to follow. [20]

John M. James had contributed his land for the log structure of Flat Lick Church. Brother James Fears served as Flat Lick's first pastor. Fears accelerated Flat Lick through the Great Revival into the formation of the Tate's Creek Association in lower central Kentucky. Founder Charles Westerman from Tennessee returned home soon after Flat Lick's founding to establish other churches of his own. Brother Elijah Barnes, known affectionately throughout the country knobs as Old Daddy, was another founder of Flat Lick. He was a highly respected example of piety and devotion. In this "Mother Church" of all central Kentucky churches, Rev. Joe Martin James served six years, following Pastor Stephen Collier whom Westerman had brought from Tennessee.

Joe was well on his way to achieving the success of Jerry Vardeman for seeding churches and growing congregations. But Joe stumbled badly. Joe's congregation at Flat Lick progressively tired of the unexpected and surprising turpitude Joe made of his private life. Despite his extraordinary gifts, Joe's personal life shook his church to its foundations, leaving no one un-afflicted. Finally, Rev. Joe's congregation turned against him.[21]

EVERYONE RECOGNIZED REV. JOE HAD A PREDILECTION FOR ALCOHOL, EXCEPT REV. JOE HIMSELF. Among the James, Joe certainly was not the first to evidence such a problem. Even Joe's namesake, Gen. Joseph Martin, had earned a reputation for "debauchery," however of the kind known for taking a single drink only, not for the wholesale drunkenness practiced by Brother Joe.[22] In night's candle light, when the James family recounted stories about the War of the Revolution, Joe's father sometimes spoke of his brother Joseph James the Younger, whose own reputation encountered a problem with spirits.

Capt. Joseph James the Younger stood in command of three hundred of the Stafford County Militia. They were camped at Richland Plantation across from Mt. Vernon on the Potomac River when Lord Dunmore and Capt. Andrew Hammond sailed up to William Brent's plantation at the mouth of the Aquia River. John Parke Custis reported to his stepfather, Gen. George Washington, about Joseph James and the evening's events.

"A Capt. James with the militia were stationed there who all got drunk, and kept challenging the Man of War to come ashore, and upbraided them with Cowardice. Hammond sent 150 Men who landed about 10 o'clock...the Militia were asleep after their drinking Frolick and did not discover the Enemy until they landed and their vessels began to Fire. Capt. James desired his Men to shift for Themselves and ran off without firing a Gun...Capt. James is to be held for Cowardice." [23]

The *Virginia Gazette* reported, *"Captain James of the Stafford Militia was blamed for the disaster at Richland and was court-martialed on September 20, 1776."* [24] Drinking may have been a predilection of Capt. Joseph James the Younger, but cowardice, blame, or persecution was not.

Justices at the Stafford County court house heard the depositions of multiple witnesses. A week later, the *Virginia Gazette* reported their conclusion. The destruction to William Brent's Richland plantation was *"owing to the militia not being better armed and disciplined."* Witnesses attested that Capt. James had held his ground, though all but fifteen of his men had fled. They reported the British *"approached under a constant fire of the canon and swivels from a gondola, two sloops, and nine boats."* About *"Capt. James deficient in spirit as has been frequently alleged,"* the court found that he was not. The trial of Capt. Joseph James the Younger would not be the only legal proceeding to test the acts and character of James family members. A variety of allegations and legal proceedings lay in waiting, from then well into the family's future in modern day.

Unlike Joseph James' combative survival, Brother Joe's addiction subsumed him. Joe may not have emulated the preaching style of his father's mentor Elijah Craig, as his father had wished, but Joe certainly found other characteristics in old Brother Craig to imitate.

Although a generation apart, Brother Craig and Rev. Joe were of a similar background. Neither one had formal schooling. Both had brothers in ministry who were of more stable temperament, better accomplished, and more adept with the development of church structure.[25] Brother Craig first held prayer meetings in a tobacco barn.[26] Rev. Joe held evening prayers with Brother Jerry in the tenant log cabins that dotted John M. James' fields and bridle trails.[27] In addition to his preaching, Craig engaged in multiple businesses, including the manufacture of bourbon. At the bottom of the hill from his home, Rev. Joe operated a store from a log cabin on Flat Lick Creek. Back in the knobs, Joe manufactured the whiskey he sold in his store house. Craig laid out a new town he called Lebanon, later renamed Georgetown.[28] Rev. Joe established Shopville, east of Somerset, not far from the Flat Lick church, reflective of the family's lingering lore of Shropshire in England on the Welsh border.

Elijah Craig fearlessly challenged authority - an example not lost on Joseph Martin James either. Craig preached brazenly as an un-ordained commoner with no license. His success threatened the gentry and the Anglican establishment. A sheriff and posse were sent to seize him. Craig was not hiding. He was plowing his fields. Three magistrates arraigned Craig in Culpeper Court. Hearing no arguments, they ordered Craig to jail. Bound in public stocks for a month, Craig preached defiantly in his restraints to all passers-by, until he was released.[29] Elijah Craig accepted himself as a rebel preacher, who was made by authorities into an outlaw preacher.

Still well respected for the sincerity of his preaching, Craig remained an irritant, even among his own. His chronic confrontations were exacerbated by his compulsive land speculation. His "petulant fault finding" with fellow preachers proved Craig no peacemaker. He became a terror to fellow Baptist ministers. Setting aside his affair with God, in his affairs with men Brother Elijah Craig proved fearless, confrontational, and rebellious.[30]

When the separate Baptists broke into conflict with the regular Baptists, Elijah Craig seized their disruption to unleash a new controversy. Craig maintained preachers should not hold themselves above their congregations. After all, they addressed each other as brother and sister. Craig pleaded persistently with ministers to be more like their congregants. Craig insisted, preachers should become bi-vocational. They should sustain themselves by a business or profession. They should not live or prosper off those to whom they ministered.[31] The idea was radical.

When Flat Lick Church was founded, Brother Elijah Craig owned more than 4,000 acres of land, eleven horses, thirty-two enslaved persons and businesses including paper manufacturing and rope manufacturing from the abundant hemp in the region. He operated a shop selling hardware and spirits together with William West. In his store Craig invented a more popular and much improved whiskey, called bourbon. For all his shortcomings of rebelliousness and radicalness, Elijah Craig demonstrated complete integrity. He planted one foot firmly in his faith. The other stood among his flock. Elijah Craig's prosperity inured to both.

Georgetown College

Giddings Hall

Elijah Craig turned from educating his peers to enlightening youth who might better hear him. In Scott County, Craig acquired 1,000 acres on which he platted the new town of Lebanon. He posted an advertisement in the *Kentucky Gazette: "Education. Notice is hereby given that on Monday, 28ᵗʰ of January next, a school would be opened....where a commodious house, sufficient to contain fifty or sixty scholars, will be prepared."* [32] The school was named Rittenhouse Academy, later renamed Georgetown College.[33] John M. James subscribed two of his own family to be educated at Georgetown College.

Like Elijah Craig, the bi-vocational Rev. Joseph Martin James established a grist mill on Flat Lick Creek. Joe also operated a blacksmith shop. While Joe's father certainly was becoming fi nancially as well established as Craig, Rev. Joe himself was not. Joe set the enslaved among the James family to build a new Flat Lick church constructed of stone. Joe also employed the same stone mason, David Carson, to build Joe a stone residence on Flat Lick Creek, upslope from his log cabin store.

Rev. Elijah Craig remained controversial all his days, to his end when his son-in-law, Rev. Josiah Pitts, the son of Rev. Younger Pitts who married Frank and Jesse's parents, finally executed Craig's estate.[34] Like his father's mentor, Rev. Joe turned fearless against his peers, too. Controversy of a different nature devastated Rev. Joe and his family of twenty-one children, when Joe succumbed to the alcohol he made and sold.

TWICE MARRIED, REV. JOE HAD FATHERED SEVENTEEN CHILDREN ALREADY WHEN HE TOOK UP WITH A YOUNG GIRL FROM HIS CONGREGATION, NAMED PERMELIA ESTEPP. A month following the birth of their first child, Joe took the girl to adjoining Laurel County, where he married her.[35] No doubt, Joe intended to legitimize his child with Permelia, but Joe willfully ignored the reality of his actions. His marriage to Permelia Estepp was bigamous. Rev. Joe was still married to his second wife Rhoda May.[36]

Joe's namesake, Gen. Joseph Martin, once had come the same. Martin was still married to the Cherokee woman Betsy Ward when he also married Susannah Graves. The Native Ward maintained Martin's frontier holdings on the Holsten River, while Graves looked after Martin's permanent home in Virginia, a story often retold by Joe's father. Betsy Ward left the Holsten to attend to her dying mother in North Carolina. When she returned to Joseph Martin in Virginia, she was warmly welcomed by his second wife Susannah Graves, not as his lawful wife, but rather as communal family.[37] Rev. Joe was a fool if he held a like expectation of his wife of thirteen years, Rhoda May.

Like Gen. Martin, Rev. Joe also had married a superior woman. Rhoda May descended from a family of German scholars and teachers. She was a severely stern, no-nonsense kind of woman, but not near as forgiving or accommodating as the wives of Gen. Joseph Martin. When Joe unwittingly imitated his namesake, Joe apparently did not fully perceive the maelstrom he unleashed upon his wife, children, or church.

Rev. Joe set up a home for Permelia Estepp across Flat Lick Creek within direct view of his home with Rhoda May. In every year for the next four years, Rev. Joe proceeded to father additional children by both wives. On one bank of Flat Lick Creek, he lived in his alcoholism with the naive and youthful Permelia Estepp. There he fathered a child with her. The next two years, struggling in recovery on the opposite bank of the creek under the unyielding discipline of Rhoda May, Joe fathered two more children by her. Finally Joe returned to his alcoholism and Permelia to father two additional children. Up to his fifty-seventh birthday, Rev. Joseph Martin James brought twenty-two children into the world among his wives Martha "Betsy" McAlister, Rhoda May, and Permelia Estepp.

As Rev. Joe became totally intolerable to his community, shame fell upon the entire James family.[38] Ultimately, Rev. Joe's congregation and family no longer could bear his impropriety and outrageousness, let alone how they were being forced to deal with it. Joe's self-destruction saved them further trials.

"But, alas, for the frailty of human nature! In his old age, he yielded to the seduction of strong drink, and was disgraced. This led on further to the heinous crime of adultery. The poor old man became an outcast, and his sun went down in a dark cloud..." [39]

Flat Lick Baptist Church dismissed and defrocked Rev. Joseph Martin James. Joe's brother in-law, Rev. Robert McAlister by Joe's first wife Betsy McAlister, assumed Joe's duties as pastor.[40] After graduating Georgetown College with Frank and Jesse's father Rev. Robert Sallee James, Joe's son Rev. John James followed Robert McAlister as Flat Lick's pastor. The young Rev. John James would partially redeem his father's soiled reputation by pastoring devotedly without blemish, first in Adair County at Russell Springs, then later in Columbia, Missouri. Pastorships followed him in Kentucky's Hart and Barrow Counties, and lastly in Paris, Texas where Frank James lived nearby in his retirement. Rev. John James fulfilled the promise of his father's failed talent, dying in Paris, Texas in 1902. Unlike his disreputable father Rev. Joe, Baptist history recognized Joe's son Rev. John James as *"an eminently Godly minister."* [41]

Joe's wife Rhoda May accepted her husband's fall from grace with a dose of historical, if not genetic, understanding. Ostracism was familiar to her May family. Drunkenness and exile had brought them to America.

In Germany in the winter of 1700-1701, Rhoda's great-grandfather George May and his brother John found themselves ostracized in the University Student's Rebellion. Excessively drinking crambambuli, the brothers' stupor voiced seditious opinions against Germany's crowned heads and potentates. In a riot that followed, five hundred of their fellow

Rhoda May 1806-1889
Widowed second wife of Rev. Joseph Martin James

students were arrested and imprisoned. The May brothers were part of fifteen who escaped.[42] George and John May donned sailors' uniforms and took immediate passage to America, landing in Philadelphia the following year. Wherever they settled in America, the brothers were referred to by the slur *"Black Dutch."*[43] Rhoda's grandfather Jacob May, who fought in the American Revolution, migrated afterward into the Kentucky frontier in 1783. He settled on lands on Hanging Fork off Dick's River, adjacent to the neighboring lands of Capt. Joseph James the Younger and Gov. Isaac Shelby.[44]

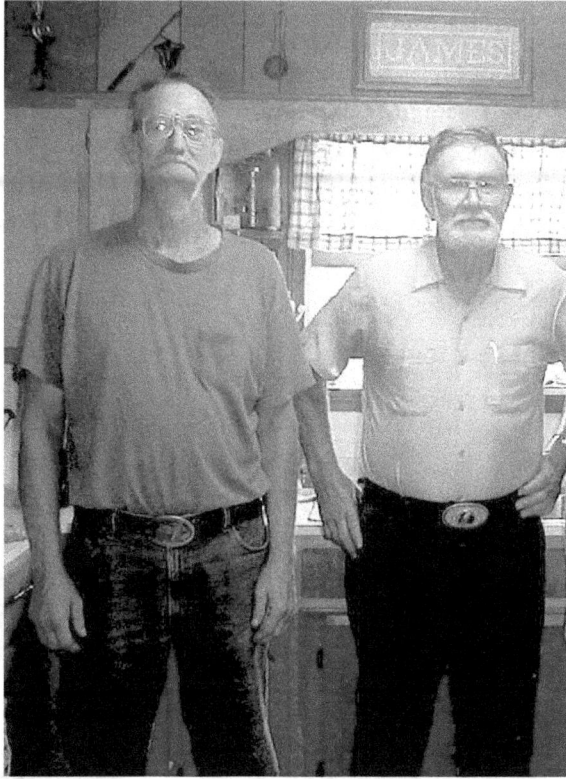

Brothers Ernest Smythe & Raymond Edward James
After 150 years, they still bristle under the stigma "the bastard bunch"

Shortly after his expulsion, Rev. Joseph Martin James died on March 29, 1848 at the age of fifty-seven. He left the forty-two-year-old Rhoda May a widow, tainted in reputation for the next forty-one years remaining in her life. He also left her ten orphan children to raise without support as a single mother. Rev. Joe left Permelia Estepp in the same condition with three additional orphans, all under three years of age. Generations of the young widow's progeny would suffer the sins of their father. Spurred by an in-law family of the James, the progeny of Permelia Estepp and Joseph Martin James were stigmatized by their community as *"the bastard bunch."*

ONE BY ONE, THE JAMES FAMILY BEGAN TO SCATTER. The ostracism of Rev. Joseph Martin James burdened the entire James family in a most repellent way. Each one felt Brother Joe's sting.

Among Joe's children by his first wife Betsy McAlister, the eldest son Henry stopped teaching school and migrated with his brother Joseph McAlister James to farm lands Mack acquired in Pesotum, Illinois. There, Henry resumed teaching. Later Henry moved onto Texas, returned into Oklahoma Indian Territory, and finally settled at Gibson Station, today's

Samuel Chaudoin 1813 – 1893
& wife
Sarah "Sallie" James 1817 – 1898
Daughter of Rev. Joseph Martin James & Martha McAlister

Rev. Joseph Martin Shadowen 1848 - Unk.

Son of Samuel & Sally James Chaudoin,
who preached for a lifetime under the blemish of his disgraced grandfather
whom he never knew

Waggoner, Oklahoma where he died. Joe's eldest daughter Sally stayed in Pulaski County as the wife of Samuel Chaudoin Sr. It became less and less recognized among the community that Rev. Lewis Weaver Chaudoin, Samuel's granduncle, had married Jesse and Frank's grandfather William James. Sally's sister, Elizabeth, was the first to go with Henry to Mack's lands in Pesotum in the fall of 1850 with her husband Squire William Lee.[45] There, Squire William and Sally James Lee entered the history book of Champaign County as the first white people to settle there.[46] Her brother George W. James left Pulaski County and reverted to living in Crab Orchard in Lincoln County. There he built an unusual reputation as a generous and considerate banker. His burial high on a hill overlooking Crab Orchard measured the distance he maintained from his father's soiled reputation. Joe's son William served the Confederacy, but disappeared in Missouri. Daniel Morgan James, named after Col. Daniel Morgan in the War of the Revolution, also followed his brother to Illinois where he lived outside Danville, after first helping Mack settle land Mack acquired in Indiana in a new town called Goodland.

Family of Rev. Martin Nall James 1833 - 1911

Of the next batch of orphans Rev. Joe left to the widowed Rhoda May, Cyrenius Waite James took his family first to Illinois to Mack's plantations in Douglas County. In the Civil War, Cy served for the Union in Company B of the 79th Illinois Volunteers under Allen Buckner. Cy was wounded at Murfreesboro, captured and imprisoned in Marietta, Georgia. While in prison Cy envisioned his daughter's ghost the night she choked on a grain of corn and died.[47] Following the war, Cy took his family from Illinois to Texas, walking the distance, limping on his cane. While camping in Oklahoma, Cy's son John was apprehended by the Choctaw. The meeting would lead to a lifelong friendship between John and the Choctaw. After serving the Confederacy, Rev. Martin Nall James elected himself as a Baptist missionary, moving his family first to Macon County in Missouri, but finally settling in Monroe County. The youngest son Andrew was wounded at Tullahoma, fighting for the Union in Company F of the 2nd Kentucky Cavalry. Following discharge, Andrew went to Indiana or Illinois, never to be heard from again. Martha Ellen James followed her other half siblings to Mack's farms in Illinois. Mary Harriet James, age eighteen, remained at Shopville to defend the family farm during the Civil War, alone with her widowed mother Rhoda May. In a newspaper interview, Mary Harriet later stated her encounter on the eve of the Battle of Mill Springs,

"My mother and I were home alone one day, when a passing Regiment started to take our horse. My mother begged them to leave it. Just then the Captain rode up and said 'Lady, which side do you belong to?' My mother said, 'Sir, you have asked a hard question, for I have two sons on each side.' At that, the Captain called his men and rode away leaving our horse." [48]

Sisters Mary Harriet & Susan Harriet James

After the war, Mary Harriet James married the returning veteran Daniel J. Owens. Owens had fought in Company M of Kentucky's 7th Cavalry of the Confederacy and was taken prisoner and incarcerated seven months in Ohio. Confined with Owens was David Hunt James, a cousin who lived in

Family of Edward Perry James 1847 - 1931

Lexington, Kentucky. David was captured with John Hunt Morgan. Daniel and Mary Harriet James Owens eventually departed for Decatur, Illinois. Mary Harriet's sister, Susan Harriet James, remained at home in Shopville to marry the elegant, intelligent, and handsome teacher Joseph Allen Herrin. He had served for the Union with Andrew James when young Andrew was shot.[49] Descendants of Joseph Allen Herrin and Susan Harriet James continue to occupy the original settlement lands of John M. James today in Pulaski County. Edward Perry James lived in the stone house built by Rev. Joe's slaves, but eventually he relocated his family to the town of Berea. There he built a new home of his own, away from the rest of the family. The youngest son Daniel lived briefly in Pike County, Illinois, before returning home to Shopville.[50]

Of Rev. Joe's three children orphaned as "the bastard bunch" to the disgraced Permelia Estepp, the eldest John Thomas James served in Company B of the 12th Kentucky Union Volunteer Infantry. He fathered nine children, naming one Permelia in honor of his debased mother. As if by dictate of fate, the child only lived to age three. John Thomas James himself was killed tragically, too, when he was run over by an automobile in 1923. His pants had become hooked on the engine crank of a car in Somerset. He was pulled beneath the car and dragged to his death. Rev. Joe's second child by Permelia Estepp, Lucy Frances James, married Alexander M. Barclay. They, too, moved to Missouri. The couple had two daughters who married, but neither daughter bore any children. Rev. Joe's youngest child by Permelia Estepp, Joel M. James, fought for the Confederacy, married a Barclay girl in Missouri, and then disappeared.

Judge John Thomas James 1844 - 1923

The stone home built by Rev. Joseph Martin James

Side view before the Civil War & front view today

Personal disgrace complicated by the divisions of the Civl War broke apart this James family. More embarrassment and stigma was yet to come after the war. For the time being, Baptist history remembered Rev. Joseph Martin James, the father of these twenty-two orphaned children, with a measured dose of kindness. Despite the grief Joe inflicted upon his family and community, his church politely and forgivingly memorialized Joseph Martin James in their history, forever silently, as *"talented but erratic."*[51]

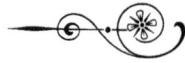

Joseph McAlister James 1818 - 1905

aka Joseph McJames

Chapter Three

Goodland

Following Rev. Joe's death in March of 1848, Joseph McAlister James divorced himself from his father's ignominy. Leaving his father's stone house in Pulaski County, Mack drove his horse and buggy several miles north to Danville in Boyle County. There he adopted his new identity as Joseph McJames.

D anville is the birthplace of the Kentucky Commonwealth. In the summer of 1784, Mack's grandfather John M. James stood among others in attendence as Judge Harry Innes drafted the petition to partition the District of Kentucky from Virginia. The separation opened Kentucky as an official frontier, west of the nation's founding Virginia Colony. Later, Judge Innes stood accused in the Spanish Conspiracy that charged the Judge's sole purpose in seeking division was to enable Innes, James Wilkenson, and other supporters to profit by selling the independent district to Spain. When John M. James served in the Kentucky legislature in the early 1800s, John defended the honor of Judge Innes.[1] The efforts of John M. James achieved exoneration for the judge. In years to come, the honorable Innes name affixed to the grandchildren of John M. James, when Admiral Chapman Coleman Todd married John's great granddaughter Anna Eliza James. The couple named their second child

Harry Innes Todd. Admiral Todd was a great grandson of Harry Innes.[2]

When Mack first arrived in Danville, the small town already claimed many firsts. Danville was the first capitol of the Kentucky District of Virginia. It was a seat of intellectual enlightenment, and also of Presbyterianism. Established outside of Danville in 1783, Transylvania College was the first college in the West. John Bradford, who married Mack's cousin Elizabeth James, was chairman of Transylvania's Board of Trustees.[3] The first Kentucky court house was erected in Danville in 1785 by Isaac Hite, a business acquaintance of John M. James. The first U.S. Post Office west of the Alleghenies was built in 1792. In the same year, the first Kentucky constitution was signed at Danville. The first law school was founded in 1799. Centre College was established in 1820. Centre's initial classical curriculum was intended to prepare Presbyterians for ministry. Among the students enrolled at Centre in 1853, when Mack resided in Danville, was Charles Bruce Younger, a native of Liberty, Missouri, and a first cousin of the Younger family, with whom Mack's grandfather John M. James had been neighbors in Crab Orchard. Younger transferred to Centre from St. Joseph's, a Catholic college in Bardstown, where he had been enrolled since returning from the Mexican War. Among Younger's classmates was Thomas T. Crittenden, who later as Governor of Missouri would plot to capture Jesse James.[4]

Mack's selection of Danville was deliberate. Mack purposely sought to detach himself from his father's community of Baptist preachers. In Danville, Mack intended to re-align himself with the Presbyterian community of his grandfather Rev. Joseph McAlister, on his mother's side. Mack set up a modest tailoring shop, as did his grandfather McAlister following the Revolution. Mack also became Danville's first cemetery sextant, affixed to the Presbyterian Church on Main Street.

In the brilliance of Danville, Mack broke with the bindings of his past completely. He extended the same benefit to his enslaved, who accompanied him. Almost a decade before the outbreak of the Civil War, Mack set free his slaves in Danville.

Mack had heard the persistent debate about slavery in his father's Baptist church. For two generations, the most able and pious of Baptist ministers in Kentucky opposed slavery, to the point of retarding the growth of their own ministries.[5] Even before Mack was born, the Baptist association judged it *"improper for ministers, churches, or associations to meddle with emancipation from slavery, or any other political subject, and as such, we advise ministers and churches to have nothing to do therewith."* For two hundred years, every generation of Mack's family in America had owned slaves. While their enslaved were welcomed to worship at Flat Lick Church in its balcony, segregated from the general congregation, in its silence the church positioned itself not to support abolition. Even Brother Jeremiah Vardeman, the husband of Mack's Aunt Betsy, advocated against emancipation when he stood before the Tate's Creek Baptist Association.

As Pulaski County's presiding judge-executive, Mack's grandfather John M. James had governed the entire enslaved population of Pulaski County. Mack's uncle, Capt. Harry James, was the slave patroller for the eastern half of the county. He enforced the slave code with his brother-in-law Jack Griffin, who patrolled the western half. If Harry or Jack found a slave at an unlawful gathering, or holding personal property without written permission from a master, at will they could inflict ten lashes of the whip. If they obtained a magistrate's permission, up to thirty-nine lashes might be inflicted.[6] In 1810, Capt. Harry owned two male and five female slaves of his own.

John M. James himself owned no less than twenty-seven slaves, often up to a hundred. They tended both his home and fields.[7] However, the second largest slave holder in the Cumberland region was Sheriff Josiah Evans, the uncle of Mack's wife Elizabeth Vardeman James. The largest slave holder in Pulaski County was John M. James' esteemed friend, Cyrenius Waite, a merchant from Massachusetts who established Waite's Hill overlooking the central business district of Somerset on the road up and out from town. Joseph Martin James had named one of his sons Cyrenius Waite James after the notable family friend. Waite always possessed more than one hundred enslaved people. They built him the community of Waitsboro on the Cumberland River. Pulaski County had earned a reputation for being the most stringent with its population of slaves. They also made Pulaski County one of the Commonwealth's most productive agrarian producers.[8]

Slavery was a turbulent issue within the James family, causing division that scathed each member of the James family. When the Baptist minister Rev. Alexander Campbell confronted the Baptist community, Campbell stated the relationship between master and slave was not necessarily sinful, but it was not expedient to the advancement of society. His Baptist sect became identified as Campbellites - to which at least one James family member, Dr. Samuel Evans James, subscribed. Others, like Mack James, also embraced enlightened progress, more than remaining affixed with a tradition that had become a corrupt practice.

Further division among the James over the issue followed. In Lexington in 1831, Henry Clay defended the right to petition for slavery's abolition. In the same year, the patroller Capt. Harry James departed his Pulaski County home for Hickman County in the westernmost part of Kentucky, taking his slaves with him. He then crossed into Missouri. Within five years Mack's cousin Burton Allen James departed with his slaves from Logan County for Mathias prairie that became Mississippi County in Missouri. Four years later, Frank and Jesse's grandmother, Sally Lindsay, left for Missouri with her new husband Robert Thomason and Thomason's enslaved. Their wagon train was the last of the Thomason family to vacate Kentucky. Thomason's family had been vacating their Georgetown lands for half a decade. All removed to Missouri.

Between Georgetown and Stamping Ground at Blue Springs, Thomason's neighbor Vice President Richard Mentor Johnson, under whom Thomason had served in the War of 1812, consternated the contentious issue further. Johnson surprisingly took another of the Johnson family's slaves as his second wife.[9] Johnson's fate as a future United States President was doomed when he introduced his first wife, Julia Chinn, to Washington D.C. society. Julia was a mulatto slave, whom Johnson had inherited from his father. She died of cholera in the 1833 epidemic, after which Johnson married a second wife from among his family's enslaved, who possessed a Lightfoot surname.

In 1842, Mack's cousin Robert Sallee James and his new wife Zerelda Cole set out for Missouri with seven newly acquired enslaved persons of their own. Robert Sallee James had no income yet. The acquisition of his enslaved, calculated at an 1843 value to be $7-10,000 in modern currency, is presumed to have been made by gift of family and faithful supporters, culled from the surplus of slaves then inhabiting the Commonwealth.[10] The gift was intended to assist Robert in establishing his mission in Missouri. Putting the enslaved immediately to work upon arrival at his new farm, Robert was expected to return to Georgetown to complete his education before establishing his mission in the West.

When Mack freed his slaves in Danville, he financed them in establishing their own farms in the bottom lands outside town off

Main St., Danville, at the Northwest Corner of Third St.

Clark's Run.[11] He also donated land for a church on the rise of the hill, financing its construction, too. The St. James Baptist Church remains functional in the 21st century as a Methodist church.[12]

Freed from the enslavement of his family notoriety as he was of his own slaves, Mack thrived in Danville's progressive climate. Off Main Street on north Third Street, backing up to the Boyle County courthouse built by Isaac Hite, Mack built James Hall.[13] From his grandfather, Mack had learned the value of real estate location. In Somerset, John M. James had acquired a key block of the town center for himself when he laid out the town and its square. When John became Pulaski County's first judge-executive, the acquisition afforded John an instant sale for the site of a new county courthouse. John M. James' close friend John Sallee subscribed to purchase an adjacent Somerset city block. As a simple merchant holding no political office, Sallee would take years to resell his individual lots.[14]

From his grandfather, Mack also had learned success derives from being of service to one's community. Mack developed James Hall into Danville's principal community center. His two story building housed the Danville Post Office and Central National Bank on the first level, plus an additional store. At various times Mack sold these commercial spaces separately, like condominium ownership interests. James Hall, which he retained under his own ownership, occupied the entire second level.[15] Mack's social center on Third Street became home to civic meetings, events, balls, commencements, and political events. Each June, Centre College held its Commencement

Ball, as did the Danville Colored School. An annual ball was held on each birthday of George Washington. On the 4th of July, speeches at James Hall lasted all day.[16] During the Kentucky State Fair, James Hall hosted the Fair Week Ball. All throughout the year, the hall hosted fund-raising bazaars, spelling bees, roller skating, and senior dances.

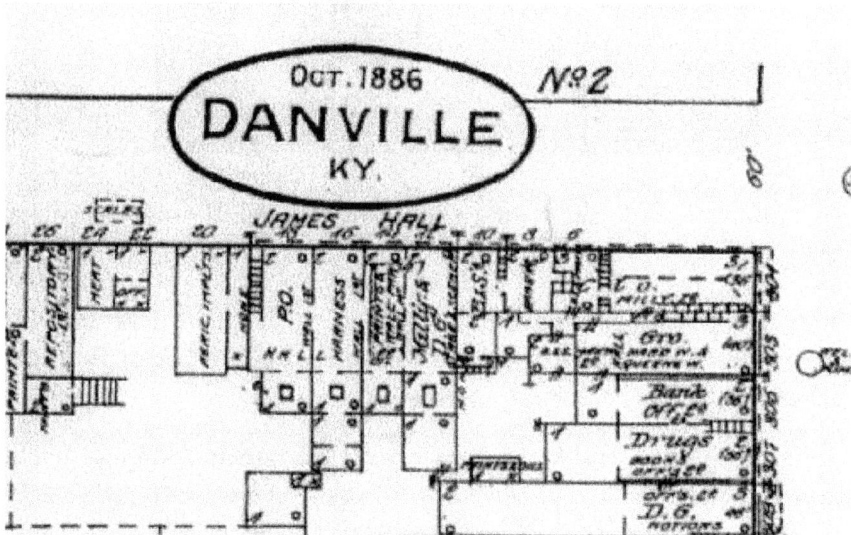

James Hall

On Third St, at the northwest corner of Main St.

Between community events, James Hall played host to traveling theatrical productions. Impresario Pat Laughlin imported shows from Europe.[17] Local talent was always proudly exhibited, as was popular Chautauqua presentations. The Danville Philharmonic Society organized at James Hall under A. M. Burbank of the music department of Caldwell College. A traveling repertory theatre routinely arrived at James Hall from Cincinnati to entertain Danville's residents and farmers.

When the city fathers organized the Danville Town Hall Company to compete against the aging James Hall, Mack refurbished James Hall as a professional opera house. He installed an innovation - permanent seating. He commissioned a new tableau backdrop to be painted by Edward H. Fox, a relation of the prominent and popular attorney Fountain T. Fox, whom Charles Bruce Younger campaigned to defeat when Fox ran for the state legislature against Albert Gallatin Talbott. Mack's cousin, A. J. James of Pulaski County, studied law with Fountain Fox in his Danville home at 240 N. 2nd St.[18] Mack's new theatre attracted John Whitcome Riley of Indiana who recited his poetry, and Gen John B. Gordon who recounted "*The Fall of Atlanta.*" Despite Mack's improvements, when the Danville Opera House produced the opera *The Mikado*, everyone referred to the opera playing at Old James Hall.[19] [20]

Next door to the Boyle County courthouse on the northwest corner of 4th and Main Streets, Mack acquired the aging Fields House.[21] The old inn was first built in 1793 as the Black Horse Tavern owned, built, and operated by Jeremiah Clemens Sr., a first cousin of Samuel Langhorne Clemens.[22] When Sam Clemens had become world famous as Mark Twain he had visited Louisville. Later, Twain reminisced about the time he encountered a stranger in Louisville.

"Guess you and I are 'bout the greatest in our line," the stranger remarked to Twain.

I began to wonder as to what throne of greatness he held, thought Twain, who then asked, "What's your name?"

"Jesse James," replied the stranger.[23]

The Fields House was long called the Clemens Hotel, though old timers persisted in calling it the Black Horse Inn.[24] The name Black Horse Inn bore an unpleasant association for Mack, reminding him of the inn in Woodford County where Frank and Jesse's mother, Zerelda Cole, was born. The old Cole family inn had a violent and unsavory reputation. The boys' mother had witnessed her uncle Amos Cole killed there. Conveniently for Mack, locals identified a property more by a place's former name or former owner, ignoring completely its current name or current owner. Regardless, Mack sought to rebrand his hotel, as he had his personal identity.

The Fields House obtained its name in 1856 when W. M. Fields acquired the property from Charles Caldwell, who had owned it between 1820 and 1840.[25] In 1875, W. M. Fields [26] sold Fields House to Columbus B. Saunders, whose son Clay would marry Mack's daughter Mary Ellen James. When the old hotel burned early in 1876, Mack's son-in-law appears to have died as a casualty of the fire. Mack paid the costs of Clay Saunders' burial in Danville's Bellevue Cemetery. Then Mack rebuilt his hotel as an impressive

The St. James Hotel (r)

Northeast corner of Main & Fourth Sts. next to the Boyle County Court House

three story, brick structure, with twenty-five rooms, one interior bathroom, and commercial stores.[27]

On the 4th of July in 1877, Mack hosted the grand opening of the St. James Hotel. Mack invited Jeremiah Clemens Jr. who was born at the inn in 1791 and was a son of the original owner-builder, to christen the new hotel. Old timers immediately began to refer to the completely new St. James Hotel as the Old Clemens Hotel.[28] Today, the hotel's site is a public park where summer concerts are held. The site was donated to the City of Danville by the descendants of Daniel Weisiger Jr. who operated the Weisiger Hotel in the 1800s on the northeast corner of Main and Ann Streets in Frankfort. Weisiger descendants also operated the Weisiger Hotel in Danville.

The triangle of the St. James Hotel, Isaac Hite's Boyle County courthouse, and James Hall placed Mack James in the heart of Danville. At no time was this more evident than after the bloody Battle of Perryville.[29] Danville's heart was opened to the war casualties, as the town opened its public structures for hospitals and emergency services.

War's end did not bring the end to hostilities. Danville was visited on January 29, 1865 by William Clarke Quantrill and his band of guerillas, including Frank James, the Youngers, and the Pence brothers.[30] Capt. William L. Gross, who manned the Union telegraph at the Danville train station,

Weisiger Park
Site of the St. James Hotel today

wired his superiors. *"Thirty-five guerillas, under Captain Clark, all dressed in Federal uniform, entered Danville this morning. They robbed some of the citizens and one boot store and left on the Perryville Pike at 11:15 a.m. They claimed, at first, to be Federal troops, Fourth Missouri Cavalry, but there is no doubt they are guerillas in disguise. They gutted my office pretty effectually."* [31] Reports were made that a book store also was plundered.[32]

Immediately, Danville native Gen. Speed Smith Fry rode in pursuit. At Perryville, the guerillas swung north toward Harrodsburg. Maj. James H. Bridgewater pursued a northern route to Harrodsburg from his home in Stanford. Bridgewater's wife was a Pence, and cousin to the Pence brothers Bridgewater was chasing. Bridegwater caught up with the guerillas several miles west of Harrodsburg as they slept in the two homes of Alice Van Arsdale and John Adams. In a cold, snowy, middle-of-the-night shootout, four of the guerillas were killed, and nine others captured, including Jim Younger.[33] Those killed were buried expediently in the frozen ground of Oakland Church Cemetery. Forty years later, Frank James, Col. Jack Chinn and his son Kit re-interred their fallen cohorts in the newly dedicated Confederate plot in Spring Hill Cemetery in nearby Harrodsburg. With Bridgewater still in pursuit, Quantrill and Frank James rode west to safety to Taylorsville in Nelson County. Quantrill sequestered himself at the farm of

Oakland Church Cemetery, now Upland Christian Cemetery
Quantrill's Confederate Plot, Springhill Cemetery, Harrodsburg

George Warfield, where on June 6th he would be found, and shot. Quantrill died a few days later in a Catholic Louisville hospital. Frank James had hid in a familiar home near Samuels Depot. When news arrived, reporting the killing of Quantrill, Frank James was found reading one of his new books.

In the years following the Civil War, Mack heard periodically from relatives about Frank and Jesse James. Their guerilla activities were relentless, and their notoriety was quickly spreading. The brothers' acts underscored Mack's lingering embarrassment over his "talented but erratic" father. The Civil War was over, but the James brothers would not allow the war to end. Much like Mack's father, Frank and Jesse James persisted in unbridled willfulness.

As children, Frank and Jesse once rolled down the hill sloping from the stone house David Ransom Carson had built for Rev. Joe, the same home in which Mack himself had been raised. The brothers then were welcomed by family in Pulaski County.[34] As veterans of the war, the brothers no longer were those childhood innocents. The brothers had made the war their own. They transformed wartime guerilla careers into exploits of political, outlaw rebellion. From then on, the James in Pulaski County remained aware and watchful of those boys.

Around 1876, in-laws of the James in Pulaski County reported the brothers had attempted to rob the First National Bank of Somerset. Five men entered the public square across from a side street from the Pulaski County Court House. Two entered the bank. When a large group of men and boys suddenly and unexpectedly appeared in the town square carrying rifles, the two men inside the bank quickly departed, followed by the three accomplices in the square. The men who suddenly had appeared in the square with their guns knew nothing of the robbery in progress. They simply were assembling in the town square for a day of hunting. The joke on the James outlaws spread wildly throughout Pulaski County, and soon was mimicked by two other nearby towns.[35]

MACK BEGAN TO VIEW HIS FUTURE FAR BEYOND THE JAMES FAMILY'S PIONEER HOME IN KENTUCKY. Progress and achievement that was accountable still propelled him as validation against family disgrace and social stigma. Mack followed the spreading railroads in his pursuit of economic advancement, investing in excess railroad lands, establishing more farms, and building more hotels.

In Newton County in northeastern Indiana at the Tivoli flag and water stop along the rails of the Logansport-Peoria Railroad, Mack brought his son Francis Marion James Sr. after the Civil War to tend and farm his land, in a new town named Goodland.

The county founders wanted to name their new county Marion in honor of Gen. Francis Marion of the American Revolution. They were particularly impressed that Mack's grandfather John M. James had been a spy for Gen. Marion, and that Mack had named his first son Francis Marion James in honor of the General. The county founders particularly were acquainted with the book *The Life of Gen. Francis Marion* written by Mason Lock Weems, a parson born in 1759 who was so zealous in his advocacy of the moral American life that he invented the story of George Washington chopping down the cherry tree. The adjacent county already had been named Jasper after one of Marion's sergeants. Taking their cue from Weems' book, in which Sergeants Jasper and Newton liberated American captives from their British guards while serving under Gen. Marion, the name given to the new county next to Jasper became Newton County.[36] Of some additional influence may have been the fact that, after the Revolution, Sergeants Jasper and Newton had made their home in John M. James' Pulaski County, and that Newton was a personal acquaintance of Mack's family.

Mack acquired a large tract off Hunter's Ditch, a branch of the Iroquois River. He laid out residential building lots for sale on East James Street from Union to Benton Streets, and further south to a tile factory built at the outskirts of town. Mack named Benton St. after Sen. Thomas Hart Benton, an influential friend of his grandfather's cousin Burton Allen James in Missouri. The street that linked his tract to the town, he named James Street.

Mack's son Marion James was the only resident of Goodland to have fought on the side of the Confederacy. Marion's original home in Goodland was a modest log cabin he built.[37] As an expression of faith and patriotism, Marion donated land for the First Baptist Church at James and Union Streets. A congregation quickly formed and grew to more than 220 faithful, making it the largest church in the regional association. Marion James also donated his Confederate guns for public display. Over time, the relics inexplicably disappeared from the town. James family lore says the town's name of Goodland arose from Mack's revulsion with the bad land of his Kentucky home, the place from where his family embarrassment sprang.

Francis Marion James Sr. 1843 – 1910

In Goodland, Mack built the Central Hotel in 1869. The large wood frame construction occupied almost a city block in length. Before the hotel was constructed, there were but ten houses in the town with a store and attached warehouse, a blacksmith shop, and a school that was open only three months a year.

After Mack built his hotel, the town was said to be putting on citified airs. People were crowding in from all directions. One newcomer from Southern Indiana said he "raised a pile, sold a heap, and had a right smart left." A Kentuckian in Goodland was seen with a "jag on" racing down the place where sidewalks yet weren't, wielding an open knife, heaping anything but blessings on a hapless citizen from Illinois. A few hours later the breach of welcome etiquette was healed. The same knife was used to cut large chunks of "plug tobaker" to put "where twould do the most service." But then moments later, "a colored gent administered condign punishment on a wild Irishman who had insulted his veracity was not A-1." [38] Mack's Central Hotel burned down in 1884. As he did with his St. James Hotel in

Goodland in 1910

Danville, Mack built the hotel anew, this time more substantially of brick. His new hotel had 30 rooms and a spacious reception office with a sample room to display an array of products a visitor could purchase in Goodland.[39]

Upon one of Mack's last visits to Goodland, he reminisced with a local newspaper reporter under giant oak and walnut trees. Mack had dug up and transplanted them from the Iroquois River when they were saplings. He recalled freeing his enslaved persons at the outbreak of the Civil War, as his son Marion went off to serve in the Confederate Army. Some enslaved, Mack said, didn't want to leave him. Those slaves he brought to Goodland to farm his lands. Among them was James Pittigon who became Goodland's town barber. Pittigon established a reputation for himself as a noted town character.[40] In his newspaper article the reporter referred to Mack as *"this fine old Kentucky gentlemen."*

In 1877 Mack traded nearly all he owned in Danville with Henry and Helen Rogers for a large ranch in Coffeyville, Kansas, and several additional ranches in nearby Labette, Allen, Coffey, and Chautauqua counties. Mack departed Danville to live on the Kansas prairie in a modest bungalow he called Maple Grove. He retained the St. James Hotel and James Hall in Danville until they sold. In Kansas, Mack imported Kentucky shorthorn to

Maple Grove

the blooming Kansas frontier.

On Coffeyville's historic day of October 5, 1892, Mack's second eldest son, Daniel Ephraim James, named after Danville's Dr. Ephraim McDowell,[41] was taken hostage when the Dalton Gang raided the Condon Bank. When Charles T. Carpenter, the junior partner and cashier in the bank, wrote his account of the famed robbery, he noted the event as "an exploit amazing enough to eclipse the fame of Jesse James..." Carpenter further noted, "...before leaving the bank, in the midst of the hail of bullets, Grat [Dalton] told us to go behind our counters and lie down to escape injury. D. E. James and John Lavan had entered the bank and been captured by the robbers." [42] Lavan was Mack's real estate broker, having arrived with Mack's son at the bank to execute a financial transaction.

In the decade prior to the Dalton Gang robbery, the *Coffeyville Star* ironically had reported, *"Our section of the country is a little behind the times in one respect. The James boys have not yet been reported as being*

The Condon Bank

The Dalton Gang

in *Southeastern Kansas...*" [43] Also the *Independence Star* had reported, *"One of the Youngers was in Coffeyville a few days ago. He appeared to be a very inoffensive sort of citizen, and participated in a prayer meeting at one of the churches while here."* [44] The unidentified Younger [45] had attended the local Methodist Episcopal Church, where Mack's son, Rev. John Robert James, a Baptist minister, would preach the following year. [46]

Mack's name was last reported in the newspaper when it was pubilshed that *"Our excellent friend Joseph McJames of Cherokee Township, was a caller Tuesday morning, and very frankly informed us that he had come to town to see the circus."* [47]

Despite Mack's public assertion as he "frankly informed" the press, in this town of Coffeyville, bespoken by ironies of the outlaw kind, Joseph McAlister James did not escape ill repute as unscathed as he would have liked. The James family member who spurned the embarrassment of his own father and family, who took every precaution to avoid being associated with those of less than reputable status, and who went so far as to trade his true identity for a disguised name, was laid to his final rest in Elmwood Cemetery in Coffeyville - buried seventy-five feet from the outlaws Bob and Grat Dalton.

John James, of Alvarado 1852 - 1927

Chapter Four

An Independent Free Man

*In Texas, one line of Mack's family who fled Pulaski County became remote from
all other lines by a geographical distance of their own making. While occasional
communication was maintained with those left behind in Kentucky, the memory
of their James family's heritage receded gradually over time. All contact was lost
for a time with those gone to Missouri, at least until John James of Alvarado, Texas
was visited by Belle Starr, Frank and Jesse James, and one of Quantrill's raiders
seeking his James kin for repatriation.*

Rev. John James, son of Cyrenius Waite James, was a founder of
Alvarado in Johnson County, Texas. John was a teacher, preacher,
and a man of many occupations. From Gerdes Jewelry store on
the northwest corner of the town square, he sold real estate. From his home
called Mountainview, he operated an orchard, a nursery, and a canning
business. Often John shipped specimen plants back to Kentucky to be
shared with relatives. John served as Alvarado's mayor for several terms, and
wrote for his local newspaper, the *Alvarado Bulletin*. Community events he
founded, like the Pioneers & Settlers Reunion, are still celebrated annually
in Alvarado today. Like his grandfather Rev. Joseph Martin James, John
James of Alvarado was remembered well for his strong and powerful good

Siblings of John James of Alvarado

William Henry James 1854 – Unk   Andrew Jackson James 1862 – 1913
Harvey James 1866 – Unk.   Sarah Ellen James-Grubbs 1866 - 1952

voice when he preached. He was a handsome man with an appreciation for women of strong femininity. He could use both his intellect and presence to effect. Unlike other James men, John James of Alvarado loved to sing, especially when he found himself in trouble.

In his youth, Johnny James never could get enough knowledge. What little learning Johnny grasped lit a fire in him for advanced education. Over his lifetime John built a library of over seven hundred books, a testament to his tenure as a lifelong student, and to his becoming an independent thinker.

"I had never been to school but nine weeks in my life but had picked up a fair education and had read the New Testament…While Father was gone to the [Civil] *war I grew out from under his rule and influence so that when he came home I felt in me a feeling of rebellion against him and was never willing for him to be my boss as I called it, so in the summer after I was 16 I left home – 'ran away'."*

During the Civil War, Johnny's father, Cyrenius Waite James, volunteered to serve the Union in Company B of the 79th Illinois Infantry. Cy was first captured at Murphreesboro. Returning to action, Cy was wounded in the leg at the Battle of Lovejoy Station in Georgia. On June 12, 1865, he was mustered out with his company at Nashville, Tennessee as a Corporal. Up to his final pension appeal, left pending upon his death, Cy James suffered continually from the depredations of the war. A short man of 5 foot, 7 inches, Cy needed his tall son Johnny to help him farm.

"I hired to a man to herd cattle, so I did not have much to do but put all my spare time reading my Testament. I planned to get myself plenty of clothes and then go to school for I wanted to get an education. I wanted that above everything else.

"Of course I loved my dear mother and the children, wanted to see them and went home in the fall on a visit intending to go back to Philo, Illinois where a man offered to board me and send me to school for my work of nights and mornings, but Father begged me to stay home and promised me an education. So I stayed, but in account of our financial condition and father's feebleness, from hardships and exposure to war, I never got to go to school. And more, I had never went to school but nine weeks, and that was to Uncle Henry by a chip fire light." [1]

Johnny's teacher, his Uncle Henry James, was the son of Joseph McJames. Uncle Henry first brought Johnny's family to Illinois to work a new plantation Mack acquired from excess railroad lands. In Kentucky, Illinois, and Texas, Henry James developed a reputation as an old fashioned but excellent school teacher. Henry taught Johnny how to educate himself.

"I sayed with my father and learned to love him again and done all I could for him, but read and studied all the time I could. I loved the Sunday School and Prayer meeting and debating societies and sing schools and became active in all that work. And I loved the girls too and had several previous sweet hearts that I hated most of to leave when we came to Texas. But I learned to write by writing back to several of them for over a year after I came here."

In 1869 Cy removed his family from Illinois. With cane in hand, Cy limped with his family to Texas to settle in the Illinois Community of Wise County. Entering Indian Territory, seventeen year old Johnny James encountered his first experience with the Native-American people, who would come to influence his life.

FROM HIS FIRST ENCOUNTER WITH INDIANS, JOHNNY JAMES WAS READY TO BE THEIR EDUCATOR, IF NOT ALSO THEIR PUPIL. One morning on the trek from Illinois to Texas, Johnny was sent from his family's camp to forage for food. Johnny happened upon a Choctaw encampment nearby. From the brush of a creek bed, Johnny spotted no man among them. But the Indian maidens quickly spied the young boy, surrounded him, and brought him into their camp. Johnny became nervous and agitated. As was his custom when he felt threatened or unsure, Johnny burst into song. He sang the Baptist hymns he had learned in his Kentucky sing school, with all the insistent meter and intestinal force he could project. His mother later recollected, "Johnny sang all the way to Texas." The next morning, the Choctaw chief arrived at the James camp, immediately expressing a desire to purchase the boy for the Indian maidens. The women wanted more of Johnny's spirited tempo-driven hymns, which sounded so much like their own.

John James later wrote the story in his book *My Experience with Indians*.[2] Much in his book was extracted from the weekly column he wrote over the years for his Alvarado hometown newspaper.

" 'I want boy. I make him heap big chief.' Father answered, 'The boy don't want to stay with you.' I spoke up quickly, saying, 'Yes, I do,' but mother said, 'No! No!'... Seeing that mother was weeping, I said, 'I do not want to stay.' but I really did want to stay, and had it not been for mother's tears, I would have done so."

The chief, whose Anglo name was Charley LeFlore, urged Cy James to remain and settle in Choctaw Territory. *"You stay with us. We make you heap*

Choctaw Village, Indian Territory, Oklahoma

big house, we give you land and cattle and horses and make you heap big rich, like Missionary Buckner." [3]

The reference to Missionary Buckner surprised Johnny's family. Ironically, Chief LeFlore was referring to Rev. Henry F. Buckner, the eldest son of Rev. Daniel Buckner, a pastor at the First Baptist Church back in Somerset, Kentucky, a church once pastored by Cy's father, Joseph Martin James. Henry Buckner left Pulaski County in 1848 to become a missionary between the Creek and Choctaw tribes. His brother Rev. Robert Cook Buckner later established the Buckner Orphans home in Dallas, Texas in 1879.[4] Johnny's mother recalled Daniel Buckner. He had baptized her in Pittman Creek in February of 1852, when she was pregnant with Johnny. Two months later, Johnny was born.

Cy James dismissed Chief LeFlore's petition, and proceeded with his wife and children to enter Texas. Walking onward, young Johnny James always knew that someday he would return to the Choctaw. *"I never got away from the feelings and impressions of that day, and fourteen years afterward, I was back among the Choctaw Indians doing mission work..."*

Arriving at the Illinois Settlement in Texas, Johnny James accelerated his education, learning to write. Quickly growing in maturity, Johnny soon became a teacher like his Uncle Henry.

John James
The teacher in his new clothes

"During the summer, our first summer here after I was 18, the neighbors fixed up an old log house with split log seats and a plank on pegs in the wall for a writing desk and put me in as teacher over about a dozen children, but my school was a success from the start.

"It gave me a chance to study and I would study every evening after school was out every lesson that was to come up the next day so I kept one day ahead of my school. I taught four schools at that place and my salary grew from $20.00 up to $75.00 per month, and at the end of the fourth school I had carried my advanced classes up into such high branches as higher arithmetic, algebra, physical geography, philosophy, and astronomy and bookkeeping. I had not only taught a good school but had educated myself during the two years or four schools that I taught there. So I kept on teaching for eighteen years, the last three years as a mission teacher to the Indians, where I learned to love the Indians and learned their language and can talk it yet." [5]

Choctaw Academy of Vice-President Richard Mentor Johnson
Between Stamping Ground & Georgetown, Kentucky

As a teacher on the Texas prairie, John James well recalled the Choctaw Academy back in Kentucky founded by Vice-President Richard Mentor Johnson between Georgetown College and Stamping Ground.[6] The school was at Blue Springs,[7] a short buggy ride to Lindsay farm back in Scott County, where Frank and Jesse's parents were married. Johnson had created the academy to educate Native-Americans, following the Battle of Thames in the War of 1812, in which Johnson claimed he had killed Tecumseh.[8] Prior to their removal from Mississippi, the Choctaw also knew well of the Choctaw Academy. The *Louisville Public Advertiser* of November 5, 1825 reported that Col. Johnson had received twenty-one Choctaw children from

Mississippi to be educated at the academy. In 1831 a Choctaw named John James at age fifteen had been enrolled in Johnson's school.

John wrote further about his log cabin school in Texas, not yet as civilized as R. M. Johnson's, and still surrounded by frontier violence.

"In July of 1872, I was teaching a small country school in the southeast corner of Wise County, Texas, about three miles east of where Rome is now located. At that time there lived in that spare settlement, two families of half-breed Indians. One of the families, named Brock, had a cabin built on vacant land. He had no field or stock, except a few riding ponies. He was not liked by any of the white people. Two grown daughters were in the family, but they never went out, neither did any of the family work for the white settlers, and they were regarded as harborers of thieves, and other bad characters, and helped the wild Indians to locate and steal stock from the white settlers. At that time the wild Comanche Indians raided on the white settlements almost every light moon.

"The other family whose name was Dawson was liked by all who knew them. Nick Dawson and family worked hard, making small crops and helping their white neighbors. He was sending four of his children to my school, three girls and one boy, from the ages of sixteen and down. Dawson was killed by the Comanches in one of the raids near his home. The daughters were very beautiful."

Unknown to John was the fact that Nick Dawson was born at Wood Farm in Woodford County, Kentucky. The family of Nicholas Henry Dawson had moved first to White County, Tennessee, before proceeding to Texas. On his mother's side, Nick's family was Cherokee. Nick who had been born in the same area as Zerelda Cole-James was a first cousin of her sons, Frank and Jesse James. As a descendant of Dr. John Woodson himself, Dawson also was a cousin to Tuck and Wood Hite, and Drury Woodson Poor. Dawson was even more closely related, however, as a third cousin to John Singleton Mosby, his grandmother Frances Cannon Mosby-Dawson being a first cousin to Col. Mosby.

Nick Dawson's namesake was his uncle Nicholas Mosby Dawson, who also was born in Woodford County. He was among the first the Dawson family to enter Texas about 1834 when he settled in with a relative in Texas, William Mosby Eastland. Two years later they joined the Texas Revolution against Mexico. Nick joined Company B of the First Regiment of Texas Volunteers with the rank of Second Lieutenant. Among his volunteers was Jackson Bunyan Bradley, the future father-in-law of Johnny James. Following

Nicholas Henry "Nick" Dawson 1838 - 1870

the Battle of San Jacinto, Capt. Nicholas Mosby Dawson led a company of fifty-three men. At Salado Creek near San Antonio, Dawson found himself surrounded by the Mexican Cavalry. Nicholas Mosby Dawson was slaughtered in what history recalls as the "Dawson Massacre."[9]

John's school house neighbor, Nick Dawson surrendered his life, for the safety of Texas settlement. As the eldest child, Nick was the sole support of his siblings and widowed mother. With his wife, children, and extended family, Nick also had adopted an orphaned Choctaw boy. Nick established his ranch in an area through which local tribes often traveled, the same location in which John James had his log cabin school. Attacks were common in the area. Nick's body of multiple accumulated wounds offered visible testimony and evidence. Nick was widely respected by his neighbors for his defense of them.

One day Nick went in search of a fine mare he had turned loose to range. At a distance Nick spotted a body of cowmen on horseback gathered inside thick brush. Riding toward the cowmen to inquire if they had seen his mare, Nick soon discovered he faced about forty-five Indians. Nick was chased for three miles. The Indians used their superior hunting tactics to corner him. They forced Nick's horse to ascend a steep hill. When his horse flagged, Nick Dawson was captured. That night, Nick's orphan Choctaw boy awoke. The boy cried out, "Uncle Nick is dead. The Indians scalped him." The next day, Nick's remains were found. Nick Dawson had been shot upon his capture, scalped, and butchered.[10]

John James had lived in Texas less than a year, when he learned of his neighbor's killing. Until then, John thought the violence of the Texas prairie as something romantic. He wrote in his diary of riding all day in search of water, unable to stop to search on foot, because no shrub could be found to tether his horse. Suddenly, his horse halted, frozen still. Unable to coax his horse further, John saw why. Staring directly into John's eyes were the predatory eyes of a panther. With his mortality in the balance, John James still viewed the creature with awe. But for once, John did not burst into singing Baptist hymns.

Within months of Nick Dawson's killing, Nick's daughter Fannie married Professor Griffin Ford, who taught at a school established by Jackson Bunyan Bradley. John wrote in his book,

"Prof. Griffin Ford, a well-known teacher here in Myer's Community in 1870 and '71 married the oldest, Fannie, in 1873. She had been a widow now for many years, and lives in Montague County, East of Bowie, Texas. My own brother George married the next oldest, Miss Sallie, about 1876, when she was only 15 years old. Dear Sallie lived only one year afterwards and died in my home..."

With much warmth, John recorded the dying words of his sister-in-law, Sallie Dawson-James. *"Just before she passed away, she said to her young husband, 'George, the angels have come for me, don't you see them, right there?'. And her last words were, 'Glory, glory!'."* [11]

Within two years of the slaughter of Nick Dawson, children of Native-Americans were among the students John James taught.

"It was at this school one afternoon, that two young Indian women rode up to the door of the log school house, jumping off their ponies, they hobbled them out to graze, and bringing their beautiful beaded blankets (they had no saddles) to the door, I invited them in, and made room for them, just to the right of my desk.

"They were plainly, though neatly dressed, and the lighter colored girl said to me, that she had heard of my school, and as she had never been in a school, she came to see how a school was conducted. This she said in good English. She was real

good looking, and about my age, 20. The darker girl said nothing, and did not seem to be interested in anything.

"Time for recess soon came, which gave me an opportunity to talk to the girl, who said she was Cherokee half-breed. That her father was a U.S. Army officer named Star [sic], at one of the reservations in the Indian Territory, and that her mother was a full blood Cherokee, who belonged to a roving band of that tribe. She told of how she learned to talk English from white men, who often traveled with them on hunting excursions into the western territory and the panhandle of Texas.

"She also said that she could read, and had read some in a Bible, that had been given to her mother by a missionary by the name of Buckner, the Creek Nation, and that she liked to read about that wonderful man named Jesus. I called in some of the larger boys and girls and we sang several songs. She joined in and helped in some of them, saying she had learned them at the mission stations. Having a small pocket Testament with me, I gave it to her, and she thanked me for it, saying she would read it every day.

"I called school, and they stayed with us until the work of the day was finished. Their ponies having fed quite a distance from the house, I sent two of the larger boys to bring them back. Seeing that the school girls were looking at their blankets, she told them how they were made. The heavy cloth from bear-grass fiber, and that the beads had been bought at the Indian agency, and of how long a time it took them to make.

"On leaving, she told me her name was Bell Star. She also told the other girl's name, which was Indian, and I do not remember it, (we afterward learned that she was one of the Brock girls,) and I should perhaps have forgotten her name, but several years later, I read in the papers of the noted band of desperados composed of Indians and whites, led by the noted 'Bell Star.' From the published descriptions I read of her, I have always since believed that she was the Bell Star, who visited my school in Wise County, Texas, in July, 1872." [12]

History today recalls Belle Starr under her birth name of Myra Maebelle Shirley, born in Carthage, Missouri. At the Carthage Female Academy, Belle Shirley excelled in reading, spelling, grammar, arithmetic, deportment, Greek, Latin, Hebrew, and music, learning to play the piano. As a teenage spy in the Civil War, Belle reported Union troop positions to the Confederacy. One of her childhood friends in Missouri was Cole Younger by whom she had a child. Her family removed to Scyene, Texas in 1864, shortly before Confederate guerrillas burned Carthage to the ground. Her

Myra Maebelle Shirley 1848 - 1889

aka Belle Starr

older brother John Shirley, whom she called Bud and who fought with Quantrill, was killed.

When meeting John James, Belle was married to James Reed, a former guerrilla of the war, who fell in with the Starr clan, a Cherokee Indian family notorious for whiskey, cattle, and horse thievery. Reed shot a man in cold blood three years prior to their meeting for the accidental shooting of his brother. Reed and Belle fled to California, but returned to Texas two years later after Reed was caught passing counterfeit money. Later in 1874, Reed and Belle were accused of robbing a wealthy Indian farmer of $30,000 in gold coins, after which the couple parted. In January 1880, Belle married Sam Starr. Belle is said also to have married Bruce Younger later that same year in July. With Sam Starr, Belle rose to national notoriety. She was murdered

Emily Wren "Emma" Shirley 1872 - 1953

Daughter of Paul Porter Shirley & Anne Marie Kuykendal

Wife of Everett Elbert "Elo" James 1876 - 1915, son of John James of Alvarado

Home of Will Aylette Shirley 1870 – 1958

Husband of Lucretia Grace Deborah "Dee" James 1874 - 1966
Daughter of John James & sibling of Elo James

in 1889 at the age of forty.

Belle Starr's father John Shirley was born in Virginia, lived in Indiana, and died in Scyene, Texas in 1876. Her mother Elizabeth Hatfield Pennington was born in Louisville, Kentucky. She also died in Scyene in 1894. That same year and again two years later, two of John James' children would marry into a Shirley family. Lucretia Grace Deborah James, known as Dee, married Will Aylette Shirley of Horsecave, Kentucky. Dee's younger brother Enoch Elbert James, known as Elo, married Emma Wren Shirley, a cousin of Will Shirley. Emma's Shirley family came from Adair County in Kentucky and before that from Spotsylvania County in Virginia. Among their Shirley and James descendants, their family lore claims to present day a kinship to Belle Starr, although the precise familial link never has been established.

Caradine,

North Side Square,
SHERMAN, TEX.

Stella, Florence, & Ella Shirley
Siblings of Emma Wren Shirley

In 1884, John was invited to teach at the Choctaw school, Stockbridg
Academy, in Eagle County in Indian Territory. John previously had been
invited years earlier by Judge James Hudson, a Choctaw. Hudson died
in 1875, but his invitation to John was long standing. The school later
became the Eagletown School in McCurtain County.

Stockbridge Academy

The Choctaw Academy of John James

Stockbridge was founded by Cyrus Byington of Stockbridge, Massachusetts, who named the Choctaw school after his birthplace. Byington migrated to Mississippi in 1821, where he became a missionary to the Choctaw. Finding the Choctaw had no written language, Byington created a grammar, dictionary, and speller for their language, which was helpful to John when he learned to speak the Choctaw language. In 1832, Byington followed the Choctaw in their removal on the Trail of Tears to Oklahoma. There, for the following thirty-one years, Byington preached and taught among the Choctaw. Byington died in 1876.

John arrived sometime in 1884, to teach many Choctaw children who would become his lifelong friends. Among John's students were the children and grandchildren of Judge James Hudson, some of whom John accounted in his book *My Experience with Indians*.

In his book, John James of Alvarado specifically introduced his Anglo James family in Texas to one Choctaw family in particular whom John had taught in Oklahoma while he lived among them.

"I wrote My Experience with Indians just as those many strange experiences occurred from 1869 to 1888 . . . that my children and grandchildren may know of them." [13]

John then proceeded to introduce the Dyer family of Elliston E. Dyer to his James family, by publishing a letter from Dyer in his book.

Hon. J. James, Alvarado, Texas

My dear old time friend:

I have just received a copy of the Cleburne Daily Times, and in it I find your picture, and note that the paper states that you spent several years among the Choctaw Indians, as a missionary...This of course calls to my mind the days of long ago, when you were at old Stock Bridge, trying to guide to the right direction, the destinies of a bunch of more or less ignorant boys and girls...Of the Choctaw tribe, I am one, and I have often thought since then, what a pity that men like you weren't scattered all over this country... [14]

Elliston E. Dyer

Flodelle Dyer   Willard Dyer
Winona Dyer   Lillian Dyer

Daughters of Elliston E. Dyer

Enclosed in Dyer's letter to John, Dyer sent family photos, some of which John also published in his book. Elliston Dyer updated John with information about himself and each of his children. Since the time when he was taught by John James, Dyer had become the collector of royalties under Choctaw Chief Jefferson Gardner. He was elected to the House of Representatives in the Choctaw Council, and continued in that office until tribal government ended in 1906. Dyer's eldest daughter Flodelle had graduated school and was a teacher in Durant. A second daughter Winona became principal of a high school in Achille. A third daughter Willlard, whom Dyer termed "our little Injun flapper," had become an entertainer for religious and social societies. Of his brother James Dyer, Jr., Elliston Dyer informed John he was a former constable, who then became a member of the Oklahoma State Legislature.

John James had brought education and ministry to Elliston Dyer, a legacy which Dyer's children clearly inherited. Dyer's family reflected the same interests and occupations as John James' own Anglo family, especially in the fields of community development, politics, and education. John's lifelong affinity for the Choctaw is responsible for many of them embarking on paths of public service as legislators in the new Oklahoma state government, sharing in a true tradition as authentic and natural a destiny as that of any James family.

On December 29, 1894, shortly after receiving Dyer's letter, John and his wife Louisa Ellen Sutton named their next born child, Elliston Dyer James.

Elliston Dyer James 1894 - 1972

In 1999, descendants of the Elliston Dyer family were located in Idaho Falls, Idaho. Tiajuana Chochnauer, a teacher and public servant herself, voiced the Dyer family's continued pride in their legacy inherited from John James of Alvarado. Tentatively, she probed, "Don't you think we look like James?" The Dyer family of Oklahoma Choctaw, whom John pointedly introduced to his Anglo family in Texas *"that my children and grandchildren may know of them,"* believes that Elliston Dyer was born of John James, and that the Dyer family truly may be the blood progeny and descendants of John James of Alvarado.[15] Other Choctaw genealogy defines Elliston Dyer as Rev. Allston James Dyer, born of Moses Dyer and Ela-Pa-Hone. The mother of Moses Dyer being Ish-Te-Mi-Ah. No one suitable candidate among Dyer's descendants has been found to put the issue to rest with a DNA test.

John James acquired a portion of the estate of Jackson Bunyan Bradley, his former father-in-law who died in 1877. John's wife Ross Bradley had died almost a decade before Col. Bradley, leaving John with five children. With his present wife Louisa Ellen Sutton, four more children increased John's brood. There were yet three more children still to come. Thanks to Col. Bradley, now they all had a comfortable home. Col. Bradley and his family first came to Texas from Mississippi in 1851, accompanied by his brother-in-law Sam Houston Myers, a personal friend of his namesake Sam Houston who often was a guest in the Myers home. In the Myers Community of Johnson County, Bradley and Myers had built and operated a school, starting in the year of his arrival. At Mountainview, John now would continue to teach, as he developed other businesses in his growing community of Alvarado, where he would be elected mayor several times.

JOHN REFLECTED ON THE PRICE HE PAID FOR HIS LOVE OF THE CHOCTAW. Following his James nature to respect human equality came with a cost. As seemingly customary among the James, retribution was required. Like his talented but erratic grandfather, Rev. Joe Martin James, John James of Alvarado was stripped of his Baptist ministry, too. In 1903 John wrote about his estrangement in his diary, *Stray Leaves*:

"I am a Democrat but in politics, religion, and everything else, I am very liberal and kind to those who differ with me in their views. I believe there is good in all creeds and in all nations of the Earth and believe God's people do wrong in

Mountainview

keeping up separate denominational creeds instead of trying to live together in Love and Unity. I began to preach that kind of doctrine about twelve years ago. Of course that did not suit Baptists. They took my credentials away from me but I am glad of it and have never regretted it. From that day until this, I have been an independent free man, and preach and teach what I believe, and hold myself accountable to no man or set of men but God only." [16]

When requested to write additional content for the publication of his book, John's time was running out. Instead, John summarized his respect for the Choctaw and for what they taught him.

"...when I began to think of what I should add to my story, I thought of those same Indians of whom I wrote and their children, and of the wonderful progress along the lines of advancing civilization they had made which had fully justified my estimate of the Indian's moral and mental capacities referred to in former chapters. Their high ideals of virtue, honesty, truth, and abiding fidelity to that which was right and just, between man and man, regardless of what ever color.

"Under their former tribunal conditions and ancient customs, they were happy and contented people, truly religious, worshiping their Shelombish Holitopa Ma

(The Great Spirit) the white man's God, with a devotion, truly humble and consecrated, that would shame many a white man, notwithstanding their [i.e. the white man's] *superior claims religiously.*

"They were naturally loathe to give up their customs and manner of life, and take up the manner of life and ways of the white man, so many had dealt so treacherously with them, and being juberous of the white man's religion, which some professing to possess, committed so many and heinous crimes among red people. Who that knows these things can blame them from holding back, preferring the traditions and customs of their fathers?

"Looking back as we do from this date [1925], *it seems that Destiny willed a change, and that the great moral character of purity and uprightness of the Indian, had been held by their ancient tradition - in its original purity until this time, of so much impurity and chicanery especially since the great World War.*

"The Indian that never betrayed a friend, or broke a promise, or treaty and from the earliest days of the White man in America, was a true and dependable friend to the worthy white man, and had conserved all those noble qualities of honor and justice, until the hour struck for his advance. Doubtless the great Ruler of people and nations, destined that the Indian go forward and be a blessing to the people among whom it became his destiny to live, and so badly needed the beautiful trait of character the red man would give, both in precept and example." [17]

JOHN'S FAMILY TOLD OF A VISIT BY FRANK AND JESSE JAMES, DURING SERVICES JOHN CONDUCTED IN HIS CHURCH. There also was another visit by one of Quantrill's men, whose name was James. The story was repeated often by John's granddaughter Willie Grace Shirley, called Bill. She's a daughter of Will Aylette Shirley and John's daughter Dee James. Bill related, *"Mama told about Grandpa James riding on a horse one time, followed by the Jesse and Frank gang. He was very scared and to make him feel better, he sang religious songs all the way home, and they never bothered him. She told about another time when he faced the James gang. He was preaching, and they came in, left their guns in the vestibule, and sat on the back pew for a while. Then before the service was over, they left, getting their guns as they walked out the door."* [18]

In the community of Weldon, in Houston County, Texas lived John's cousin Rev. Joseph Mack James, the son of John's teacher Uncle Henry who also had settled there, before he died at Gibson Station, the terminus of the

Frank James & Rev. Joe Mack James, son of Joseph McJames

the Trail of Tears. Joe was named after Joseph McJames. Rev. Joe Mack James was a Baptist circuit minister in Weldon. Isolated on the Texas plains, he never met his namesake. He certainly never knew of the family's relationship to the outlaws. But like John's son Jackson Waite James, Rev. Joe Mack James also was the spitting image of Frank James.[19]

On April 13, 1917, *The Alvarado Weekly Bulletin* published the following story:

"A Mr. Will W. James, first cousin of Frank and Jesse James, whose fathers were cousins of Mayor James' grandfather, and who came originally from England to Virginia back before the Revolutionary War, and from there to Kentucky in the days of Daniel Boone, was visiting Mayor J. James last week.

"Mayor James says that when he caught a glance of this Mr. Will James he thought it was his brother, Wm. James, of Dallas, as they were as much alike as 'two black eyed peas,' and they soon, by inquiry established the above named relationship.

"Mr. Will W. James is the last surviving member of the James band and was with the James boys from the time he was 14 years old until their disbanding when his father moved to Mississippi, but on account of the search for the members of the James and Quantrill men, he shipped to England, where he enlisted with the

French and fought in the Franco-Prussian war. On returning to England he went to Australia with the English soldiers and fought the Bushmen into subjection, then on to New Zealand and fought the Moros, and returning to England he was sent to South Africa to fight the Zulus and then went to South America, and back to the U.S. As he so much longed to return to his native land, on which when landing, he stooped down in his gladness and kissed the sacred soil."

In Chillicothe, Missouri, on June 28, 1920, *The Daily Constitution* reported the passing of Will W. James. The headline read, *"Cousin of Jesse James Dies with His Boots Off —Aged Outlaw Who Fought All Over The World, Dead At Fort Worth, Texas."* The obituary identified Will W. James as William Wythe James.

William Wythe James

Illustration from the Kansas City Star

Upon the urging of Frank James who died in 1915, William Wythe James came to Fort Worth, seeking a comfortable place and manner in which to surrender to the United States Government. Like Frank James, Will W. James also needed to acknowledge his oath of allegiance. Will engaged the assistance of John James. A letter from Will W. James addressing John as *"My Dear Kinsman"* was published on May 18, 1917 in the *Alvarado Weekly Bulletin*. In the public letter, Will acknowledged John's help in gathering signatures for his petition. He offered his gratitude to all whom he met in Alvarado. As the *Alvarado Bulletin* continued to report about Will W. James,

"As he had never surrendered, he came to Fort Worth and there last September he surrendered and took the oath of allegiance to the U.S., as he wants to go and fight for our country, and has offered his services to President Wilson to serve anywhere and as long as he is needed. He has fought in seven wars, has been wounded three times, but as his whole life has been spent in military service, he now in his 70th year, long for a soldier's life, and so loves his native land that he now places himself upon its alter to die if need be for her cause."

William Wythe James further acknowledged in the article, *"I've been an outlaw since 1862, when General Hallock put a price on my head, along with the rest of us Quantrell boys,"* he told US Commissioner Mitchell, as he signed the Oath. *'He gave orders to catch us and hang us. Well, they caught a few of them, but they never caught me.'."* [20]

When the two met again, Will presented John with a sword in gratitude for John's assistance. Will said he acquired the weapon when serving under Quantrill. Welty Eugene Whitaker, a second great grandson of Rev. Joseph Martin James living in Pulaski County, Kentucky, stated he had met John's son Elliston Dyer James once. Elliston described to Gene Whitaker the sword he inherited from his father as not being a ceremonial or a full length saber sword, but rather more like the shorter cutting sword in common use in Kentucky in the Civil War. Elliston further stated the sword had been taken from a Union soldier when Quantrill came through Danville, Kentucky in 1864.[21] A granddaughter of John's, Billie Shirley-Mills, nicknamed Cricket, further stated Jerry James, the son of Elliston Dyer James, hastily had gathered the sword among other effects when Elliston died, together with his father's possessions. Not knowing the history he held in his hand, Jerry James then proceeded to dispose of the Quantrill sword at a yard sale.[22]

Mountainview

JOHN JAMES OF ALVARADO WAS NEARLY BLIND WHEN HE
DIED. His great granddaughter Billie Shirley-Mills recalled seeing the man
in her childhood who had nicknamed her Cricket. Still he entered a room as
an impressive figure. He stood simple and tall in black pants, a white starched
shirt, sporting a Texas bolo. Cricket's love of her grandfather spurred her to
study her family history, as she was doing when a heart attack took Cricket
after she just attended a meeting of the Society Daughters of Colonial Wars,
for which she had served as state president.

The *Alvarado Weekly Bulletin* foreshadowed what was coming John's
way. On March 18, 1927, its headline announced, *"John James resigns as
President from the Johnson County Pioneers Association on account of failing
health."*

A week later, the paper reported further, *"Owing to declining health,
J. James has sent his resignation as Justice of the Peace and the matter will come
before the Commissioner's Court at its next session. Mr. James has stated that he
has come to this action in consideration for the best interest of the office, as he
feels that it should be in the hands of a more active man. He has made a splendid
official in the place, fair and impartial magistrate and we regret to see him step out."*

*Annual family reunions, begun by John James,
continue today among the descendants of Jackson Waite James*

Finally, the headline in the *Alvarado Bulletin* in October, 1927 reported "J. James Answers the Summons of Death." Of the four ministers attending to John's service at the First Baptist Church were Rev. S. J. Howeth, the father-in-law of John's son George Dehoney James, and a James family cousin, Rev. C. M. Woodson.

Some in this family of John James are entirely oblivious about any relationship to Frank and Jesse James. Others prefer simply to bypass or ignore the subject. On his deathbed, though, one family member diverted from the family silence. John's son, Jackson Waite James never quite met with his father's approval. In fact, John James disinherited his son Jackson, for want of repayment of a loan. Jackson was a black sheep. Three houses Jackson owned suspiciously burned to the ground, some said, to collect insurance money. Jackson James strongly resembled Frank James, both physically and in his taciturn nature, especially as he grew older.

The two namesakes of Jackson Waite James were Andrew Jackson and his grandfather Cyrenius Waite James who brought the family to Texas. As Jackson Waite James lay dying in 1965, his teenage grandson, Paul Maurice James, was ushered into his papaw's room for a final visit.

Jackson Waite James Family

Knowing his grandfather was near death, the young man was burdened for what to say. All he could think to ask was the question no one else in the family ever would answer for him. "Papaw, are we kin to Jesse James?" Jackson Waite James' dying words to Jackson were, "Son, don't let anyone ever tell you different." Among the James family, the black sheep Jackson Waite James always perversely called his grandson Paul Maurice James "Little Jesse."[23]

Frank James & Jackson Waite James

In the years to follow, whenever the descendants of Joseph McJames asked about their family's relationship to Frank & Jesse James, Mack's daughter Mary Ellen James sternly voiced what had become a standard response among many of the James family lines, in some instances using the identical verbiage. The response was echoed by other lines of the James family in the same words, all of whom had dispersed throughout America and had no contact with each other for 125 years into the 21st century. The tart response of Mary Ellen James was, "You know all you need to know about Jesse James. And that's that."

Mary Ellen James-Saunders 1848 – 1906

Daughter of Joseph McJames

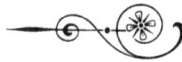

Thomas Martin "T. M." James 1823 - 1901

Chapter Five

The Highest Mental Culture

*In Missouri, Thomas Martin James kept hushed about his relationship to his
infamous nephews, Frank and Jesse James. T. M. insulated his family against
their ill repute. He concentrated instead on creating opportunities for faith and
education. He built his business, and forged an American metropolis from a
great prairie. As his stake grew, T. M. James took every precaution to safeguard
his family's economic prosperity for generations to come, protecting the social
standing he diligently earned in Kansas City as a millionaire merchant.* [1]

In his thirty-first year, Thomas Martin James and his wife Sarah departed
Westport just east of Louisville, Kentucky, headed on a river boat for
Westport Landing in Missouri. With them were their two children,
six year old John W. Crawford James, affectionately called J. C., and four
year old Luther Tilman James, whom T. M. named after his brother-in-law,
Tilman Howard West, who was waiting to greet them now in Missouri.

T. M.'s earnings as a teacher had become limited. He could sustain
himself as a bachelor, but his family was growing now faster than his
income. Kentucky was losing students. For fifteen years, migrations of self-

appointed Baptist missionaries to the Missouri and Northwest territories of Indiana, Illinois and the Nebraska withdrew entire congregations, families, and their children from the Commonwealth.[2] The exodus reminded T. M. of those rebel preachers who departed Virginia with their congregations. They left behind a stagnant population.

His prospects began to dim two years ago. T. M. then opened a general store with a partner, Waltus Gill of nearby Todd County.[3] T. M. perfected his knack for trade, that he first learned working in the store of his step-father, Rev. John Wilson Mimms. His accounts with Gill now settled, T.M. looked eagerly to Missouri and the opportunities Tilman Howard West bragged about. Tilman begged for T. M.'s help. He baited T. M. with opportunities for both teaching and commerce. Thomas Martin James believed himself now well prepared to accept the challenge.

T. M. James was the last of his orphaned siblings to leave home. Since the death of his parents, John M. James and Mary "Polly" Poor, all of T. M.'s siblings were established. His eldest sister, Mary, still operated the hotel east of Louisville where they all grew up. Her husband, Rev. Mimms, still maintained his store. He also still farmed tobacco. T. M.'s brother, Rev. William Henry James, became a minister. He, too, was a merchant in Greenville, Missouri, near the farm of their brother Rev. Robert Sallee James. Robert was dead and buried in California. His teenage boys, Frank and Jesse, still worked Robert's farm for their widowed mother Zerelda.

Mary Elizabeth, T. M.'s baby sister, was dead, too. She had married John Richard Cohorn. Hugh, as the family called him, had attended Vice-President Richard Mentor Johnson's Choctaw Academy near Stamping Ground. Hugh aspired to become a politician in Franklin County. He gave outstanding speeches. But he never got elected, possibly because he may have been of mixed blood. Mary Elizabeth suffered a crippling birth deformity of her hands. She died at nineteen, giving birth to their only child, Mary Jane.

T. M.'s other brother John tried preaching like William Henry and Robert Sallee James, but John gave it up. Instead, John opened a dentistry practice in Logan County, living quietly near his sister Nancy and her husband, Maj. George B. Hite. John held frontier life at a distance from his family. Though born to wealth, Maj. Hite was becoming a very prosperous merchant and tobacco farmer in his own right. He was not about to risk losing it all by moving Nancy and their family to Missouri.

T. M.'s baby brother, Drury Woodson James, was succeeding in California well beyond any of the family's expectations. With Tilman and T. M.'s half sibling Robert William Mimms, Drury made an exploratory voyage to California. Drury saw California's riches, and stayed. Tilman and Robert saw California's dangers, and returned to Russellville to consider moving to Missouri instead.[4] The family later learned Drury's cattle ranch probably would make him the wealthiest of all of the James orphans and their Mimms half siblings - even wealthier than Maj. Hite. Drury's communications confirmed California was still a dangerous place. Since the war with Mexico and the gold rush, murder was not uncommon. Drury and his neighbors often were required to form a posse. Some years would have to pass before Drury could safely start a family of his own. One thing was certain, Drury never would return to Kentucky.

Returning to Kentucky from California, Tilman had gathered Elizabeth and their three children in May of 1847. With Robert, they left Russellville, boarding a steamer at Bowling Green. Robert wrote they arrived in Independence, Missouri, but they settled first in Cass County at Pleasant Hill. Tilman became postmaster there. Robert was Tilman's clerk. They stayed only eighteen months.

Abandoning Pleasant Hill, Tilman moved next to Randolph Bluffs, where Col. Charles Lee Younger operated a ferry from the north side of the Missouri River.[5] Col. Younger warmly welcomed the Kentucky family, quickly recalling his old neighbor back in Crab Orchard, John M. James. While John developed his new county of Pulaski and served in the new state legislature, Younger left in 1808 to settle the Missouri Territory. After a year of fighting Indians, Younger returned to Crab Orchard. Eight years later he left Kentucky to make Missouri his home permanently. The Colonel's son, Henry Washington Younger, remained in Crab Orchard. Later, Henry accompanied the flood of missionaries who left Kentucky for Missouri in the 1830s. Missouri was where Henry would raise his family, including his sons who became widely known as the Younger Gang.[6]

At Randolph Bluffs, Robert received a letter from Drury Woodson James in the spring of 1848, summoning Robert to assist Drury's brother Rev. William Henry James at his store in Greenville. Somehow Rev. James could not grasp the knack of being a merchant. With Tilman's permission, Robert spent six months in Greenville. He returned, but two years later Robert left Tilman and his family again to join Drury Woodson James in

Col. John " Jack" Harris 1798 - 1872

Seth Edmund Ward 1820 - 1903

California. He returned to Greenville, but two years later Robert left Tilman and his family again to join Drury Woodson James in California.

With Robert gone, Tilman moved once more - this time to the bend in the Missouri River, where boundless commercial activity swamped Westport Landing. As Tilman acquired, bartered, and traded land throughout Jackson and Clay Counties, he desperately entreated T. M. to come to Missouri.[7] Tilman had developed a boarding house, a failsafe business in the burgeoning outpost of Harlem. Tilman also sorely needed the help of T. M.'s wife and children. Thanks to Tilman Howard West and T. M.'s half sibling Robert William Mimms, T. M. felt confident about a future for himself in Missouri.

ONLY 250 PEOPLE LIVED AT THE FRONTIER CROSSROADS where the steamer F. X. Oxberry deposited T.M.'s family on Westport Landing.[8] The pioneers among them would become influential to T. M.'s future. The most visible was Col. Jack Harris. He came to Westport in 1832 from Madison County in Kentucky.[9] Col. Harris operated the Harris House, a fancy boarding house built of brick. Nearby, Col. Harris lived in a two story Mansion House he built in the Greek revival style.[10] Recently, Col. Harris added his land to the new town of Harlem. Col. Harris himself was as ostentatious a landmark as anything he built.

Thomas Hoyle Mastin

1839 - 1905

Harris married off his daughters well, partitioning them to young men who enhanced his enterprises. In 1860, Mary Frances Harris married a rich fur trader, Seth Edmund Ward. Her sister Elizabeth later married Thomas Hoyle Mastin. Mastin imported prized cattle from R. A. Alexander's Woodburn Farm in Woodford County, Kentucky, next to the Black Horse Inn operated by the Cole family of Frank and Jesse's mother.[11] Eventually, the Mastin Bank owned by their son, John J. Mastin, would fall into receivership to be liquidated by Seth Ward's son.

In 1829, the Hickman family arrived from Frankfort, Kentucky. Edwin Alfred Hickman was the son of Rev. William Hickman, a wide ranging Baptist who preached the first sermon in Kentucky. Settling in Kentucky with John M. James and the Traveling Church, Hickman was a founder of the Forks of the Elkhorn Church in Woodford County. He also founded the church at Great Crossings, sometimes called the Stamping Ground Church.[12] Rev. Hickman was a personal witness to many of the persecutions that made rebel preachers of them all and forced them from Virginia. When

Rev. William Hickman 1747 - 1834

those same outcasts were called to the War of 1812, Rev. Hickman son, Capt. Paschal Hickman, was sacrificed in the Battle of River Raisin.[13] Liberty secured, Paschal's brother Edwin Alfred Hickman now looked towards opportunities in Missouri, as did T. M. James.

Edwin Alfred Hickman bought ten acres outside Westport in 1850. He established a steam mill, to grind flour and meal. The place became popular as Hickman's Mills. The farmstead later was annexed into Kansas City before the Civil War. Edwin's brother, Ezra Hickman, later became the county clerk when the new Jackson County was formed, as later did Edwin's son, William Zere Hickman.[14]

Ezra Hickman co-founded the Jackson County Agricultural and Mechanical Association with Sam Ralston, Samuel Hughes Woodson, John B. Wornall, among others. After first emigrating from Scotland to North Carolina, Sam Ralston previously made exploratory excursions northwest into the Nebraska Territory and then southwest into *Nuevo Mexico*, before

Samuel Hughes Woodson Esq. 1815 - 1881

he decided to settle in Westport in 1842. Thereafter, Ralston made his home in Independence. When Frank James courted Ralston's daughter Annie, Sam Ralston sent Ezra Hickman to spy on the young woman.

John R. Swearingen arrived from Crab Orchard, to become a Santa Fe trader like Col. Harris.[15] He made his home at Westport in 1825. Thirteen years later, Swearingen married Mary Pence. Later in Kentucky, Mary's in-law cousin, Maj. James Bridgewater, chased Bud and Donnie Pence after the Civil War, when the Pence brothers pillaged Danville with Frank James, the Youngers, and Quantrill.

A year before T. M.'s arrival, Senator Burton Allen James, brother of Joseph James the Elder of Virginia, had moved his family to Westport. T. M.'s distant cousin had been in the Missouri territory since he first moved to Mathias' Prairie in the Platte Purchase in 1836. B. A. James had a long established relationship with the Hickman family. Ezra Hickman named his first son Burton Allen James Hickman.

Born in Culpeper County, Virginia, B. A. James and his parents first left Virginia in a dearborn for North Carolina, to reside briefly in Louisburg.[16] They finally settled in Kentucky in Logan County, arriving there before T. M.'s father, John M. James. Burton Allen James grew to maturity in Logan County. He departed for Missouri after John M. James died, migrating with John's son, the slave patroller of Kentucky's Pulaski County, Capt. Harry James. When Capt. Harry died in Missouri, B. A. James married Harry's daughter Polly, Burton Allen James' first cousin.

In Missouri, B. A. James already had been a county judge in Greene County in 1843. The following year, he resigned when he was elected to the Missouri legislature. He also was a delegate to the Missouri Constitutional Convention.[17] In August of 1850, B. A. James squeezed into the Missouri Senate after a tie election vote was broken by the support of a James family friend, Sen. Thomas Hart Benton.[18] Now Benton was about to throw a political plumb and financial windfall to his protégé, securing the appointment by Congress of B. A. James as Indian agent of the Sauk-Fox reservation.[19]

The first settler to reside in Westport, long before Thomas Martin James arrived, also came from Kentucky. Rev. Isaac McCoy intended to establish a Baptist Indian mission in Missouri. Five years after the War of 1812, Rev. Isaac McCoy received his first government appointment as missionary to the defeated Indians in the Northwest Territories of today's Michigan, Ohio, and Indiana. Born in Pennsylvania, McCoy grew up on the Kentucky frontier. His wife Christiana Polk, whom he called Kittie, was a relation of President James Knox Polk.

Kittie had a personal motivation for establishing a mission in Missouri. Kittie's mother, and several of Kittie's siblings, were kidnapped previously by Indians in late summer of 1782 at Kincheloe Station in Nelson County. Kittie's son was painted with feathers and trinkets. The Indians named him "Young Chief of the Long Knife." Kittie's own fate, however, was debated by her captors, often within her earshot. Another captive, Mrs. Ashe, complained about their long trek from Kentucky to Detroit, as captives of the Indians. Mrs. Ashe was stripped to her waist and ridiculed. Her children were removed from her, and Mrs. Ashe was told to leave. As her children watched her reluctantly obey, a tomahawk thrown from a distance crushed into the back of Mrs. Ashe's skull, in full view of her children. When George Rogers Clark finally rescued Kittie, the remains of Mrs. Ashe and her children, including Young Chief of the Long Knife, lay visibly strewn over the campground. Rev. Isaac McCoy was intent upon Christianizing the indigenous peoples of the West. Kittie McCoy intended to render them her forgiveness.

Continually, Isaac McCoy rode on horseback between the West and Washington, D. C. He brought surveys. In return, he secured government approvals to acquire remote territory for the Indians, "in which the white man might not intrude his wicked commerce," as McCoy ideally wished.[20]

Physical survival was always on Isaac McCoy's mind. Five of his daughters had died. When he went to Chicago in the fall of 1825 to preach the first sermon heard there in English instead of French, McCoy deposited his three sons at Transylvania University in Lexington, Kentucky. Joseph and Charles Rice McCoy were trained as medical doctors. John Calvin McCoy was trained as a surveyor. The educations of Isaac McCoy's sons were meant to be useful to their Indian mission.

Already having established missions with the Miami Indians above Terre Haute, with the Potawatomie near Niles, Michigan, and with the Ottawa at Grand Rapids, Rev. Isaac McCoy brought to Westport dispossessed Shawnee to establish a Shawnee Mission in the West. Dr. Johnston Lykins, the husband of the McCoy's daughter Delilah, managed the mission. Later,

Rev. Isaac McCoy 1784 – 1846

Rev. Johnston Lykins 1800 – 1876
Son-in-law of Isaac McCoy

Lykins would be called upon to save the life of T. M.'s cousin, Jesse James, when he operated on the outlaw in the summer of 1865. By then, Rev. Isaac McCoy had returned to Louisville to take charge of the American Indian Mission Association. Shawnee Mission was left to Isaac McCoy's son-in-law, Dr. Lykins.

The pioneer settlers of Westport Landing were recognizable to T. M., most from stories told among his family. As the stories foretold, T. M. found his fabled, fellow pioneers overwrought with ambition.

NO RAILROAD TRAINS YET ENTERED THIS EXPOSED LAND TO WHICH T. M. JAMES BROUGHT HIS FAMILY, except for the noisy trains of prairie schooners crowding the place with their dusty business. Arriving and stocking provisions, the wagons departed as quickly as they rolled in. Attended by the Indian or Mexican greasers on foot to lubricate their wheels, the trains creaked heavily, sinking beneath the western horizon to take route on one of the three trails to Oregon, California, or Santa Fe. In and out of Westport, the wagon streams flowed continuously.

The traffic created riches. Mr. Somerville, a government emigration overseer at Fort Laramie, reported on ten days of traffic passing from Westport through Fort Laramie. "Total number of emigrants passed this post up to June 10th, 1850, inclusive, 16,915 men, 235 women, 242 children, 4,672 wagons, 14,974 horses, 4,641 mules, 7,425 oxen, 1,653 cows."[21] The next day William Switzler wrote to the *Missouri Statesman* newspaper of the riches the Hickmans were collecting. "We have just crossed at Hickman's Ferry. They are running four boats and when hurried can cross 500 teams per day. At an average of $7.50 per team."[22]

T. M. James saw this kind of wealth created before. In his boyhood he sat on the banks of the Ohio River, watching the countless flat boats packed thick with emigrants. From Virginia and Pennsylvania, they navigated hell bent for the Cain-tuc. Their palpable excitement made early Louisville founders like George Rogers Clark very wealthy. This Missouri frontier border seemed made for T. M. The teacher in him saw both lessons to be taught and learned in this place, where a fortune could be made. Despite the forecast of an imminent return of a cholera epidemic, T. M.'s optimism far outweighed the gamble.

John Calvin McCoy 1811 - 1889

Plans already were underway to develop a larger town. The rock ledge in the bend of the river on which Isaac McCoy had built his log cabin, only to see the river sweep the bend and wash it away in a storm, was but a start. Isaac's son John Calvin McCoy had a plan.

Formerly, John Calvin McCoy acquired excess railroad land east of Independence. He expected to build a town. There, he surveyed and plotted lots. He gave the plots freely to settlers willing to start a business. But an outfitting station had sprouted up about 1830 at the bend. The hamlet's postmaster, William Miles Chick, convinced Charles Bent of Bent's Fort in the Far West, and his French partner Ceran St. Vrain of Fort St. Vrain in the Nebraska Territory, to stage their freighting business conveniently from the river, rather than inconveniently inland. John Calvin McCoy abandoned his upstart town and relocated to the hamlet.

Shrewdly, John Calvin McCoy married Chick's daughter Virginia. He was a teacher to all of Virginia's brothers at his father's Shawnee Mission. Later, Chick himself became one of three commissioners who negotiated the purchase of enough safe land around Westport, where buildings would not wash away.

When Virginia and her father both died of cholera, John Calvin McCoy next married Betsy Woodson, the daughter of Samuel Hughes Woodson. The forceful lawyer and former U. S. Congressman had just arrived from Nicholasville in Jessamine County, Kentucky. He was intent upon making a fortune. Rigging elections in the West became a specialty for Woodson, who employed Sam Ralston as his operative.

Obstinate and obstructive land disputes with an old French trader disappointingly halted their development effort. When Gabriel Prudhomme finally died in 1838, the fur trader Bill Sublett from Crab Orchard, Kentucky formed a purchase group with twelve other investors. Prudhomme's 256 acres were purchased for $4,220. McCoy completed plotting the new Town of Kansas. Residual claims against Prudhomme's land lingered until 1853. At last, the *Liberty Far West* and *Missouri Republican of St. Louis* newspapers advertised for sale the first town company of Kansas.

All of the old disputes cleared, William Gregory was elected mayor. Upon inauguration, however, Gregory was revealed no longer to be a Kansas City resident. Gregory was replaced quickly by the city council president, Dr. Johnston Lykins, as the first legitimately seated mayor of Kansas City. As one of the new councilman elected to the first Kansas Town Council, Tilman Howard West proudly welcomed the arrival of T. M. and his family, showing them the new border town and introducing T. M. to the wild western community that was about to make his future.

EVERYONE WAS SEIZED BY A FEVER FOR DEVELOPMENT. THE EXPECTED CHOLERA FEVER FAILED TO MATERIALIZE. Four years after, T. M. purchased a half interest in a steam saw and grist mill Tilman operated, located at the corner of Grand Avenue and Market Streets.[23] The mill was centered strategically amid the growing population and economic activity, gainfully usurping the clientele of Hickman's Mills, sixteen miles away.

Surprisingly and suddenly as any cholera epidemic, the economic panic of 1857 instantly halted all economic investment in the developing town. Building a railroad to the town stopped. A shortage of banking liquidity froze all credit. Businessmen calmly and shrewdly paused to reassess the uniqueness of their "boarder money" economy.

Cash flow never had been a problem in Westport. Why should it?

Money always came directly from the U. S. Mint as annuities to Indian tribes. The money stayed, to be invested. Additional money for the U. S. Army always left a fair share, too, to be earned by local merchants. The constant flow of emigrants to Utah, New Mexico, or California, always left more money. As it was said, "this money is expended immediately on the border, and what little the emigrant retains after the purchase of supplies and outfit, he keeps in his pockets - for what! Why, to come down and trade again!" Silver and gold arrived from Far West mines and trade with *Nuevo Mexico*, creating the only panic Westport's businessmen wanted. When "...a train arrives, the camp formed, and everything nicely 'corralled,' the money is in town, the employees paid off, feed purchased, stock increased or renewed, paid for, and everything connected with the business of the trains transacted with great rapidity - and that makes business - a border panic - and the only panic we ever expect to see on the frontier..."[24]

The mill and saw businesses of West & James proved the border economy assessment correct. Work orders drilled through the credit freeze. Construction exploded. The mill generated consistent income year round, and soon surplus enough to open a general store at Main and Delaware Streets, then primely positioned on the levee.

The success of West & James enabled the partners to invest five hundred dollars as underwriters of a new enterprise. Perry Fuller, one of the mill's log cutters envisioned a trading post for himself. With Tilman and T. M.'s underwriting, Fuller established Centropolis on the lands of the Sauk-Fox Indians, governed by Burton Allen James.[25] Perry's trading outpost grossed sales of $50,000 in each year of its first two years. Perry later became an Indian agent himself, but soon became a target of lawsuits for fraud in Louisiana. His partnership with West & James was divested.[26] Tilman and T. M. garnered a quick and easy return of $14,000 for their short term investment. The payment, however, was made in government claims, which could not be collected until after the Civil War.

T. M. and Tilman took on a more steadfast business partner. Daniel Lewis Shouse arrived a month after T. M. from Fisherville, Kentucky, where he had operated a mercantile store southeast of Louisville.[27] Shouse's father, Daniel, proved himself a prosperous farmer there in both Shelby and Woodford counties. Shouse's older brother, William Overton Shouse, had been one of Westport's early arrivals, settling there in 1837.[28]

The Lewis name Daniel bore came from Meriwether Lewis of the Lewis and Clark expedition, which passed through Westport from Louisville in 1803, on route through Thomas Jefferson's Louisiana Purchase to the Pacific Ocean. Lewis returned again through Westport three years later, surprising all who had given him up for dead. The explorer was a cousin of Shouse's mother, Mary Lea.[29]

Like T. M., Daniel Lewis Shouse came from a large family of siblings. Shouse was the second youngest in his family. T. M. was the third youngest in his. Shouse savored education, as did T. M. Years later when Ralph Waldo Emerson visited the convention center in Kansas City that Shouse's son managed, Shouse made a point of befriending the New England Brahmin, who then visited Shouse in his home.

Following Shouse's early employment in the West & James Company, Shouse advanced as a bank clerk. Around 1859, Shouse became cashier of the Mechanics Bank, the first bank established in Kansas City, with Dr. Johnston Lykins of the Shawnee Mission as its president. Shouse remained in the position for a dozen years, until 1871 when John Bristow Wornall was elected to the Missouri State Senate. Wornall reformed the Bank of Kansas City as the Kansas City National Bank, installing Shouse as his bank's first cashier.[30]

Shouse's son, Louis Wayland Shouse whose birth was delivered by T. M.'s wife Sarah, developed a coffee and sugar plantation in Mexico. After

Louis Wayland Shouse 1867 - Unk.

first obtaining his master's degree at William Jewell College and working in his father's bank, he became U.S. Vice-Counsel to Mexico.[31] In 1896, Louis Wayland Shouse returned to Kansas City to work at the *Kansas City Times* newspaper. Four years later, Shouse became briefly associated as assistant manager of the Orpheum Theater, where Frank James himself later was employed briefly in his retirement. Louis Wayland Shouse eventually retired to a less strenuous position managing and welcoming guests to the Kansas City Convention Center.[32]

Daniel Lewis Shouse became the namesake of T. M.'s grandson, Daniel Lewis James Sr., and he in turn to his son, Dan Lewis James Jr. Shouse became a James in-law when T. M.'s eldest son, John Crawford James, married Shouse's daughter Fannie. T. M.'s relationship with Shouse proved invaluable, especially when T. M. and his brother-in-law sold their mill, and T. M. went into business for himself.[33]

A DEMAND FOR PREMIUM GOODS SEIZED KANSAS CITY. Tilman Howard West established the T. H. West & Son's Gent's Clothing & Furnishing Goods Company. Thomas Martin James established the T. M. James China Company in 1863, first purchasing a stock of warehoused queen's ware from Westport pioneer Thomas A. Smart, who had operated a grocery from a log store house on the levee since the early 1830s. Smart had taken the queen's ware in trade from a passing Frenchman. Smart warehoused the inventory, deeming the fancy items useless to frontiersmen. Young and handsome T. M. shrewdly appealed to the growing female clientele in the area, whom the old settler Smart ignored entirely. Women expanded T. M.'s prospects. They demanded he import more queens' ware directly from France.[34] Women became the centerpiece of T. M.'s clientele. From a separate store and warehouse at 551-553 Delaware Street, T. M. also sold the wholesale crockery, glassware, cutlery, and groceries required by hotels, saloons, and settlers stocking their businesses in the Far West.[35] Business development in the Far West made T. M. rich. But the women of Kansas City spread T. M.'s reputation.

Like Tilman West before him, T. M. became desperate for help. About 1876, T. M. brought his half-brother, nephew and namesake, Thomas Martin Mimms, from Logan County with his family to handle the company's shipping department.[36] Like the population of Kansas City, business for T. M. James and T. M. Mimms boomed.

With cash to spare, T. M. hunted investment opportunities big and small. On November 20, 1856, T. M. attended a meeting in Liberty to form the Kansas City, Hannibal, & St. Joseph Railway Company.[37] Col. Edward Madison Samuels, with whom T. M.'s brother Robert Sallee James was granted the charter from the State of Missouri for William Jewell College, now was soliciting subscribers to extend the railway from Kansas City to Keokuk. At the same time, the Missouri legislature approved the incorporation of the Union Cemetery Association for Jackson County. Thomas A. Smart, Daniel Lewis Shouse, T. M. and Burton Allen James, all acquired cemetery plots.[38] Before the cemetery's incorporation, the remains of William M. Chick already had been laid to rest in the cemetery location when Chick died in 1847 of pneumonia.

In February of 1869, T. M. was one of sixty-seven original members of the Kansas City Chamber of Commerce to dissolve the chamber to institute the new Kansas City Board of Trade.[39] With credit and banking relationships securely established, T. M. erected his own James Building in 1871 at 558-560 Main St. on the northeast corner Sixth and Main streets. It became his flagship store for the T. M. James China Company.[40] T. M.'s half-brother, Thomas Martin Mimms continued to handle shipping for the company from a building at 1319 Cherry St., where Mimms lived above the business.

Since he was a school teacher in Kentucky, Thomas Martin James always strived for quality in everything he did. T. M. now held his salespeople to the standard of a listed sales price for his products. He discouraged any negotiation that was formerly customary in frontier commerce. T. M. intended to insure his cash flow. But he would not diminish his reputation for integrity at any cost.[41]

His services and goods proved increasingly exceptional. Following his death, a portion of T. M.'s business and real estate would be sold easily in the 1920s by his sons to Joyce Clyde Hall and his brother Rollie B. Hall. The Hall brothers from David City, Nebraska, wanted a retail location in central Kansas City, after fire destroyed their business. Mr. J. C., the name by which Joyce C. Hall preferred to be known, subscribed to the principle of quality himself. In his autobiography titled *When You Care Enough*, J. C. Hall wrote, *"If a man goes into business with only the idea of making a lot of money, chances are he won't. But if he puts service and quality first, the money will take care of itself. Producing a first class product that meets a real need is a much stronger motivation for success than getting rich."* Hall was the founder of the Hallmark Greeting Card Company in Kansas City, whose slogan became *"when you care enough to send the very best."*

T. M.'s tradition of quality and excellence would survive him handily. Fifty years after his death, the T. M James China Company was acquired in the 1950s by the prestigious Havilland Fine China Company.

The sale to the Hall brothers proved benefi cial for the James family. For thirty-eight years, the grandson of Jesse James, Lawrence Henry Barr, worked in Hallmark's payroll department in near anonymity. His wife, Thelma Duncan-Barr, always complained her husband was penalized by the very small salary her husband received.[42] But Lawrence was grateful to hold a job in which he could remain in the background, away from public notice or scrutiny.

Joyce Clyde "J. C." Hall 1891 - 1982

Thelma further related a story of the perversely, jabbing sense of humor of J. C. Hall's brother. Rollie B. Hall was vice president and director of national sales for Hallmark. When Mr. R. B. poked fun at Lawrence, the grandson of Jesse James fell into a depression, fearing his steadfast job at Hallmark was in jeopardy of termination. Thelma wrote, *"...one day Mr. R. B. Hall found out that L. was gr andson of J. J. He was quite a kidder anyway and he made the remark. 'Well who would ever thought we'd have J. J.'s grandson working for us, and in the payroll department of all things!'."* Laurence remained secure in his job. His daughter, Betty Barr, remained employed at Hallmark most all of her life, too, as a merchandise analyst. Despite Mr. R. B. Hall's good-natured humor, Thelma Barr added, *"He used to give Betty $5.00 for Xmas when she was a little girl growing up."*[43]

By the late 1870s, the Grand Central Hotel was home to Thomas Martin James and his wife.[44] As T. M. prospered, for the first time he moved into a prominent residence, befitting a well-heeled and well-recognized businessman. The home at 1235 West 57th Street Terrace, one block west of today's Ward Parkway in the Sunset Hill residential district of Kansas City was built by the Ward Development Company. Its stately presence exceeded all of T. M.'s boyhood dreams.

COMMITTED TO BUILDING BOTH HOME AND COMMUNITY, THOMAS MARTIN JAMES REMAINED TRUE TO HIS RELIGIOUS HERITAGE. Having been raised in the Methodist church of his step father, Rev. John Wilson Mimms, T. M. joined the Baptist church at the age of fifteen of his own volition, while he still was living in Kentucky.[45] Arriving in Westport, however, T. M. found no Baptist church; so he associated himself with the Methodist Episcopal Church, the only Protestant church in the area.[46] The church was founded by William Miles Chick. Chick's son, Joseph, who operated a general store, was the church's guiding influence. Joseph seized upon T. M.'s skills as a teacher to organize a Sunday school for his Methodist church. Perceiving the school failed to flourish outside the church's small congregation, T. M. became its superintendent. He reorganized the school independently of the church. T. M.'s Union Sabbath School was opened to Methodist church members willing to unite with non-Methodist church members.

By nature, T. M. remained inclined toward his chosen Baptist faith. On April 21, 1855, less than a year after his arrival, T. M. moved to establish his own Baptist church. Unclear is whether T. M. summoned those more experienced and older than himself; or whether the energetic and self-motivated young, Sunday school organizer was himself solicited by others to create a Baptist presence.

T. M.'s co-founders for the First Baptist Church of Kansas City were

Dr. Johnston Lykins of the Shawnee Mission and his sister Julia; Rev. and Mrs. Alton Franklin and Elizabeth Martin; Robert James Holmes and his wife Mary; and the former president of William Jewell College in Liberty, Rev. and Mrs. R. S. and Elvira Thomas.[47] If T. M. himself was summoned, it was likely Rev. R. S. Thomas who buttoned him.

Rev. Robert Stewart Thomas was born in Scott County, Kentucky, home to Georgetown College. His brother, John Pendleton Thomas, was Kentucky State Treasurer under Governors Charles Scott, Isaac Shelby, George Madison, and Gabriel Slaughter. Thomas was converted, and baptized in Paris, Kentucky by John M. James' son-in-law, Rev. Jeremiah Vardeman. With family finances meager, Thomas first was schooled at Transylvania University in Lexington. Displaying proof of his intellectual acumen, funds were collected to send Thomas to Yale. Upon his return, Rev. Vardeman brought Thomas into Baptist ministry. Arriving as a missionary in Missouri, Thomas became principal of the Bonne Femme Academy in Boone County, where Warren Woodson was a teacher. Bonne Femme was established by David McClanahan Hickman, a second cousin of the family from Hickman's Mills.

Rev. Robert Stewart "R. S." Thomas 1805 - 1859

Physically, Rev. R. S. Thomas appeared the perfect missionary for the frontier. One of his students described him. *"His hair, moderately thick, hung down by the side of his head, lank, black, and oily, like an Indian's. His complexion was sallow, and he was smoothly shaved. He had dark eyes with a piercing gaze. He had a refreshing sense of humor and was fond of telling anecdotes. He knew how to be friendly and intimate with boys and yet to keep his dignity. He was a man of commanding appearance, balanced and composed, dignified, gentlemanly, and with a most benignant countenance."*

The talents of Thomas were quickly evident. Thomas was elected to the faculty of the University of Missouri. In 1852, Thomas was made president of William Jewell College.[48] Ten years after Rev. Thomas died in 1859, William Jewell College reported an endowment of $40,000 for a school of theology. The school was named for Thomas' mentor as the Jeremiah Vardeman School of Theology. Thomas' term as president at Jewell was now ending. Becoming the first pastor for the First Baptist Church of Kansas City was his next challenge.[49]

Like Thomas, Mr. and Mrs. Robert James Holmes were from Kentucky, too. They had recently arrived from Shelby County. Holmes was related to Dr. Johnston Lykins' family, as a second cousin of Mrs. Lykins, Delilah McCoy, who was the daughter of Rev. Isaac McCoy.

Among all of T. M.'s church co-founders, Rev. Alton Franklin Martin was the eldest and most experienced. He gave the organizing church its *imprimatur*. Riding a prairie schooner as a boy with his parents, Martin entered Missouri territory in 1794, earlier than any of Westport's pioneer fur traders. Martin was born on the Mississippi River in St. Louis County. As a child, Martin suffered from white swelling, tuberculosis of the joints. His parents, believing he would be crippled for life, educated him to be a teacher. He was sent to Rock Spring in Illinois where Rev. John Mason Peck, a Baptist missionary who founded the First Baptist Church of St. Louis, had a seminary. Young Martin was baptized there, and at age nineteen embarked upon a teaching career. Missouri then was *"one great missionary field,"* in which Martin became a *"Rough Rider"* for the Lord. In 1844 he rode 1,000 miles in 120 days, preaching 70 times, baptizing 26 people, organizing one church, and adding another to the four churches he already ministered. The experience he brought to forming T. M.'s church would be formidable. However, shortly after the founding, Rev. A. F. Martin withdrew to Linn County, leaving the foundling First Baptist Church of the new town of

Kansas capably in the hands of Pastor R. S. Thomas and his young deacon, Thomas Martin James.

As T. M.'s sons later would state, T. M. assumed the position of deacon *"not because he sought control, but because he was a 'servant for all.' Our Lord has taught that service was the only way that any of His disciples could attain pre-eminence."* [50] Later, T. M. James turned over his deaconship to Daniel Lewis Shouse, and his impassioned talent for recruiting church members.

Rev. Joseph Cowgill Maple, one of the later pastors of First Baptist, wrote of Deacon Shouse, *"At the time I was his pastor, there was a great inflow of strangers into Kansas City. As cashier of the leading bank, he met many of these people. He knew the older people so well that it was easy for him to mark new comers."* Maple recalled, *"There was an alley between his barn and mine. He would often call by as he was going down to the bank and say, 'I heard of some new Baptist families who have just moved to the city. Bring my horse with you at 4 o'clock and I will go with you and see them'."* Shouse subsequently became pastor of the First Baptist Church, as competition among Baptist churches developed in Kansas City.

Rev. Joseph Cowgill Maple

Like T. M., Shouse's first employment was as a teacher, at the age of nineteen in Henry County, Kentucky. At the First Baptist Church, Shouse became its model Sunday school superintendent. He was recognized for *"encouraging the weak of faith, cheering the faint hearted, and setting an example of Christian piety for all."* After a decade, Shouse replaced T. M. as the church's deacon. Shouse brought T. M. into the Young Men's Christian Association, as a director and benefactor. He advanced local, home, and foreign missions, as well as educating new ministers. He became secretary of the Missouri Sunday School Convention. For all of his good work, the life of Daniel Lewis Shouse fell short. He died at forty-six years of age on April 1, 1873, quite possibly anticipating there would be a run on his bank in a few short weeks, forcing his bank to close and enter a period of reorganization. Stressful, economic times lay ahead, but Kansas City continued to grow.

After Shouse died, T. M. donated land at Grand and Eleventh Streets upon which to build a second Baptist church.[51] The cost of the larger structure was $153,000, about half of the funds coming from the sale of the previous church. The new Calvary Baptist Church was organized on February 7, 1876, with thirty-two members.[52] Rev. J. E. Chambliss became its first pastor. T. M.'s obituary in 1901 highlighted his generosity of the moment:

"To Calvary Baptist Church alone he contributed $9,000. When, on the day of the opening service, it was announced, with a degree of satisfaction that 'All we owe on this magnificent structure is $30,000.' Mr. James arose in his pew and declared the service must not end with a dollar owing. He then said he would be one of two to make up the deficit. The $30,000 was raised during the next ten minutes. Mr. James contributed something like $9,000." [53]

Calvary Baptist Church

By 1890, the congregation grew so large that the new Calvary Baptist Church then comfortably seated 1,443 worshipers per service. Following multiple services on Sunday mornings, all of the fellowship usurped the public street, where a large, urban, communal picnic lasted well into mid-afternoon.

From 1878 through 1886, T.M. was an active member of the State Missions and Sunday Schools. The quarterly meetings held in Mexico, Missouri required attendees to pay their own expenses. While attending a meeting in 1885 of the General Association in Carthage, T. M. was entrusted with subscription funds to purchase a struggling church on Missouri's western border. The funds, however, proved insufficient to meet the costs of concluding the purchase. T. M. finalized the transaction, adding *"quite a sum to the amount of money considered sufficient at first."* T. M. did not request reimbursement.[54]

In 1887, T. M. made another trip to Carthage. His brother, the dentist Dr. John R. James, was dying. T. M. was accompanied by his sister Elizabeth and his brother Rev. William Henry James. They, with Drury Woodson James in California, would become the only surviving siblings of the orphan clan of John M. James. Dr. John's son Johnny remained at work on Uncle Drury's rancho in California, but his other children were in attendance. Dr. John James had remained devoted to the Southern Methodist Church until his parting breath.[55]

T. M. BELIEVED THOSE OF EVERY CALLING SHOULD HAVE the *"highest mental culture that might become citizens who would make our government not only permanent, but would make it impossible for ignorant and immoral men to obtain positions of responsibility in civil life."*[56]

T. M.'s vision perceived that *"the day was past when men without mental culture could lead to success the coming hosts that would soon populate this great country, so full of promise."* He saw William Jewell College was blessed with more students for ministry than any other college. Farmers even were being schooled. As a symbol of community development, Thomas Martin James illustrated his belief daily, whether he waited on a customer, hatched a business deal in the counting room, sang in a prayer meeting, or taught his class in Bible School.

For the boy who was orphaned at age three to become a mannered merchant to upper classes and subsequently a generous philanthropist, Thomas Martin James could lay his success to the education provided to him by his uncle, State Rep. Drury Woodson Poor of Kentucky. Poor insured the orphaned T. M. was educated not only in the rough-hewn, pioneer Kentucky culture of his natural father John M. James, but also in the more refined civilities and polished society of his father's Southern ancestral culture in the Old Dominion.

Drury Woodson Poor was a former Virginian himself from Goohland County, and a close friend and confident of John M. James. Poor occasionally took the bachelor T. M. with him on periodic family visits to Virginia. When T. M. became a parent himself, he'd send his own children to Eastern schools to be prepared in gentility, comportment, and social protocols. T. M. intended more importantly that his children be schooled with the most progressive education available. Kentucky's bachelors and widowers still returned to the Old Dominion, as did T. M.'s father, to find marriageable wives of refinement, poise, and bearing. When twenty-four, T. M. met and married Susan Ann Woodward in her father's Goochland County home.[57] He had ventured into Virginia on a lumber wagon. He returned to Kentucky in a buggy with his beloved new wife, Sarah.

For T. M.'s formal schooling, Rep. Poor provided T. M. the personal tutoring of J. W. Rust at Russellville. Poor committed seventeen year old T. M. to the fifteen year old Rust for a period of a year and a half.[58]

The relationship between the younger teacher Rust and older student James was more one of schoolmates, or teachers in training. Rust had only thirteen months of schooling himself. In the fashion of self-education employed by John James of Alvarado, Texas, the two young men embarked upon a program of self-directed educational development.

Rust had been brought up in Logan County, the son of poor farmers. But like T. M., Rust demonstrated a promising intellect and an eager self-motivation. Rust had resolved to become a teacher at an early age. With the help of T. M. as his student, Rust achieved his goal by age eighteen. It was noted, *"Without friends to help, or money to sustain him, he determined to qualify himself to teach, and such were his persistency, energy, tact and safacity that, by the time he had fairly reached manhood, he had earned a reputation as a teacher."*[59]

Thereafter, Rust employed T. M. as his teaching assistant. Three years later in 1844, T. M. witnessed Rust advance to become principal of Mt. Carmel Academy, a Catholic school. Rust succeeded further in a like position at Springfield Academy, Clarksville Female Academy, and Lafayette Female Institute, until in 1857, three years after T. M. departed for Missouri, Rust was elected president of Bethel Female College.[60]

For several years in the Bethel Baptist Association in Logan County, Rust employed his education to write effective circulars to be distributed among the member churches of the association, addressing issues such as "Christian Amenity and Love," "The Paramount Obligations of Christians," and "The Religious Training of Churches." [61] The principles contained in the tracts Rust wrote were actualized in practice by T. M. later in his Missouri Baptist church.

Rust's most valuable teaching contribution to T. M. instilled in him a religious egalitarianism, not too unlike that practiced by John James of Alvarado, Texas, who surrendered his Baptist credentials in deference to the innate spirituality he found evident in the Choctaw. T. M. never had to rationalize why his Sabbath School should be open to those of divergent faiths. A respect for knowledge and learning was universally the most worthwhile tool one possessed for creating success, be it in freedom, commerce, or even in faith.[62]

The rapid acceleration of Rust's career demonstrated to T. M. that advancement in life came of one's own making. Education is one's keystone tool for success. Education elevated Thomas Martin James from a lowly, emigrant tenderfoot to well-beloved philanthropist.

T. M. also recognized from Rust that the structure of a school could mold minds, more effectively if the school was dedicated to a denomination of faith. Like Rev. Robert Sallee James who was a founding trustee of William Jewell College, and like Rev. Jeremiah Vardeman who had founded the schools of theology at both Georgetown College in Kentucky and William Jewell College in Missouri, T. M. achieved greater success, becoming a trustee of William Jewell College himself in 1879.[63] Captain Oliver Perry Moss, T. M.'s third cousin who conducted an expedition against the Mormons and also was a deacon at the Second Baptist Church of Liberty, Missouri had served as an early trustee in 1853. Rev. William Henry Vardeman, a son of John M. James' daughter, Elizabeth James and her husband Rev. Jeremiah Vardeman, was a trustee in 1869.

John Bristow Wornall 1822 – 1892

Oliver Perry Moss 1813 – 1881

T. M.'s dedication for learning, scholarship, and service, would be inherited by his progeny, and passed on to their progeny in turn. T. M. followed the example of John Bristow Wornall, the president of the board under whom T. M. served. Wornall was an early Westport settler since 1844. Both John B. Wornall's son and grandson, all of whom bore the same name, served as William Jewell trustees. When T. M.'s sons, J. C. and Luther Tillman James, returned home after graduating Brown University in Rhode Island, J. C. also became a William Jewell trustee in 1915. Daniel Lewis Shouse served as trustee in 1867, as did Tilman Howard West in 1890.[64] Even the fur trader Seth E. Ward served in 1872.

Among all the Kentucky Baptist influences to tame the Westport frontier and commercialize the Kansas City metropolis, application and industriousness marked those who would leave a legacy of accomplishment and contribution. T. M. augmented those tenets to include the distinct influence of faith and education. In his lifetime, T. M. James was recognized for his endowment. What followed became a legacy for all among the James family, as well as for his community.

James Elementary School

Chapter Six

Only a Large Soul Can Do This

The harmony demonstrated among the family of trustees at William Jewell College was not so evident to T. M.'s sons, John Crawford and Luther Tillman James, when the brothers took their education at Brown University in Rhode Island. The end of the Civil War left much rancor unresolved. After the war, the brothers' cousins, Frank and Jesse James, transformed their partisan campaigns into well publicized outlaw exploits. If anything at all was learned at Brown, J. C. and Luther learned that being a family relation of outlaws attracted suspicion, caution, and distrust. The rest of their lives would be spent defeating the handicap.

C lass Day dawned for John Crawford James as a gloomy morning. J. C. first entered the sophomore class of Missouri University three years after the Civil War in 1867. He transferred to the sophomore class of Brown the following year. J. C. relished history and political economics. His grades put him at the head of his class. His final exams completed in June of 1871 with graduation a few days hence, school administrators granted J. C. and his fellow seniors a single day to exercise their achievement over the under classes. Dissension, however, ruled the day. One third of the class refused to participate. Cliques, secret societies, and fraternities, all besmirched with the residue of the Civil War became a discordant evil at Brown.

The day's first address attempted to set a moderate tone. Class president J. M. Gould of Bangor, Maine, exhorted a liberality of viewpoints through thoughtfulness. D. W. Hoyt next read the poem *The Real and Ideal*, the closing lines admonishing graduates that character development spelled true success. Lunch was followed by a sunny game of baseball, in which the Boston Red Stockings attracted the largest audience to witness a ritual chastisement of the graduates, measured by a bruising 24 to 3 victory.

T. M. James Fine China Company (R) & Commerce Bank (L)
545 Delaware St. – 1863

Late in the afternoon, the *Address to Undergraduates* by E. W. Hendrick throttled those remaining, with "a quaint racy flavor, tinged with the lawless exuberance of Western thought and expression." As evening approached, the graduating class strolled to supper between Chinese lanterns that cast their figures against the College's crumbling walls as luminous phantasmagoria, soon to disappear from the scene. Supper ended on an appropriate note of congenial grace.[1] The education of John Crawford James was complete.

Leaving his brother Luther at Brown to complete two more years of study, J. C. boarded a train for Western Missouri with his Bachelor of Arts degree in hand, prepared to assume the employment waiting at his father's side in T. M. James & Sons.

Two years later, J. C. married Fannie Shouse, the daughter of Daniel Lewis Shouse. The couple started a family. Vassie James was the couple's first born child of their three daughters. In between Vassie and the youngest daughters, Fannie and Helen, arrived Thomas Martin James II, and then Daniel Lewis James Sr. As his five children grew, J. C.'s growing brood ranked him as a respectable Victorian.

The fast rising arc of his professional success always mystified the modest J. C. He readily recalled the day he was elected to the Kansas City Board of Education. *"On June 19th, 1884, I stepped into the yard of my home for the morning paper. A man said, 'Congratulations.' I then learned I had been elected to the school board."*

J. C. had intended to become a lawyer. As a boy, he swept floors in Daniel Lewis Shouse's Mechanics Bank. He became a teller and learned to keep the bank's books. T. M. sent J. C. to subscription schools, but he also provided J. C. with private tutoring.[2] In his spare time, J. C. studied Greek and Latin under the lawyer J. V. C. Karnes. In the evenings he studied mathematics under Karnes law partner, Henry Newton Ess and his wife Phoebe Jane Routt, who was a teacher.

Mrs. Ess proved a stronger influence on young J. C. than did her husband, or his law partner. When Phoebe Ess joined the Tuesday Morning Study Club in 1882, she proclaimed herself an "advanced thinker." She was a founder of the Kansas City Athenaeum, the Women's City Club, and the Susan B. Anthony Civic Club. Later she founded the General Federation of Women's Clubs, channeling her zeal for social reforms through more than thirty clubs and movements. As a fearless opponent to poverty and injustice, Phoebe Ess periodically appeared before J. C. when he headed the Board of Education, petitioning her former student for school playgrounds and art classes, and protections for widows with children. She established the Jackson County Parental Home for Girls, advocated prohibition, campaigned to improve prison conditions, and together with J. C.'s daughter

Phoebe Routt Ess   J. V .C. Karnes, Esq.

Vassie James made Jackson County one of the first Missouri countries to adopt woman's suffrage.[3]

JOHN CRAWFORD JAMES REBUFFED INVITATIONS TO JOIN THE BOARD OF EDUCATION. He believed he had not been trained for a position of public trust. Recalling the factionalism he experienced at Brown, and reading the sensational reporting about his bellicose cousins in the news, J. C. was slow to be persuaded. What swayed him ultimately was evidence that the board was equally balanced between Republicans and Democrats. Board policy strictly avoided the disastrous partisan politics that demoralized most government office holders. The quiet J. C. admired the Board for refraining from "the display of oratorical powers." The Board's motto was taken from George Elliott. "Where one has nothing to say, he need not give wordy evidence of the fact."

Taking his oath of office, J. C. was seated on the Board of Education. With him sat Henry C. Kumph, a robust German, knowledgeable of Goethe and Schiller. Kumph believed physical training taught industry, truthfulness, and discipline. E. L. Martin had been mayor of Kansas City. Martin scrutinized the budget, and focused on bringing black children into schools. Robert L. Yeager was raised to have a judicial temperament by Judge John T. Redd. Yeager never allowed the board to "do the right thing in the wrong way, at the wrong time." In the war, Yeager had served in Sterling Price's army. Gen. Frank Askew served in the war, too. In a dry sense of humor, Askew provided the Board a command of building construction with military precision. Completing J. C.'s associates was Gardiner Lathrop, a lawyer. His father, John C. Lathrop, was formerly the president of the University of Wisconsin, and subsequently the first president of the University of Missouri. A Yale graduate, Gardner Lathrop brought a lofty sense of educational betterment. However, at the start of each meeting, Lathrop always served humorous appetizers to align his fellow board members at a starting point of camaraderie. The term of John Crawford James would outlast any of these men, among whom he first sat with uneasy trepidation.

Over twenty-four years, J. C. dutifully served on sub-committees for finance, building, teachers' examinations, and the High School & Teacher's Institute. He served as both member and chairman, until finally J. C. was elected President of the Board on November 19, 1908. When his mentor, the lawyer J. V. C. Karnes, was brought onto the board, J. C. formed a keen suspicion of professional reformers in education, religion, and theories of government. Instead, J. C. and his former tutor Karnes plumbed the depths of education for ideas that were "fresh, original, and replete with wisdom." Ever present was the question, what will make children thoughtful, industrious, and self-respecting citizens, fully qualified to take their place in society?

When he ended his twenty-seven years of service, J. C. wrote down his accomplishments and put them into perspective.

"I have seen the school grow from small beginnings, from 9,000 pupils, then to 36,000 now in 1912; from 147 teachers to 973; from seven small buildings to seventy-two splendid school structures; from a small high school with 241 pupils to four magnificent high schools with an attendance of 5,000. Our library, insignificant then, now is in an appropriate building, housing 110,000 volumes." [4] For all his years of service, J. C. James accepted no pay.

His seven years as president was memorialized when J. C.'s name was affixed to the James Elementary School at 5610 Scarritt Avenue. His successor J. M. Greenwood wrote of J. C., *"With men accustomed to broad and statesmanlike views, Mr. James...brought into the Board high ideals of manhood, womanhood, and childhood, - a true Christian spirit, and he would listen to the wants of little children from the humblest home, or its parents, with infinite patience. He is true and loyal to his convictions, clear-headed, truthful, frank, sympathetic with the sufficiency and struggling of others, kind and unselfish. It is always the possessor of the polished, cultivated mind that attracts him. The charm of cultivated simplicity went straight to his heart. Refinement of the mind and solidity of character he placed far and above the accidents of birth or fortune. He faced each new day with the joyous freshness of a little child, because he ever has an abiding faith in humanity and of the loving kindness of the Creator. Out of the depth of his innermost soul he always spoke and acted. With these sympathetic qualities, he brought into the inner circle a calm, warm judgment, a wide observant experience, and flexibility in discussion that marks the mind in search of truth, not made rigid by narrow, microscopic vision. During all these years, he stood for every safe educational movement that had been taken by the Board. A rare quality of mind, which he possesses in high degree, is that of self-acknowledgment of a mistake in judgment whenever one was made. Only a large soul can do this with good grace."* [5]

In his resignation letter, J. C. proudly noted, *"No scandal has ever attached to the Board or any of its members, and to a rare degree it has enjoyed the confidence of the people."* [6]

IN HIS BUSINESS CAREER, J. C. ADDED A WHOLESALE OUTLET TO T. M. JAMES & SONS at 607 Wyandotte Street, while he maintained the lucrative retail store on Grand Avenue. J. C.'s nephews, Crawford Martin and William Heberd James, eventually became J. C.'s secretary and treasurer in managing the firm, bringing another generation into the family trade.[7] Within five years of entering his father's company, the firm was grossing more than $400,000 per year.

His father's social and financial relationships advanced J. C.'s career further. T. M. obtained directorships for J. C. in the National Bank of Kansas City of Joseph S. Chick, and later the City National Bank.[8] In 1897, J. C. and his two sons were appointed directors of the new Kansas City, Missouri Gas Company, headed by the banker Robert M. Snyder of the Mechanic's Savings Bank, which employed Daniel Lewis Shouse.[9]

In May of 1891, J. C. and his father hosted an International Convention in the commodious auditorium of their Calvary Baptist Church. Businessmen

Joseph S. Chick   Robert McClure "R. M." Snyder

from across the nation were hosted in the private homes of T. M., J. C., and other Kansas City businessmen. J. C. became a director of the Commercial Club of Kansas City, out of which grew the Chamber of Commerce, and subsequently the Kansas City Board of Trade. More than 800 members touted, "Make Kansas City a Good Town to Live In."

A billion dollars in checking revenue now cleared Kansas City's banks. The Commercial Club boasted, "We are not handicapped by any ting of factionalism" - a clear refrain of the painful border struggles and Civil War. The scope of the Club's dedication expanded beyond business alone to include civic improvements of street paving, improving sanitary conditions, clearing air pollution, reducing tax and postage costs, providing railroad transportation, arranging city land acquisition and paying for acquired Indian lands, and dealing with tariffs and land titles. The Club's reach also extended deeply into the South to improve the port of New Orleans, upon which Kansas City trade flourished.[10]

Since his youth, J. C. was well acquainted with the Missouri River. Only fourteen years old when the Civil War broke out, J. C. was too young to go to war. T. M. did not allow his son simply to run off to war, as did J. C.'s cousins, Frank and Jesse, who lacked a father's discipline. Instead,

J. C. purchased newspapers from steamboats docked on the Kansas City waterfront. J. C. then saddled up and rode inland to sell news accounts of the war for a profit.[11]

Three years after J. C. returned from Brown, Jefferson Davis came to Kansas City on a speaking tour. The previous year, Davis had turned down the presidency of newly forming Agricultural and Mechanical College of Texas, the forerunner of today's Texas A. & M. University. Davis also graciously sidestepped election as a Mississippi Senator. Instead, Davis traveled to England where he met with British businessmen. They formed the Mississippi Valley Association. The British firm promoted emigration to the South and European trade through the port of New Orleans. Jefferson Davis became their spokesman. Davis drew 10,000 to 11,000 people at each stop in Missouri. T. M.'s family ties to Frank and Jesse James insured J. C. a position where he could hear every word Davis spoke.

Davis recalled his time in Missouri. "*Well do I remember your country when it was not such a teeming population as it is now. I knew the wild hills about the headwaters of the Meramec when very few were living there - when the population was what would be called rude - hunters and miners, with here and there a little scrap of cultivation; but within the homes, within the rude tenements they inhabited with the latch string always on the other side, there was heart and hospitality within...That was the day then heroic men and women occupied the land.*"

Jefferson Davis

1808 - 1889

Issues of the recent war were deftly sidestepped by Davis. *"I have come, my friends, not to discuss with you any of those vexed questions which have agitated the country, and still may disturb the minds of a certain portion of people. I come to you to rise to a higher plane, and if there still be those in whose hearts malice and hate and non-charitableness disturb the judgment, let us withdraw from such and pass over to the other side, where, sitting in the abode of brotherly love, we can confer together as to what will best conduce to the prosperity and permanent welfare of ourselves and our posterity."*

Often appearing as rambling, Davis extolled the virtue of the robust agricultural life of the Mississippi Valley. *"Agriculture is the great pursuit of our people. Agriculture was the first, and I behold it to be the highest occupation of man...The mechanic arts, commerce, and the liberal professions all go hand in hand to aid the farmer in the progress of his work."*

Davis then came to the bond that the river provided among people. *"We are one. Whatever the devices of man may do, whatever the passions of men may do, whatever statecraft and local policy may do to keep you divided, I say still the people of the Mississippi Valley are one, held together by that great artery which extends from the frozen regions of the North to the perennial flowers of the South."*

Moving in on his sales pitch, Davis well might have set Mark Twain thinking about how the Mississippi River might be symbolized as the primary artery of the heart of America in his stories of Tom Sawyer and Huckleberry Finn. Davis highlighted the Mississippi River as the most cost efficient means to direct trade through the international port of New Orleans. River transport was superior to paying the high costs charged by railroads and profit consuming middlemen to transport the commerce of the Valley to Eastern ports. *"The people of England, the manufacturers and the moneyed men of England, are anxiously looking to the trade of the Mississippi Valley."*

Davis got down to cash and brass tacks. *"You will have no more specie, if the present things exists, ten years hence than you have now. But if you will export, as you are able to do, a hundred millions more than you import, then the world will pay you in specie, and specie will aggregate in your country. There will be those who say, 'Oh, we have got too much currency'."*

He drove home his hard sell. *"In 1874, taking the statements of the Bureau of Statistics...The active circulation of Great Britain per capita was $21.34;*

of France, $41.92; Germany, $17.87, and now we come to this country, bloated by an inflated currency, bloated so high no man can tell whether he has his pockets too full or not...And what is this active circulation per capita in the United States? $14.33, far less than either of those great commercial countries with which I have compared it." Davis concluded, *"unless we have the currency of the world, we never can compete with other countries in exports."*

The *New York Times* of September 11, 1875, reported that Davis' speech also advocated, *"that foreigners be freely and cordially invited to settle among them. He also urged the necessity of education for everybody, from the highest to the lowest, and advocated the establishment in the Mississippi Valley of at least one great university."*

Throughout his business life, J. C. became an active promoter of the ideas he heard that day from Jefferson Davis. After J. C. had achieved most of his accomplishments in the field of education, the Missouri River Valley Improvement Association was formed in 1906, through which federal government expenditures were sought to improve river channels and build dams.[12] John Crawford James advanced protections for the waterway to New Orleans that would grow Kansas City commerce.

NEWSPAPERS REPORTED J. C. DIED of bronchial pneumonia at the age of eighty-four in January of 1933. Immediate family members were his pall bearers. One obituary listed J. C.'s honorary pallbearers, highlighting J. C.'s close ties to those who shaped Kansas City commerce, culture, as well as its rising skyline, now elevated higher than any of T. M.'s dreams when he first arrived at Westport Landing.[13]

At his death, J. C. was a director of the Fidelity National Bank & Trust. His fellow bank officers were cited as honorary pallbearers. Henry C. Flowers was the bank's founder, and W. D. Johnston its vice-president. Lester W. Hall was its attorney and second vice-president. Together with John Crawford James, these bankers had acquired the old post office and federal building at 909-911 Walnut St. On its site, they erected a thirty-two story office building in 1930 and 1931. Together, too, they succumbed to the Great Depression that liquidated their bank and its high rise enterprise. The foreclosed building later was acquired by President Harry S. Truman to be used for government offices. Truman kept his own office in the building. The edifice of Kansas City pride has been added since to the National

909-911 Walnut St.

*Tallest building
in Kansas City
when built*

Register of Historic Places, a testimonial to the vision of J. C. and his honorary pallbearers.

Also among his honorary pallbearers was Robert Alexander Long, originally from Shelbyville, Kentucky, who became a lumber baron in the Far West. His R. A. Long Building, erected in 1924, stood sixteen stories tall, and housed his United Missouri Bank. Long made frequent contributions to J. C.'s educational causes, producing building funds for a high school, a library, and a YMCA. Alfred Gregory, an attorney and additional honorary pallbearer, also funded construction of The Street Boys Club, J. C.'s program for disadvantaged youth.

R. A. Long Building

J. B. Reynolds, another honored pallbearer, was president of the Kansas City Life Insurance Company. He erected his first commercial office building in 1824, when Kansas City was "The Athens of the West." As Kansas City became the second largest city in the West behind San Francisco, Reynolds chartered the Bankers Life Association in 1895. The bank insured cash flow put in service to Kansas City's development.

Others honorees included Wallace Campbell Goff, who established the Grain Exchange. James Franklin Holden was president of the Kansas City Southern Railway, which tied Kansas City trade to ports in the Gulf of Mexico. In his long railroading career, Holden managed the accounts for the St. Louis & San Francisco Railway, was vice-president for the Choctaw, Oklahoma, & Gulf Railroad that crossed Indian Territory where he created the town of Holden, and Holden managed the freight of the Chicago, Rock Island, & Pacific Railway. William Malcolm Lowery founded an engineering firm in Kansas City. Ernest Hemingway later was Lowery's house guest, where Hemingway completed writing *A Farewell to Arms*. William A. Repp founded the J. H. North Furniture Company. In partnership with Charles P. Duff, he formed the Duff & Repp Furniture Company. Also honored was Dr. Ralph Major, J. C.'s physician.

Two distant family members also were among J. C.'s honorary pallbearers. John Venable Hanna of Kansas City was a distant cousin to J. C. through their mutually shared family in the Morton family of Kentucky and the Woodsons of Virginia. William Pendleton "W. P." Tutt also was a distant relative, Tutt being a direct descendant of Joseph James, the Younger, the brother of J. C.'s grandfather, John M. James.

J. C.'s BROTHER LUTHER TILMAN JAMES GRADUATED BROWN IN 1873. Like his brother before him, Luther brought home a strong distaste for division and factionalism. Though he, too, returned to work at T. M. James & Sons, Luther found deeper purpose in his dedicated work outside of his father's company.

Five years out of Brown, Luther Tillman married Mary A. Heberd. Her grandfather, William T. Heberd migrated first from Homer in Cortland County, New York to Connecticut. When the Northwest Territory was opened to settlement following the War of 1812, Heberd then moved to Vincennes, Indiana. In Vincennes, Heberd opened a harness and saddle

Luther Tilman James 1850 - 1916

shop. He also operated a general merchandise store named Burtch & Heberd, with his father-in-law William Burtch. When Burtch died, the firm became W. T. Heberd & Son, bringing Mary's father William into the family business, and later her uncle, Ulysses Heberd. Mary's father married Irene Hanna of Georgetown, Kentucky, Irene's father having been Rowland Hanna, an immigrant from Downpatrick, Ireland. In September of 1867, William Heberd and his brother Ulysses with others established the first private bank in Indiana. The Vincennes Deposit Bank operated privately and successfully until 1879, when the bank was voluntarily dissolved, following Mary's marriage to Luther Tillman James.[14] The couple began a family that grew to four children. The youngest of their children, Marjorie James, remained unmarried all her life. She was known to collect her Heberd and Hanna family history, but not any of her James family history. In the early 1970s, Marjorie took a vacation in Peru. There, a skiing accident left her paralyzed for the last ten years of her life.

THE PRIMARY INFLUENCE UPON LUTHER TILMAN JAMES WAS HIS UNCLE, REV. WILLIAM HENRY JAMES. The same year Luther came home from Brown, his uncle wed Jesse James to their cousin Zee Mimms. Though he had explored California in 1849 with his brother Drury Woodson James, William Henry stayed in Clay County, Missouri. He formed his own town of Greenville, a more stable enterprise, he thought, than panning for California gold. He petitioned to open a post office.[15] In the decade prior to the end of the Civil War, however, his enterprise was ravaged by the growing factionalism. His wife, Mary Ann Varble, who had born him seven children, died before the war. By war's end, Rev. William Henry James closed his store, no longer able to afford his property taxes.[16]

He removed to Kansas City. There, Rev. William Henry James affiliated with the Methodist Episcopal Church South, the very same church that during the war recaptured the school of Frank James' future wife, Annie Ralston, from the Methodist Episcopal Church North, after the school had been appropriated by the northern church faction at the beginning of the war. Periodically, Rev. James preached a circuit.

Rev. James married a second time to the widowed Mary Ann Gibson Marsh. Her home had been burned by Federals in July of 1864. The couple was married two months later. Sometime thereafter, Mrs. Marsh separated from Rev. James to live with her son, James L. Marsh, a deputy court clerk

Rev. William Henry James 1811 - 1895

for Platte County.[17] Upon his sudden death, she lived with her son Gibson.

Ultimately, Rev. William Henry James found his calling administering to the indigent and poor of Kansas City. In the 1870s, while in his sixties, he was operating a boarding house for the poor, with four of his nine children, Mary, Laura, George, and Luther James. The boarding house required charitable contributions to sustain it.[18] Luther Tilman James responded to his uncle's need.

In the 1890s, the health of Rev. James progressively failed. He lived with his daughter Mary and son-in-law George Kirkpatrick until his death on November 14, 1895.[19] Luther Tilman James was determined to insure his uncle's legacy of charitable community service to the poor.

The Kansas City Provident Association initially arose from the need of local businessmen to rid the city streets of vagrants and beggars by transforming them into employed workers. The non-sectarian relief society had been established in 1882, administering tests to employ badly needed lumber yard, masonry, and laundry workers. Machinery workers also were included. In return for work, vouchers for meals and lodging were dispensed. An office was maintained to collect county, municipal, and private contributions.

In 1902, Luther Tillman James was elected treasurer of the association. He served freely without pay among twenty other directors, who represented the city's leading industries and professions. Representing the city's spectrum of faith, the board even included a rabbi. The first year's budget of $20,000 serviced 2,132 individuals and 569 families.[20] The next year, the Association found itself competing against the Associated Charities. Solicitations from each confused the public. As remedy, each month thereafter Luther Tillman James, as treasurer, informed the Associated Charities of its previous month's deposits and expenses. This arrangement continued for the next seven years, until the Kansas City Provident Association was transformed into the Kansas City Board of Public Welfare.[21]

The Board was the first of its kind to be established in the nation. All philanthropic work in Kansas City fell under the Board's auspices - social problems, legal aid, the city's quarry, farm, and women's reformatory, public censorship, factory inspections, and parole of minor offenders, charity endorsements, and social agencies.[22] Thereafter, the Board's officers were appointed by the mayor of Kansas City.

While serving the Provident Association, Luther Tillman James worked under its board president, Edward William Schauffler. As a medical doctor, Schauffler believed he once had treated Luther's infamous cousin, Jesse. Born in Vienna and raised in Constantinople, Schauffler's father had been a missionary to Turkey. Schauffler was only sixteen when the famed British Cavalry, made famous as the "Light Brigade" in a poem by Alfred Lord Tennyson, camped near his family's home. He joined them in the Crimean War. The following year he was sent to America, to Williams College in Massachusetts. After the Civil War, he completed medical studies and traveled west to find a position. Dr. Schauffler settled in Kansas City in 1868. One day after a robbery by the James brothers, the new medical doctor in town was summoned from his home and placed in a carriage with drawn curtains. He attempted to peer out, but was restrained by a revolver put to his face. He was told he was "on a surgical mission and not one of sightseeing." Upon arrival he was escorted into a cellar, and through an underground tunnel that entered another house. There Schauffler extracted a bullet from a wounded man, and wrapped his wound in bandages. When returned home, he was warned of the wisdom of silence. Luther Tillman's fellow director, Dr. Schauffler, maintained Jesse James was one of the first welfare cases he treated in the West.[23]

Charles J. Schmelzer

Luther Tilman's vice-president of the Provident Association was Charles J. Schmelzer, son of a German born manufacturer who owned the Schmelzer Fire Arms Company. When first arriving in America, Schmelzer's father first worked at the Colt armory in Hartford, Connecticut, that produced the Navy revolvers favored by the James brothers. Schmelzer's father traveled through Nebraska and Kansas to Colorado, selling firearms as he stood beside stacks of buffalo skins piled outside of trading stations. In Leavenworth, his father spent $75,000 to open J. F. Schmelzer & Sons, an arms and sporting goods store in which Charles worked with his brother Herman. In Kansas City, Charles J. Schmelzer opened the Schmelzer Arms Company at 710-712 Main Street a few doors away from T. M. James &

Sons, but later relocated his business to a new "up-town" store at 1214-1218 Grand. The *Kansas City Star* reported on April 5, 1908, that Schmelzer just returned from New York. He advised young men to "Stay West." Schmelzer was intent upon retaining the talent that made Kansas City a progressive community. In 1910, his drumbeat elected Schmelzer president of the Kansas City Chamber of Commerce.[24]

WHILE LUTHER TILLMAN JAMES SERVED THE PROVIDENT ASSOCIATION, HIS SON WILLIAM HEBERD JAMES SR. ENTERED CENTRAL HIGH SCHOOL. In 1899 Heberd, as he was called, then entered Yale University with his cousin Daniel Lewis James Sr. Graduating Yale in 1903, Heberd advanced his education with a four month tour of Europe, before entering the family business. Writing later to the *Yale Alumni*, Heberd noted about his visit to the Panama Canal, "My only recent experience was a visit to the big ditch where I found out how small one poor man really is." According to Heberd's granddaughter, Virginia Jacques Church, "That he left Yale early was probably due to the demands of the china business and furthering his education in this field." Virginia added, "One time he told me he wanted to be an architect, but the family business came first, and he was trained to be heir apparent."

At home in September, Heberd promptly married Aileen Stevens, the daughter of a local real estate broker. She was best known locally as the girl who drove a White Steamer car down the broad boulevard where only horse and buggy had gone before. Her father, Edward A. Stevens, had just completed building a large family home, near the stately stone mansion of Herman Schmelzer. The Stevens' mansion was unique for having a ground level room built solely to house the White Steamer. E. A. Stevens suddenly died, shortly before he was to give his daughter's hand in marriage. Heberd and Aileen married, and then moved into the new home, living together with Aileen's widowed mother and her brother, William P. M. Stevens.[25] Aileen's brother periodically took refuge in the home, whenever his real estate deals collapsed. W. P. M. Stephens usually recovered from his periodic losses quickly, making his residencies short.

In the decade to follow, Heberd and Aileen had three children, Virginia Aileen, Eleanor, and William Heberd James Jr.[26] Heberd often quoted the book *Ivanhoe* by Sir Walter Scott to his children, "as easily as reading a daily newspaper," said his granddaughter Virginia.[27] Heberd and Aileen both

William Heberd James Jr. 1916 – Unk.

Aileen Stevens-James 1886 – 1936

could issue *Ivanhoe* quotations. "He taught all his children the value of an education, and my mother [Virginia Aileen James] graduated one year earlier than her classmates."[28]

In 1938, William Heberd James Jr. graduated Dartmouth, and married his girlfriend from Sarah Lawrence College, Burleigh Wolferman, who graduated the same year. The couple had four children, one of whom became a doctor. The Wolferman family was known to the James both in business and social circles. To the public, Burleigh's father Fred Wolferman was popularly recognized as "The Muffin Man." Wolferman's English Muffins had become a popular luxury food, widely advertised by Wolferman's slogan "Eat Good Things." Burleigh's grandfather Louis Wolferman had emigrated from Germany to Milwaukee, Wisconsin, but soon after arrived in Kansas City, where the Wolferman business thrived. Burleigh settled into domestic life with Heberd Jr. Her sister Barbara Wolferman headed for the stage lights of Broadway. There, Barbara began as a casting agent, casting the hit Broadway musicals *Pipe Dream* and *Me & Juliet*. Barbara then produced her own hit play *Blue Denim*.

Eleanor "Ellie" James-McCrae 1911-Unk.
Daughter of William Heberd James Sr. & Aileen Stevens

Virginia Aileen James-
Jacques

*Daughter of William Heberd
James Sr. & Aileen Stevens*

Virginia Aileen James (Front Row, third from right), Mt. Vernon College
*Also in her class was Eleanor Pendleton Chinn,
granddaughter of Frank James' associate Col. John Pendleton "Black Jack" Chinn*

Virginia Jacques Church & husband Arthur Burdette Church (c)
With her parents Horton Jacques & Virginia Aileen James

As Heberd Sr. and Aileen advanced the James family's emphasis on education, especially with their repeated incantations from *Ivanhoe*, the couple was creating an unexpected literary legacy, still evident today. Heberd's daughter Virginia had a daughter of her own, Jacqueline Aileen Church-Simonds. Jacqueline is the publisher of Beagle Bay, Inc., a publishing house for feminist literature. She also is the author of the novel *Captain Mary, Buccaneer*. An advertisement for *Captain Mary* subtly reflects the family's *Ivanhoe* legacy, if not also the James family legacy.

"This adventure of greed and romance will carry you to a distant time when violence was the norm, and the difference between the good and the bad was the flag they flew from the masthead. Captain Mary is more than an ordinary pirate; she is both principled and ruthless, a robber baroness and a generous patron. She is as much loved by her allies as she is hated by her enemies who will stop at nothing to destroy her and her empire. But those seeking Mary's head best watch out for

their own, for in Captain Mary they will find a worthy adversary and deadly foe."

As author, Jacqueline Simonds states she had no conscious plan to reflect any outlaw heritage of the James. Readers of the advertisement for her book might believe otherwise. Of her author daughter, Virginia says, "Jacki graduated with high honors from University of Maryland, though I don't think she can quote *Ivanhoe*, which her grandmother Virginia Aileen James [Heberd's wife] could do into her late eighties."

Author Jacqueline Aileen Church-Simonds

Luther Tillman James died on November 21, 1916, a month after his grandson William Heberd James Jr. was born. On January 20, 1932, Luther's youngest son, Woodward Shelton James, then forty-three years old, was one of more than a hundred charter members who formed the Native Sons and Daughters of Greater Kansas City, self-described as "an organization dedicated to the recognition, preservation, and restoration of Kansas City's unique and rich heritage."

The third generation of the descendants of Thomas Martin James was preparing to recapture a fading history of the James family. Though the effort of the Kansas City community had moved towards historical preservation of its founding families and their history, the force within the James family was not yet ready for the legacy of Thomas Martin James to be fully memorialized. No known item of recording within the lineage society would tie the families of T. M. James or his grandson Woodward Shelton James to Frank and Jesse James.

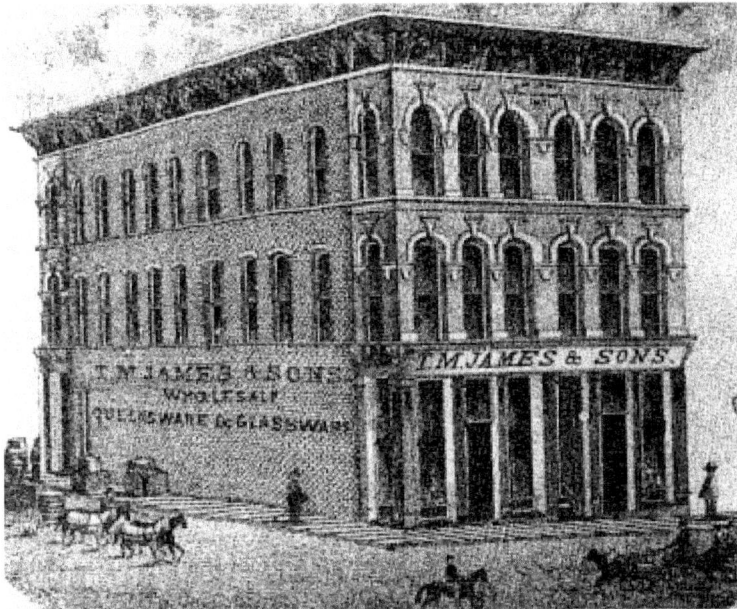

T. M. James & Sons, 1896

The descendants of T. M. James had much more of a legacy yet to develop to insure the James family's integrity. No one among them could have guessed, however, how far women in the James family would advance the family interest and its progressive identity. Captain Mary was born of a legacy and soul in the James family that was about to grow much larger.

Vassie James

Vassar Graduate 1897

Chapter Seven

Breaking Barriers

The first daughter to be born to John Crawford James challenged the educational foundation stones of both her father and her grandfather, T. M. James. Numerous women among the James were strong and forceful matriarchs. Most exercised their influence, staying within accepted social conventions for womanhood. Except for Frank and Jesse's mother Zerelda Cole, few James women publicly confronted powerful interests or government. J. C.'s daughter, Vassie James, challenged both, and further challenged their male dominance. Her influence left a legacy of leadership and activism lasting generations.

Vassie James graduated Vassar College in 1897, president of her class.[1] She became a Vassar regent. Her attendance at Vassar was predestined by her mother, Fannie Shouse, from the day Fannie insisted John Crawford James name their daughter Vassie after Fannie's *alma mater*. Fannie Shouse graduated Vassar's first class in 1874.[2] Honoring her mother, Vassie James gave her own daughter the name of Frances, and sent a third generation named Fanny to Vassar, too.

When a daughter of Vassie died, two large college scrapbooks of Vassie's were found among her effects. Vassie's scrapbooks depicted the discontent and *ennui* of her classmates, as they approached a time of seminal change for womanhood. *"Of information, I have none, since I've neither married, nor am I engaged, don't care a cent about voting, and have not even had an operation or been to Europe."* Another classmate complained, *"I do nothing of consequence beyond taking care of Louise...I wish I had more news but I have found a comfortable rut and am peacefully jogging along it."* One classmate wrote of her career, *"... nothing new and interesting to tell. The same old busy round of teaching and home duties sounds so very tame."* [3]

Such was not the destiny of Vassie James. Educated to challenge societal shortcomings, she joined the suffragette movement. Vassie James was the first woman in Kansas City to engage political forces. She became the first female delegate to the Democratic National Committee, the forerunner of the Democratic National Convention. Beyond politics, Vassie still managed a real estate development company, and produced her own legacy in education for future generations.

VASSIE MARRIED MISSOURI STATE REPRESENTATIVE HUGH CAMPBELL WARD, a year after she graduated from Vassar. Her father-in-law, the old Westport settler Seth Edmund Ward from Virginia, had been a buffalo hunter and Indian agent in the Far West. By 1848, the elder Ward had $1,500 cash in hand to form a matching partnership with a Frenchman, William LeGuerrie, to trap and trade fur. With provisions acquired on ten month's credit lent by Albert Gallatin Boone, a grandson of the Kentucky explorer Daniel Boone, and his partner James B. Hamilton who themselves were traders at Council Grove on the Kaw Reservation, Ward returned to Westport the following year with five wagons, loaded with 6,000 buffalo robes.[4] He sold his inventory in New York and was wealthy. In the Far West, Ward befriended Robert Campbell, whose name he gave to his son. Campbell established Fort Laramie in Wyoming Territory with Bill Sublett from Crab Orchard in Kentucky. Ward became the exclusive suttler for the fort. Over fifteen years, he commuted between Fort Laramie and Westport, before marrying Col. Jack Harris's daughter, Mary Frances. Vassie's husband, Hugh Campbell Ward, was born in 1863. In 1870, Seth Ward commissioned the artist George Caleb Bingham, who had married Dr. Johnston Lykins' widow Mattie Livingston, to paint a portrait of seven year old Hugh. In

Hugh Campbell Ward
1863-1909

Husband of Vassie James

1873, Seth Edmund Ward retired from trading and was appointed president of the Mastin Bank, owned by his wife's nephew, Thomas Hoyle Mastin.

Most of his life, Hugh Campbell Ward maintained a membership in the Society of Colonial Wars, a lineage society that celebrated his father's patronymic name of Seth Ward, and his family's deep roots in Colonial Virginia. Hugh's fifth great-grandfather was the Seth Ward of Sheffield plantation in Virginia's Chesterfield County. He had been a justice in Henrico County, then a county sheriff. He served in the Virginia House of Burgesses between 1761 and 1768, establishing the governing structures of the early Commonwealth.[5] Generations of the Ward family bore the name of Seth Ward. Hugh's father even gave the venerated name to his first born child, Hugh's much older half-brother by his father's Sioux consort, Wasna.

Vassie's husband was educated first for seven years at William Jewell College, expecting Hugh might become a Baptist minister. As an orphaned child, Hugh's father was deprived of an education entirely. Hugh was sent next to the East to continue his education. Hugh graduated Harvard, after which he obtained a law degree from Washington College in St. Louis.[6] Returning to Kansas City, Hugh opened a law office with attorney Frank Hagerman. Soon he became a high powered, corporate attorney.[7]

Early success led Hugh to straddle both law and politics. In 1893, Hugh was elected to State Legislature of Missouri. He served as vice-chairman of both the judiciary and municipal corporations committees, and was a member of the committee on constitutional amendments. His judiciary experience later led him to the chairmanship of the Judiciary Committee of the Kansas City Court of Appeals.

Having served as State Representative, Hugh next was appointed receiver of the problematic Mastin Bank, where his father once was president. Thomas Hoyle Mastin Jr., a former Lieutenant Colonel on the staff of Jefferson Davis, had started the bank with William Rodney Bernard, a U. S. geological surveyor who engaged in a mercantile business with Albert Gallatin Boone. Bernard also had married one of Col. Jack Harris' daughters, Susan Simpson Harris. Under Mastin's son John J. Mastin, the former banking firm of Bernard & Mastin became the Mastin Bank. Bernard withdrew from the bank to profiteer by transporting U. S. Army, Indian, and camp supplies to Fort Union in New Mexico, and Forts Doragi, Sill, and Laramie. Still a resident of Westport, Bernard later engaged in silver mining in Montana.

William Miles Chick
1794 - 1847

The failure of the Mastin Bank was precipitated by earlier failures of the First National Bank of Kansas City, operated by William Miles Chick, and the Commercial National Bank. The three corresponding banks were once the leading banks in Kansas City. The run on Chick's banks was tripped when the correspondent banks ran dry. Chick complained, *"I do not see how the depositors can lose a penny...Our deposits at one time were about $4,000,000, but they have been drawn down so that they are now between $800,000 and $1,000,000. I cannot tell what our assets are exactly, but they are between $2,000,000 and $3,000,000. They are largely in mercantile...loans."* [8] Their domino failures accelerated the Kansas City Savings Association of William Stone Woods into prominence. The banks of W. S. Woods would face its own crisis in the Panic of 1907. Under Hugh's receivership, the deficiency was laid to the Mastin Bank's heavy investment in the local water company, and not too surprisingly to underwriting Bernard's distant mining ventures in Montana.[9]

Untangling the mess took Hugh Campbell Ward four years, but his effort secured him credentials as a premiere authority for solving complex banking problems. Hugh was still processing the Mastin Bank failure, when he was appointed receiver of The Metropolitan National Bank collapse.[10] For four years, the quaking world of Kansas City banks was entirely in the hands of Hugh Campbell Ward. Having calmed the landscape, Hugh established Kansas City as the fifth largest banking city in the nation, following New York, Chicago, Philadelphia, and Boston.[11] It's easy to see why Vassie James found him attractive.

THE MARRIAGE OF VASSIE JAMES TO HUGH CAMPBELL WARD FLEW METEORICALLY, THE BEAUTY OF WHICH EXPIRED TOO SOON. Hugh and Vassie were married on October 26, 1898. He was thirty-five. She was twenty-three. The couple enjoyed little more than a decade together.

That same year, Hugh was called upon by Gov. Lon Vest Stephens to serve Kansas City on its new Police Commission. Stephens had just entered office.[12] Hugh had been commissary general for Stephens when the Missouri National Guard was organized.[13] Shortly before Stephens left his governorship, Frank James ran for Sergeant at Arms of the Missouri State Legislature. Despite Stephens' tepid, last minute support, the legislature slapped down Frank James' bid.

Frank James

Gov. Lawrence "Lon" Vest Stevens

When Hugh retired from the Police Commission in 1902, then governor Alexander Munroe Dockery instituted districting of schools. To Vassie's satisfaction, the reformer also provided increased educational funding. Dockery was a Baptist deacon, whose father, Rev Willis Dockery, was born in Garrard County, Kentucky. He was not a rebel preacher of the Traveling Church like John M. James, but Dockery fell under their influence. Throughout Missouri, he established Baptist missions. They became the political constituency that elected his son Lon Vest Stephens as governor.

While still on the Police Commission, Hugh Ward sought out a law partner among his political friends. In January of 1899, Herbert Spencer Hadley became the junior partner of the law firm Ward & Hadley.[14] Each partner earned a handsome living, averaging an income of $15,000 to $20,000 each per year.

Herbert Spencer Hadley   Agnes Lee-Hadley

Hadley's wife, Agnes Lee, was a Vassar graduate like Vassie. The two wives started bearing children, as if competing against one another. Hugh Campbell Ward Jr. was the first born to Vassie and her husband, followed by James Crawford Ward. Their only daughter Frances, named for Vassie's mother Fanny Shouse, was born in 1903. In the same year, Hugh lost his father. The Hadleys bore three children also. As business tumbled into Hugh's law office, Vassie playfully tumbled with their children at home.

Law, politics, and a high profile trial interrupted the cycle of child bearing. In 1905 the Republican Party nominated Hadley for Attorney General of Missouri. Hadley did not expect to be successful in his bid. The rabid political reformer from the Democratic Party, Joe Folk, seemed assured of election. Folk won, as expected. But surprisingly, Hadley a Republican was elected, too.

As Hadley's first test in office he was pitted against Hugh Ward's first law partner, Frank Hagerman, who represented the weighty Standard Oil Company. Hadley set out to bust Standard Oil's monopoly. Doing so, Hadley gave Hagerman such a competitive run that the firm of Ward & Hadley was thrust into the public limelight.[15]

Hadley became a rainmaker. Business poured into Ward & Hadley. In 1908, Hadley was appointed as assistant to the city attorney for Kansas City, thrusting him into the spotlight of the Republican Party. Added to the client roster of Ward & Hadley were the Commerce Trust Company, the National Bank of Commerce, and the Kansas City Home Telephone Company. Hugh Ward became both counsel and director of the Kansas

William Stone "W. S." Woods
1840 - 1917

City Railway & Light Company, as well as the soon-to-become-notorious Kansas City, Mexico & Orient Railway that took John Wayland Shouse into business ventures in Mexico.[16] The next January, Hugh brought Ellison A. Neel into the firm to assist with the overload, expanding the firm's name to Ward, Hadley, & Neel.

The Bank Panic of 1907 struck the Commerce Bank, where Hugh sat on its board of directors. Vassie had just become pregnant with John Harris Ward, the couple's last child. Scandal threatened Vassie's future.

W. S. Woods was the Commerce Bank's founder. Like Hugh and Vassie's families, Woods came from a Colonial family in Albemarle County, Virginia. Like T. M. James and Seth Edmund Ward, W. S. Woods was a child orphan, too. When an orphan's school was hit by a devastating fire, W. S. Woods paid off the existing mortgages, and re-established the orphanage as William Woods College.[17] T. M. had known Woods when both were young competitors in the mercantile business. Woods had first established the Kansas City Savings Association, which he then reorganized as the Commerce Bank. With his nephew C. Q. Chandler II, Woods created a network of banks, spanning from Kansas City, through Oklahoma Territory and Texas, into New Mexico. In all, Woods controlled eighteen banks.

William Thornton Kemper Sr.
1866 - 1938

A year before the panic struck, Woods hired William Thornton Kemper Sr., as vice-president. Kemper, too, had owned a mercantile company, after starting out as a shoe store janitor for his father. Like Hugh Ward, Kemper had served on the Kansas City Police Commission. He was a defeated mayoral candidate, but Kemper remained active in the Democratic Party. Kemper was a recognized rainmaker in the banking business. However, Kemper's investment of Commerce Banks's funds in the defunct Kansas City, Missouri, and Orient Railway which extended into Mexico's Copper Canyon, felled the bank to its knees.[18]

Kansas City banks already had been wracked by the repetitive bank runs of 1873 and 1893 that contributed to the untimely death of Daniel Lewis Shouse. The attempt by the United Copper Company to corner the copper market created the 1907 panic. Banks that lent to the scheme fell like dominos. When New York's Knickerbocker Bank failed, the third largest in the nation, bank runs became a contagion across the country. With $19.5 million liquidated from its deposit coffers in six weeks, the National Bank of Commerce no longer was sustainable. The U. S. Office of Comptroller of the Currency stepped in. Depositors were paid out. The bank was re-capitalized, and later was returned to its owners.[19]

Mindful of the mortal toll taken on D. L. Shouse when Shouse was cashier of the National Bank of Kansas City right before it failed, Hugh Ward opted to retire from his directorship in Commerce Bank.

The summer of 1909 was planned by Hugh and Vassie as a time for recovery, relaxation, and hopeful avoidance of imminent disaster. Near Gloucester, Massachusetts, the family retreated to a cottage at Bass Rock.[20] Their children, ages three to nine, proudly displayed for sunbathers their new one year old brother, John Harris Ward. As Vassie and the children played, Hugh was called back to Kansas City. On the train, Hugh suddenly fell ill.

The problem of the Metropolitan Railway Company of Kansas City pressed in on him. In 1902 the company extended its line from James Street in Kansas City over the James Street viaduct to the stock yards.[21] Now the company requested an extension of its franchise for forty-two years. Forceful political opposition was gathering a majority. They charged undue influence through the railway's 5,000 voting employees, and political manipulation of the mayor and city council in the election. In the opposition's cross hairs was Mayor Thomas T. Crittenden, son of the former Gov. Thomas T. Crittenden Sr., responsible for ending the life of Jesse James.[22] The junior Tom Crittenden had been a friend and ally of the junior Jesse James. Tom Jr. defended Jesse Jr. when he was charged with train robbery. Tom also attended Jesse Jr.'s wedding. As the summer of 1906 heated up, it was unclear if Hugh Campbell Ward could clinch the railway franchise in time to save Tom Crittenden's political career. Despite feeling badly ill, Hugh made every effort.

As July turned into August, Hugh made a donation of $25,000 to the

Thomas T. Crittenden Jr.
1863-1938

Friend of Jesse James Jr.

Young Women's Christian Association, before he boarded a train to return to Vassie and the children. Hugh telegraphed Vassie, alarmed about his deteriorating condition. She instructed him to meet her in New York City instead. There Vassie entered Hugh into a sanitarium at 247 West 76th St. Hugh suffered a stroke there on a Sunday morning. Much like Daniel Lewis Shouse, Hugh Campbell Ward died unexpectedly - working on a failing bank, precipitated by a national economic debacle, and also at forty-six years of age.[23]

VASSIE INHERITED THE WARD INVESTMENT COMPANY. Only thirty-four years old, Vassie James found herself president over the firm's extensive property holdings and real estate development portfolio. The task left to her was daunting. Vassie's husband did not leave her without his help and support, however. His absolute disgust for any sham or subterfuge left Vassie a clearly visible path forward that was well prepared, orderly, easy to grasp, and ready to be actuated. Her husband's foresight took her breath away.

When his father Seth E. Ward died six years earlier, Hugh had inherited almost 500 acres of his father's first settlement purchase in Westport. Seth Ward originally purchased the land from Charles Bent, who built and operated Bent's Fort in Colorado. Ward's land now lay within the Kansas City limits, making it ripe for development.

Home of Hugh Campbell & Vassie James Ward

Albert Ross Hill 1869 – 1943
Second husband of Vassie James

When he was stricken, Hugh was embarked upon the ambitious development project. He needed expert help. Hugh had approached an earnest, twenty-seven year old director of the Commerce Bank, Jesse Clyde Nichols, to employ name architects to design and build an enclave of luxury homes for Kansas City's emerging mercantile, political, and upper classes. The "green" banker, as Nichols described himself, was brought into Commerce Bank by William T. Kemper, and was younger than all the other bank directors by a decade. Nichols, however, perceived that "the best part of this directorship was the fact that it enabled us to borrow from a big bank, and it was always a great satisfaction that W. T. [Kemper]...never turned us down."[24] Like Vassie, the wife of Jesse Clyde Nichols was another graduate of Vassar.

Vassie seized the real estate assets and its development opportunity as a springboard for her own educational and political legacy. She retained J. C. Nichols to proceed with the visionary planned community. She added a golf course for her son, James Crawford Ward. Vassie also directed Nichols to include a memorial to her late husband in the plan. The memorial for Hugh Campbell Ward became Ward Parkway.

Vassie hired her future second husband as her company's general manager. Albert Ross Hill of Nova Scotia, a graduate of Dalhousie University, later acquired his doctorate degree from Cornell. His prior marriage to Dalhousie classmate Alice Sime Baxter landed the young couple teaching positions, bringing them from Canada to the University of Nebraska. Agnes gave up her mathematics career in Nebraska when Hill later became Dean of Teachers at the University of Missouri.[25] Later, Hill also became president of the University. Agnes died in 1898 at age forty-six, leaving her husband a widower. Having waited a full decade after Hugh Ward passed away, Vassie James married Albert Ross Hill, bringing her considerable financial enterprise to the marriage, and from the marriage expecting to realize her goals for education.

Vassie already had founded the Kansas City Country Day School for boys and the Sunset Hills School for girls. As a widowed mother concerned about educating her three sons and only daughter, Vassie drew twelve prominent Kansas City businessmen to underwrite the Country Day School for Boys in 1910. The school was housed in the old home of Westport pioneer and William Jewell College trustee, John B. Wornall, at 61st St. and Wornall Drive. Hugh Ward had purchased the Wornall estate right before

Pembroke Hill School

his death. The stately residence also had been employed as a Confederate hospital in the Civil War, making the home worthy of historic preservation. Despite Hugh's passing on August 15, 1909, Vassie opened the school without delay for the impending scholastic year. Within three years enrollment grew from twenty to fifty-two students.

In 1913 Vassie duplicated her efforts to establish the Sunset Hills School for Girls, constructed on a spacious campus overlooking the Kansas City Country Club she built. Quietly, Vassie recognized she was preserving a portion of the battlefi eld from the Battle of Westport, the very same battlefi eld upon which Frank James fought in the Civil War. In 1926 an additional eight acres of the battlefi eld was preserved when Vassie sold some acreage to Mrs. Ella Clark Loose for $500,000 through her Ward Investment Company.[26] Jacob Loose, founder of the Loose Wiles Biscuit Company that makes Cheezit crackers, had died. With the land purchase his wife founded Loose Park in his memory. Vassie then built a residence for herself adjacent to the park at 800 W. 52nd St.[27] In 1982, the two schools which Vassie instituted were merged. They thrive today as the Pembroke Hill School.

Jacob & Ella Clark Loose

SOCIAL COMMITTMENT THRUST VASSIE INTO POLITICS AND FEMINISM DURING WORLD WAR I. Her husband, Dr. Hill, was vice president of the American Red Cross, in charge of foreign operations. In Paris, France, Hill established a headquarters for a permanent Red Cross Commission. Pleas were broadcast across America for donations of clean clothing, in good repair, for refugees of the war.[28] Vassie took a leadership role in spreading the Red Cross efforts.

Her commitment evolved into active political engagement. Vassie sold Liberty Bonds to underwrite the war. She became close friends with Eleanor Roosevelt. Vassie impressed the President's wife. They formed a personal bond. With Eleanor's influence, Vassie was one of five selected to represent the interests of women at the League of Nations Peace Conference in Geneva, Switzerland in 1919. When women's suffrage finally was achieved, Vassie organized the Jefferson Democratic Club to involve women in Kansas City politics. Eleanor supported Vassie's maneuver to become the first woman to attend the National Democratic Convention. Vassie was appointed to the National Women's Committee for Mobilization for Human Need. Later Vassie served as president of the Kansas City League of Women Voters.[29]

Dr. Hill was retired from his presidency of the University of Missouri in 1934 when a Kansas City mayoral election offered an opportunity to clean up the politics of Kansas City government that increasingly had become corrupted, long after Hugh Campbell Ward had served on the city's Police Commission.

A radical student, Joseph C. Fennelley, only 29 years of age, pitted social reform against the political machine of Big Tom Pendergast. Fennelley was educated at the University of Virginia. He was an expert golfer, though not as competitive as Vassie's son, Jim Ward. Fennelley golfed often with Jim at the Kansas City Country Club. Fennelley and his golf buddies had cleaned up Cincinnati politics. Fennelley alleged that twenty-five Kansas City policemen had criminal records, the acting police chief had served a term in a penitentiary, there were 8,000 ghost voters on the city's voting rolls, gambling and vice were rife, and that Kansas City had become a hangout for the criminal riff-raff from the Midwest, including Charles "Pretty Boy" Floyd, Tommy Holden, George "Machine Gun" Kelly, and an obscure bank and train robber from Minnesota named Jimmy Keating, whose son subsequently would marry into the James family. The young man assured Vassie and Dr. Hill that "boss control would remain as long as the young women and men sat quietly at home and allowed the bosses to rule."

Vassie accepted Fennelley's challenge to mobilize educated youth and women. Seeking to run a slate of candidates, Fennelley formed the Citizens-Fusion Party. At sixty-four, with no hardscrabble political experience, other than the kind found in academia, Hill was recruited to run for mayor. Despite the fact that Dr. Hill had a dozen college degrees, his educational expertise proved itself outweighed by the brutality that Kansas City politics had become. As *Time* magazine printed lurid reportage reminiscent of the former news reported about the deeds of Jesse James, election day turned bloody.

"Sprawled across the sidewalk in front of a Kansas City polling place lay the body of William Findley, Negro election worker, blood on his face, a bullet in his brain, spats on his feet. Slumped in a heap lay Lee Flacy, deputy sheriff, pumped full of buckshot. To his bride of a fortnight went news of her widowhood by radio: 'A shooting at 5824 Swope Parkway - Lee Flacy killed -.' A mortal head wound crumpled Larry Cappo, sleek little gangster, onetime prizefighter, night-club headwaiter, in the back of a wrecked sedan. Few doors away Pascal Oldham, 78,

*hardware merchant, was locking up his store when he turned to see a car flash by,
to hear guns crackle. A stray bullet drilled clean through his head. Hours later he
died in a hospital. Slugged and beaten with blackjacks, brass knuckles, gun-butts
and baseball bats were a housewife, a Kansas City Star newshawk, a candidate for
the City Council, a chauffeur, a policeman, and five other persons."*

By a plurality of 59,566 votes, Big Tom Pendergast's violent and
brutal political machine cut down the candidacy of the gentlemanly Dr.
A. Ross Hill. Though not victorious, Hill's candidacy finally did mark the
beginning of the political demise of Pendergast's machine, as the bloody
election fallout attracted national scrutiny.

T .M.'s long tradition of disassociation from the violence of the James
brothers bore down on Vassie and her husband. Dr. Hill retired to private
life, dying nine years later. Hill had proved an excellent step-father for
Vassie's children by Hugh Ward, especially John Harris Ward who was only
ten years old when Vassie and Hill married. In 1951 on the University of
Missouri Campus, Vassie attended the dedication of Hill Hall, named in
honor of her late husband. The building since has been put on the National
Register of Historic Places. Vassie outlived Hill by nine years.[30]

The only time Vassie James was known to come close to linking
herself even remotely with the violence of her cousins, Frank and Jesse
James, occurred seven years prior to the election, on June 3, 1927. Then,
as Mrs. A. Ross Hill, Vassie appeared before the George Edward Pickett
Chapter of the United Daughters of the Confederacy in Kansas City. The
organization reported that "Mrs. A. Ross Hill gave a most interesting address
on 'Jefferson Davis,' recalling that her grandparents, the late Mr. and Mrs. T.
M. James, were friends of President and Mrs. Davis and Mr. and Mrs. James
had exchanged visits upon several occasions." [31] Never acknowledged was
the fact that Sarah Knox Taylor, the wife of Jefferson Davis and daughter
of President Zachary Taylor shared ancestral relationships with the James
family still residing in Kentucky, going back several generations.

Dr. Hill and Vassie produced no progeny. A birth announcement
appearing in The *Oakes Times* newspaper of Dickey County, North Dakota,
however, gave public notice that on December 9, 1920 "a baby girl was
born last week to Mr. and Mrs. Ross Hill." An historical reprint of the
announcement also was published in the *Recorder Herald* newspaper of
Salmon, Idaho, on September 16, 1998, further identifying the site of the

Hill Hall, College of Education, University of Missouri

birth as occurring in Morongo, in Keystone Township. A survey of the 1920 census for the location reveals no enumerated resident by the name of Hill, leaving an intriguing mystery as to whether Dr. Hill and Vassie are the actual subjects of the birth announcement, and what may have become of the infant.

Regardless, the gene pool Vassie inherited from her James family was passed to those who carried the surname of her husband, Hugh Campbell Ward. Also passing to Vassie's children, grandchildren, and great grandchildren were many of the hallmarks that Vassie's life came to represent. In the years prior to and following the death of Dr. A. Ross Hill, Vassie James had plenty of time to enjoy her children and grandchildren, as she watched the James family's legacy for education thrive and grow in ways that appeared fresh, creative, imaginative, and powerful to Vassie James.

Vassie James-Ward-Hill
1875 - 1953

Vase of Flowers, Painting by Jan Van Huysum

Chapter Eight

Underrated Men &
Unleashed Feminists

*When Vassie James sent her daughter Frances to Vassar, she created a tradition
that insured a third generation of the James family's women a superlative Eastern
education with all its benefits. More Vassar graduates from the James family
were yet to come. From this tradition founded by Vassie James sprang a legacy of
social, political, and philanthropic contribution, the breadth of which Vassie James
herself could scarcely imagine.*

Vassie's daughter Frances Ward graduated Vassar with a Bachelor
of Arts degree in 1925. Expecting to work in her mother's Ward
Development Company, Frances advanced her education at the
Cambridge School of Architecture in Massachusetts.[1] However, like her
mother, Frances Ward became an architect to her husband's success. In the
process Frances sublimated her own remarkable success.

Two years after graduating Vassar, Frances married Williams graduate George T. Olmsted Jr. of Evanston, Illinois. As a college athlete, Olmsted broke a world's record when he was captain of the swim team at Williams. He served on the student council, and was editor in chief of the *Williams Record*. Olmsted thought he might become a teacher. That ambition made him particularly appealing to both Frances and Vassie. After a decade of apprenticeship in the paper trade, however, George Olmsted instead became president of the S. D. Warren Company, a paper manufacturer in Boston. His self-made success later made him founding chairman of the American Paper Institute.

At the Warren Company, Olmsted enjoyed unfettered access to the Cumberland Falls Library, which the Warren family privately owned and maintained for their employee's use. Advising Susan Cornelia Warren, wife of the mill's founder Samuel Dennis Warren, Frances and her husband petitioned the firm's board of directors to transfer the library to a foundation together with sustaining funds. Today the Warren Memorial Library in Westbrook, Maine is a public library open to everyone.[2]

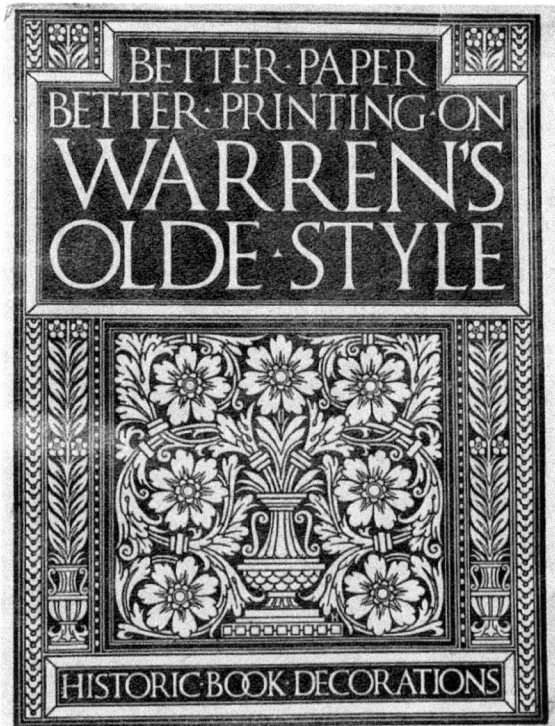

Vassie's son-in-law and daughter guided Mrs. Warren further in her contributions establishing the Westbrook Community Hospital, the Cornelia Warren Community Foundation, and the Westbrook High School gymnasium. From their own personal funds, George and Frances Olmsted added $100,000 to develop the high school's athletic field.[3]

In his career, George T. Olmsted was either director or trustee of a variety of financial institutions, including the Boston Safe Deposit & Trust Company, New England Mutual Life Insurance Company, the Provident Institution for Savings, Suffolk Savings Bank, and the Boston United Fund, sometimes called The Williams Program or the Williams Capital Fund, which raised funds for Williams College. Olmsted became an inveterate recruiter of students for Williams. In World War II, he also was employed at one dollar per year, raising funds for the War Production Board.[4]

Occasionally, Olmsted's business acumen put him at odds with his mother-in-law, Vassie. Olmsted resisted unionization at the Warren Company. Over a decade under his leadership, Warren Company employees repeatedly rejected unionization. Where Olmsted, Frances, and Vassie always agreed was in their mutual support for education.

For eleven years, *Financial World* magazine cited George T. Olmsted for writing the best corporate annual reports. Olmsted wrote Warren's *Annual Report* personally by hand. Lippincott Publishing Company requested that he write a manual. He never did, claiming what he had to say would "whip over the head of the average chief executive officer." Olmsted decried government, saying the Securities & Exchange Commission "had imposed so many specifications...that you couldn't very well write what I used to write."[5] Olmsted's career was capped with an honorary Doctor of Laws degree from the University of Maine, and another honorary Doctor of Laws degree from Bates College.[6]

In 1993, George and Frances established an endowment to support superior teaching. The Olmsted Award at Williams College supports secondary school teachers and faculty from across the country in the development of professional or curricular programs and tools. The honors are awarded annually.[7]

George and Fannie didn't neglect support for students, either. Six years later, their endowment established a summer science camps at Williams College for elementary students. As Williams advertises, "Mix

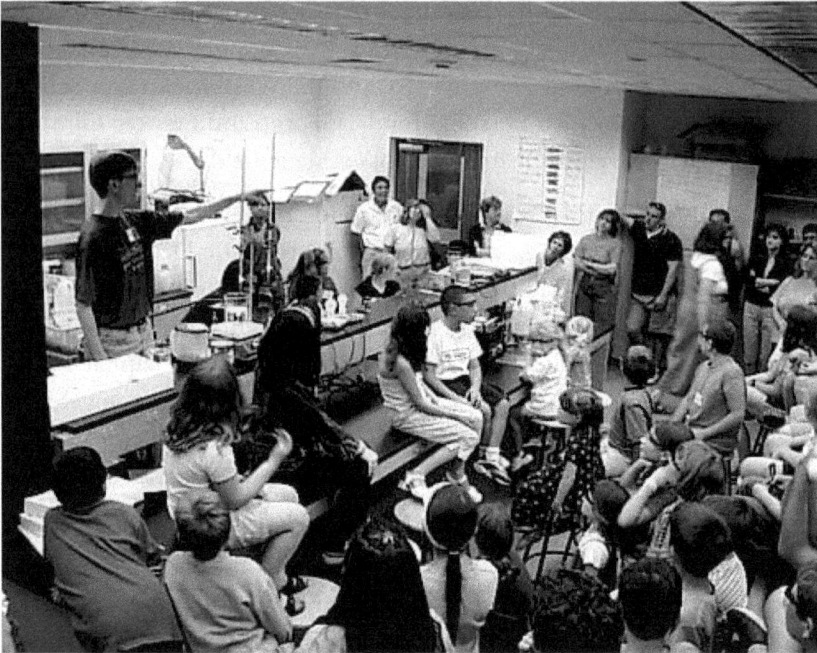

Williams College Summer Science Camp
Founded by George T. & Frances Ward Olmsted

inquisitive youngsters, cabbage juice, eggs, balloons and 'mysteries;' add a duo of energetic Williams College chemistry professors and a team of dedicated elementary teachers from local schools, and the result is another highly successful Williams College Summer Science Camp...The kids come to understand that if you have a question...you can try to answer it yourself."[8]

Olmsted and Frances were the parents of three children, Virginia, Joan, and George Olmsted III. In the same year that daughter Joan married Dr. James Franklin Oates, Vassie died. But Vassie would have approved of her granddaughter's choice. Dr. Oates was a graduate of Phillips Exeter. He had attended Princeton and graduated from Cornell University Medical School.

Had she lived longer, Vassie might have been more impressed by her granddaughter's father-in-law. James Franklin Oates Jr. had garnered nine honorary degrees. He was an alumni trustee at Princeton, where he graduated, as did his father. He was an honorary trustee at Williams, and a life trustee of Northwestern University, where he obtained a law degree. Mr. Oates, Jr. started as a litigator for utility, oil, and railroad interests. He became Chairman of the Peoples Light, Gas, and Coke Company of Chicago, after which he was president and CEO of the Equitable Life Insurance Company. Oates wrote several books, about the relationship between corporate and community culture.[9] He sat as director to numerous financial as well as cultural institutions, including the Hubbard Street Dance Group in Chicago, and was a life trustee of Chicago's famed Goodman Theater.[10]

VASSIE'S SON, JAMES CRAWFORD WARD SR., ALSO ATTENDED WILLIAMS COLLEGE. His interest jumped back and forth between the golf links and his investment banking career. Because of the education he lacked, Frank James' son Robert could not keep up with his cousin.

Stumped for a way to razz James Crawford Ward, his fellow students shortened his middle name to Craw. Those impressed by Craw's athletic ability called him Jamie. As Jamie scholastically proved himself, Craw was respectfully nicknamed Jim. In Williams' 1923 yearbook appeared the dumbfounded forecast about Jim, "if we do not hear from Jim in the future, something is wrong with the universe."

Vassie puzzled herself over what might become of her son, too. Jim spent too much time on the links of the Kansas City Country Club. Jim also was much too friendly with his cousin Robert Franklin James, Frank James' son.

Bob James resided at James Farm in Kearney. Bob never attended college. His father's life was too peripatetic for Bob to obtain any stable education. Bob demonstrated no motivation or career direction or interest. For several years, Bob subsisted as a modestly paid grain clerk in offices in St. Louis and Chicago.[11] Like Jesse James Jr., Bob never could escape his father's stigma, even among his own family.

Frank James requested Bob return to the deteriorating James Farm and farm it. With little income, Bob became diverted, golfing in Kansas City with his cousin, Vassie's son Jim. The more golf lessons Jim gave Bob, the more obsessed Bob became with the game. Together, Bob James and Jim Ward enthusiastically sold memberships to the country

Robert Franklin
"Bob" James
1877-1959

Son of Frank James

club. Suddenly, Bob earned some meaningful income. After his father died in 1915, Bob decided to give up farming altogether. Imitating his Kansas City cousins, Bob James constructed his own three-hole golf course at James farm. He invited players he had met. Players though avoided James Farm and its reputation. His father's stigma was indelibly attached to the farm, and in turn was re-attached to Bob James. Bob lacked the education and personal initiative that would make his enterprise at James Farm a success. Bob's golf course failed.

At Williams College, Jim Ward did not appear to be a serious student. Not at all like his future brother-in-law and schoolmate George T. Olmsted. Jim studied for a degree in athletics. He played baseball and football, but he excelled in golf. In his sophomore year, Jim was part of a team of U. S. college golfers who defeated the British at Greenwich, Connecticut. He appeared first to be headed for defeat in the opening round. Although his score equaled the two year amateur record and the professional record for the course, in the final hole he failed to sink a two foot putt. Jim lost to the Scottish-American golf star Harry Scharff. Three days later, though, the Americans defeated the stars from Cambridge University, winning two out of three rounds.[12]

As she fought disappointment, Vassie underrated her son. If anything, Jim was an over-achiever by heritage; if not in fact another underestimated over achiever among his family.

Confounding expectations, Jim Ward did not fail to fulfill the family promise. By graduation, Jim was president of his class, and president of his Class Day. His fellow students identified him as, "Chairman of Everything ad infinitum - a conscientious, hardworking, and respected good fellow and gentleman...who has not lost contact with the rest of the world." Vengefully tweaking those who consistently underrated him, Jim Ward perversely listed his future occupation as "Undecided."

The first decade of Jim Ward's business career was spent in Kansas City. Jim secured a banking position with the National City Company of Kansas City. After a few years, he moved eastward and was employed as a manager of the First Boston Corporation. Moving to St. Louis in 1937, Jim became a partner in the securities firm of Reinholdt & Gardner. Very shortly thereafter, Jim accepted an exciting invitation to become a partner in G. H. Walker & Company.[13]

Unknown to Jim was the fact that his partner's wife was a relation of his own. The Walker's children were his distant cousins. The firm's founder, George Herbert Walker, descended from an English immigrant. But the family of his wife, Lucretia Wear, had a number of ties to the James family in colonial Virginia and Kentucky. Among Lucretia's great grandparents were Abraham Field and Mary Ironmonger, who were also the fourth great grandparents of Jim Ward. Among Lucretia's great grand uncles was George Rogers Clark, under whom John M. James once

George Herbert "Bert" Walker

Lucretia "Lullie" Wear

served in the Northwest Territory. When Jim joined the Walker firm, Bert and Lullie, as the Walkers called themselves, had a grandson and namesake serving in the U. S. Navy. George Herbert Walker Bush later became president of the United States, as did his son George W. Bush.

In 1943, Jim Ward left the Walker partnership to become senior vice-president of the Third National Bank of Nashville. He took up residence at 4119 Harding Place, a short walk to the Belle Meade Country Club. There, James Crawford Ward Sr. remained a lifetime resident and member.

VASSIE'S GRANDSON, JAMES CRAWFORD WARD JR. KNOWN AS JAY, WAS SENT TO PREP SCHOOL IN CONCORD, MASSACHUSETTS, AND THEN TO PRINCETON. Like his father Jim Ward, Jay also was underestimated when he first attended Middlesex School. Described as "the pudgy man from Nashville," his yearbook at Middlesex satirized Jay as having "Light blond hair and a cherubic face [that] concealed a mind teaming with evil intentions." His "quick coordination and natural trickiness" earned him broad recognition as "the only boy in the class who could throw a spit ball

James Crawford "Jay" Ward Jr.
1933 – 2000

behind his back with any degree of accuracy." If Jay's great granduncle Jesse James could have shot as well, he might have avoided his own assassination.

Jay definitely was not his father's athlete. Playing baseball, Jay was thrown out at first base time after time. A leg injury prevented him from becoming a football star. Jay played better as a morale builder. As a writer

Jay composed stirring football reports for his school's *Anvil* newspaper. Jay also was an associate editor of the *Middlesex School Yearbook*, and a photography editor, much admired and acknowledged for the quality of excellence displayed in his photographs. Although a member of the movie committee, Jay disclaimed all responsibility for anything being shown.

At Princeton, the pudgy cherubic Jay majored in political science, and graduated in the class of 1955. His senior thesis was titled, *Formosa in United States Policy.*[14] His thoughts of a political career, or public service, for whatever reason evaporated. Instead, Jay followed the money trail. Returning to Nashville, Jay Ward founded his own securities firm, trading and selling municipal bonds. Over thirty years, he established a national reputation for himself among the "muni" fraternity. On the sale of his company to Hilliard, Lyons, Inc. Jay remained as senior officer in the company.[15]

Genevieve Underhill Ward
& husband
Edwin Barnes Tucker

Granddaughter of
Jay Ward & Caroline Hilton

Once divorced and once widowed, Jay married a third time to Caroline Hilton of Nashville. Caroline's brother, Robert C. Hilton, was president of the investment firm, Autumn Capital, and a director of the Cracker Barrel Old Country Store restaurant chain. As president and CEO of Home Technology Healthcare, Jay's brother-in-law led the company to its listing among the Forbes 400 Best Big Companies for three succeeding years.

Jay Ward's Princeton obituary acknowledged his wide popularity and his devotion to Princeton, but did not neglect to mention his exuberance for life.

When Jay's father died at the age of seventy-two, the reputation of Jim Ward "as one of the finest amateur golfers in Kansas City history" remained his principal memorial. Jim Ward still was holder of the course record.[16] Twice Jim Ward was the Missouri State Champion amateur golfer. Jim maintained memberships in the St. Louis Country Club, The Cumberland Club, and the Belle Meade Country Club in Nashville. More than fifty honorary pallbearers were identified in his obituary, most all of whom were his golf and business associates.[17] His grandsons, Stephen Watkins and J. C. Ward III honored him as members of the Society of Tennessee Golfers.

THE CAREER OF VASSIE'S YOUNGEST SON, J. HARRIS WARD, looked at first like it might not get off the ground. The Great Depression impacted even people of means.

John Harris Ward grew comfortably into his manhood among matriarchal and feminist influences. John's father died when he was only a year old. Vassie didn't remarry until nearly a decade later. Encouraged by Vassie and his sister Frances to marry a Vassar graduate, John married Mary Godwin Van Etten, the daughter of a timber, lumber, and furniture tycoon from Grand Rapids, Michigan.[18] Mary was a freshman at Vassar when Frances graduated. As John pursued his career, Mary directed its resulting philanthropy.

Before completing his master's degree at Harvard in 1932, John and Mary were married. In those desperate Depression times, Mary sold student summer jobs in Europe while John completed his education. John was assured a job with Allied Chemical Company awaited him in the fall. Meanwhile, the couple took their postponed honeymoon in Europe, but their return was delayed by a seaman's strike. Coming home, John found the job promised to him has been filled by another in his absence.

Several attempts followed to secure permanent employment. Retreating to Kansas City, John's family connections parked him in the Westport Avenue Bank. One of his Harvard professors called on John to join the National Recovery Administration in Washington. In 1935, John finally secured a financial position with the Guaranty Trust Company of New York. There, a New Dealer named W. Averill Harriman lured John to his investment banking firm, Brown Brothers, Harriman, & Company. It is not unlikely that Vassie may have secured the arrangement through her political connections with Eleanor Roosevelt. John thought Harriman hired him to be an investment banker, but Harriman used John to administer his Sun Valley real estate development project instead.

Pursuing a position as a company treasurer, John moved Mary to Chicago in December of 1937 to accept a position with the famed department store Marshall Field & Company. John had a letter from its Chairman of the Board J. O. McKinsey, hiring John as Field's assistant treasurer with a very attractive salary. John and Mary arrived a few days early and rented a house for $125.00 per month, much more than John would pay did he not have a job. On the day John was to report to work, the newspaper reported McKinsey's death. McKinsey's successor elected to hire his own staff and suggested John return to New York.

"I explained I had already moved my family here and we liked Chicago. Finally, he sent me to the Edison Company to talk to Willis Gales, then financial vice-president. I was hired as a financial analyst. But don't let the title fool you. I was a clerk, and the pay was considerably less than the amount McKinsey had offered." [19]

From January 16, 1938 to April, 1941, John worked for Edison before being loaned to the War Production Board for six weeks. As World War II dragged on, John's six weeks engagement turned into two years. John started as a captain in the Army. By war's end, he was major of the Strategic Bombing Survey, based in England and Germany. Mary worked in the Lend-Lease Administration, later renamed the Foreign Economic Administration.

The war finally over, John resumed his work at Edison in 1945. John advanced through the company ranks, just like his cousins employed at T. M. James & Sons. In January of 1948, he was made company secretary. Three years later John became vice-president and secretary, then vice-president and treasurer. In 1955 he was made executive vice-president; and in 1957 John was appointed to Edison's Board of Directors.[20] Now formally recognized as J. Harris Ward, John had full charge of all financial activity and total control of the giant utility.

As the Atomic Age dawned, the principles of the James family trade were applied by John at the Edison Company. Under John's leadership, Edison's post war spending on infrastructure exceeded $1 billion. John recognized that "the electric utility business is a glamorous business...but the average college boy doesn't think so. He is thinking in terms of space

John Harris Ward
aka J. Harris Ward 1908 – Unk.

Mosaic by Seymour Adleman

age. We have to do a real selling job." As John advanced the utility toward nuclear power in 1960, John maintained close relationships with schools and faculties, to harvest the very best talent for his company. "Above all, we are seeking leadership capabilities." [21]

John defined his company's progress in the tradition of T. M. James. "You could say that the day to day job is the pursuit of excellence. We have to be determined that we are going to have the best utility in the county – and we had better have that idea because, while we are described as a monopoly, we are in a highly competitive industry." [22]

When William Clark wrote about John in the *Chicago Tribune* of October 17, 1960, Clark pointed out, "Ward is quietly articulate. He is direct and sincere. He does not seek persons not to overpower them with conversation, but he is an immensely capable employer of the English language when the occasion arises." When Clark first met John, Clark thought John was an attorney. John responded, "I'm not an attorney. But everyone who has been around Washington for a while gets to be sort of a curbstone lawyer." [23]

Prior to his retirement in 1973 as Chairman of the Board the Commonwealth Edison Company, John additionally served as a director of the Northern Trust Bank, International Harvester Company, the Union Carbide Corporation, and the New York Life Insurance Company from 1960 to 1973.[24] He also served as director of The National Association of Electrical Companies, was a member the advisory board of the Ford Foundation's energy policy project, and sat on the Executive Committee of the Federal Power Commission.[25]

Locally in Chicago, John was elected to the Board of Trustees of the University of Chicago, serving from 1956 to 1974.[26] He also was a member of the Citizens Board of Loyola University, a Jesuit school. He was a member of the Board of Governors of the Metropolitan Housing and Planning Council of Chicago, and a director of the Illinois State Chamber of Commerce. Among his civic activities, John was a member of the Committee for Economic and Cultural Development, the Committee on Urban Progress, the Chicago Central Area Committee, The Chicago Merit Employment Committee, and the Leadership Council of Metropolitan Open Communities.[27]

AS JOHN HARRIS WARD IMPRINTED CHICAGO'S CORPORATE CULTURE, HIS WIFE MARY VAN ETTEN IMPRINTED THE CULTURAL LIFE OF CHICAGO, the effects of her accomplishments lasting long after both John's and Mary's demise.

Mary's mother-in-law Vassie already was active in the post-Depression, Roosevelt era politics. Vassie's feminist success rubbed off on Mary. Once John's employment was secured, Mary and John had two children. David Harris Ward was born in 1937. He became an attorney. John Anthony Ward, called Tony, was born two years later. As Mary raised her two boys, she followed Vassie's example in the years following the war. Mary became active in the League of Women Voters. Mary also became Illinois Radio Chairman and chaired the women's Drive for Educational Television, the forerunner of today's popular Public Broadcasting System (PBS).

Mary met a friend whom Vassie often talked about. Margaret Sanger was considered a rebel of the early 20th century. Like Vassie's father J. C. James, Sanger's father taught her to be a critical and independent thinker. Sanger's mother died at age forty-eight, after eighteen pregnancies that sapped her life. Sanger worked among the poor of New York's Lower East

Woman's Suffragette Movement

Margaret Sanger 1879 – 1966

*Founder of the American Birth Control League,
Forerunner of Planned Parenthood*

Side. On a daily basis, Sanger witnessed suffering at its root. She considered social sufferance not only as a health issue, but also as one of class subversion. Sanger turned to the liberal political culture for remedy. She mastered becoming a union organizer. She learned the techniques of public protest and of its powerful beneficial effects.

Margaret Sanger suffered arrest for her protests. She published a newspaper, *The Woman Rebel*, banned by the U.S. Post Office as obscene. Her birth control manifesto *Family Limitation* made her an outlaw in violation of the Comstock Act, for disseminating information about contraception. Sanger fled to Europe, but returned to face trial. Her daughter's death in the middle of her trial won over public sentiment. Charges against Sanger were dropped. From the 1920s forward, Margaret Sanger ceased her illegal acts, seeking instead the support from her opponents. What resulted in 1942 was the formation of the Planned Parenthood Federation of America. As Vassie lay ill and dying in 1952, Mary traveled with Margaret Sanger to Bombay, India where they met with Gandhi. Margaret Sanger became one of the first presidents of the International Planned Parenthood Federation.[28] Mary Ward later was made president of the Chicago Chapter of Planned Parenthood.

Mary stated birth control was one of the world's most important causes. That alone didn't stop Mary's feminism from accelerating a multitude of other causes in small ways that produced big results. To educate women for leadership in civic participation, Mary founded "Know Your Chicago." The series of local civic tours highlighted Chicago neighborhoods, industry, and cultural institutions. The program evolved over the years into the Graham School of General Studies at the University of Chicago. Mary then created the women's board for the Chicago Lyric Opera, leading her to appointments to the boards of the Chicago Public Library Foundation, The Chicago Symphony Orchestra, and the Chicago Council on Foreign Relations, the Field Museum, and the Chicago Art Institute.

In 1961, Mary instituted the "Bright New City" lecture series in urban environmental design. The same year, she was President of the University of Chicago's Women's Board. Becoming a Trustee of the University and serving together with her husband, Mary also was Chair of the Visiting Committee to the Department of Music. Mary founded the department's Jazz Archive, now housed in the University's Special Collections Research Center. She raised $200,000 to save and preserve the landmark Laredo Taft

Mary Godwin Van Etten-Ward 1907 - 2002

Studios, today called the Midway Studios, housing the University's Committee on the Visual Arts. She also served on the board of the International House.

Awards began to follow. Mary was made a Life Trustee of the University of Chicago. In 1970, Lake Forest College in the community where she and John lived awarded her an honorary Doctor of Humane Letters degree. In 1986, the Illinois Public Humanities Council recognized Mary's role in contributing "to public understanding of the role of humanities in transforming lives and strengthening communities," giving her its Public Humanities Award. Mary received other awards from the Harvard Club of Chicago, the YWCA, and the Chicago Chapter of Multiple Sclerosis Society. Recognizing Mary as founder and Chair of "Bright New City," the Metropolitan Planning Council of Chicago gave Mary the Burnham Award in 1988 for improving the livability of the communities she shaped.

Mary died in 2002 at age ninety-four. When John died on July 28, 1974, Mary remarried sometime after to Dr. Peter M. Wolkonsky, a University of Chicago graduate who served as chief resident of internal medicine at Columbia Presbyterian Hospital in New York and later was medical director of the Standard Oil Company of Indiana, today known as AMOCO. Her memorial service filled the huge theatre of Chicago's Lyric Opera House.

Upon Mary's demise, the Chicago City Council adopted a public resolution, accounting eleven paragraphs of Mary Ward Wolkonsky's lifetime achievements. Each year now, Chicago's Friends of Downtown bestows the Mary Ward Wolkonsky Award for lifetime achievement. In 2010, the award was given to Richard M. Daley, Chicago's longtime mayor who used his terms of office to vastly improve the social, economic, cultural, and political climate of Chicago as a progressive city. At the University of Chicago, the J. Harris Ward Fellowship Award furthers a student's graduate education with a $4,500 stipend, with no restriction on a student's chosen field of study.

THE TIES OF VASSIE JAMES TO EDUCATION, COMMUNITY DEVELOPMENT, AND POLITICS required the same impeccable discretion for her descendants as it did for the descendants of Thomas Martin James. Public writings about J. Harris Ward never referenced the tainted James side of his mother's family. Instead, John always was referenced as the son of a distinguished attorney and legislator from Kansas City, despite the fact John's father had no measurable influence upon John because he died when John was one year old.

When Barbara James, granddaughter of J. C. and daughter of T. M. James III, was left widowed by her husband Milton M. McGreevy, no mention appeared either in the Kansas City press about Barbara's family relationship to Frank and Jesse James. The reporting focused solely upon the couple's bequest of two hundred works of art - all paintings, master prints, and drawings the couple had assembled, and then granted to the Nelson-Atkins Museum of Art in Kansas City. The donation included a Caravaggio painting of the Italian Baroque period.

The collection started simply enough in 1930 when Barbara was given $500 by her mother to purchase an ink and chalk wash of a floral still life, titled *Vase of Flowers,* by the 18th century Dutch artist Jan Van Huysum. The *Vase of Flowers* portrait depicts a lush floral arrangement, among which slumps a single, broken-stemmed carnation with its stunted offspring, under the cautious gaze of cherubs - a representation not too unrecognizable to the family of Barbara James.[29]

Her Caravaggio painting risked an unwitting revelation about Barbara's family. Caravaggio, as an artist and an outlaw, was consumed by social issues of the lower classes. A killer himself, Caravaggio elevated the underclass to the attention of the ruling classes. Inside of him resided a sub text of restless religious influence, consumed by social concern.

John in the Wilderness

Painting by Caravaggio

Caravaggio's painting of *St. John the Baptist*, subtitled as *John in the Wilderness*, was commissioned by a papal banker, intended to be placed in the bankers' private chapel. The artist sent the patron a copy, holding tightly to the original for himself. One critic described the bequest, as if subliminally analyzing Jesse James as *John in the Wilderness*.

"It seems, indeed, as if Caravaggio instilled in this image an element of the essential pessimism of the Baptist's preaching, of the senseless tragedy of his early martyrdom, and perhaps even some measure of the artist's own troubled psyche." [30]

With no overt reference to the benefactor's hidden relationship to Jesse James, however, the sub-text remained hidden and went entirely unnoticed by society.

Through descending generations, the nefarious reputation of the outlaw Jesse James had been quarantined successfully at James Farm. There, the public eye could be diverted without inflicting any harm upon the James family, nor upon their social community.

The isolated relic of James farm was in no way perceived like the celebrated art of the criminal artist Caravaggio. James farm was no artistic depiction. The farm provoked no intellectual inquiry, raised no serious criticism, nor provided any insights or cultural interpretation of its outlaws and their cultural significance for the nation. James Farm became solely a recreational amusement attraction. As a public venue, James Farm entirely ignored the art of the outlaws' business. It disregarded what meaning, significance, and lessons might be derived from an understanding of their historical perspective. James Farm provided no deeper cultural sustenance than was contained in a commercial souvenir - precisely as the James family and the Kansas City community had preferred and intended.

The donation of the James family farm to Clay County was made by the great grandson of Jesse James, Henry Lafayette Barr, who simply wanted to be divested of his great grandfather's notoriety and past. The contribution did not come from a highly respected philanthropic family, like Milton McGreevy who was a diligent broker in the securities firm of Harris, Upham, & Company.[31] With the stigma of Jesse James securely quarantined in the amusing distractions of James Farm, the shield protecting the family of Thomas Martin James, his daughter Vassie, and all of their descendants remained protected and intact.

LIKE VASSIE'S CHILDREN, THE CHILDREN OF BARBARA JAMES-MCGREEVY ADVANCED VASSIE'S FEMINIST LEGACY. Barbara's daughter Gail McGreevy-Harmon combined her mother's interest in community philanthropy with Vassie James' interest in education. As a *cum laude* graduate of Radcliffe College, Gail and her husband James Harmon established a fellowship at Harvard, providing grants for public service. As a law partner in the firm of Harmon, Curran, Spielberg, & Eisenberg in Washington D. C., Gail established a career as an expert attorney, "providing strategic advice to foundations, charitable and lobbying organizations, and political action committees." She became a lecturer, writer, and commentator on non-profit issues.[32] Gail also became a board director for the D.C. Library Foundation, St. Mary College of Maryland, and the National Partnership for Women and Families. With respect for her mother who was jailed in 1936 for her civil disobedience while demonstrating on behalf of birth control, Gail also served on the board for Population Services International, better known as Planned Parenthood.

Barbara James-McGreevy 1905 – 1996
Daughter of Thomas Martin James III & Gertrude Jones

Her children (L-R): Barbara Ann McGreevy-McNay, Gail McGreevy-Harmon Thomas James McGreevy, & Joan "Jean" McGreevy

Gail McGreevy-Harmon, Esq.

Gail's oldest sister, Joan McGreevy-Green, calls herself Jean. A Vassar graduate with a degree in history, Jean became a trustee of the Jacob L. Loose Foundation, and the Westport Fund, for which she also served as board member and secretary. Like her great grand aunt Vassie, Jean broke another female political barrier, becoming the first woman member of the City Plan Commission of Kansas City. She later served on the city's Municipal Art Commission, progressing to a seat on the International Relations Council. Jean served as a board director of the Johnson County National Bank, and for the E.S. & R.A. Long Ellis Foundations. In her eighties, Jean adapted to the internet age, blogging a *Peace Letter* in 2007 as an anti-war advocate against the presidential administration of her distant cousin, President George W. Bush.[33] When the nation was mired in the devastating Great Recession of the early 21st century, Jean's writing proposed remedies.

Joan "Jean" McGreevy-Green

"I have a suggestion for the use of some of Kansas' and Missouri's share of the federal stimulus dollars. This proposal would help low-and moderate income people get to jobs, doctors, and stores in our spread prairie city. At the same time, I believe that this project would reduce carbon emissions and the particulates that aggravate asthma for many innercity children and adults, thus improving health...I suggest that Kansas and Missouri allot stimulus dollars to convert the public transit fleet into small buses, which would run more frequently on more routes and be fueled on natural gas. Natural gas, which is plentiful in our country, is cheaper and less polluting than diesel and gasoline." [34]

Jean shuns interviews like her sister, especially regarding anything having to do with Jesse James. Instead, Jean sidesteps her James kinship to proudly assert her kinship to the explorer Meriwether Lewis, claiming her Lewis descent from her third great grandmother Fannie Shouse, a cousin of the Lewis family.

Gail and Jean's brother Thomas James McGreevy, named after T. M., was killed at the age of fifty-eight in a scuba diving accident off the Netherlands, Antilles. He was educated at Harvard College and Harvard Business School.[35] At home in Santa Fe, New Mexico, he was managing director of Smith Barney Harris Upham & Company. Like many men among the James family, Thomas James McGreevy found himself drawn to strong willed, independent thinking women, if not also to a woman who was utterly attractive in a brassy, flashy way.

In 1959, Thomas James McGreevy married Mollie W. Paine, a New York actress. Her father Hugh Eustis Paine was a founder of the securities firm Abbott, Proctor & Paine. Mollie was a recurring actor on the soap opera *Ryan's Hope*. Off screen, Mollie avidly collected Pop Art. Mollie said of herself, *"I was always looking for the limelight...I wore micro miniskirts when they were in. I was a real 'who can we shock at the country club' person."*

Mollie's penchant for shocking people was more strongly stated when she was ordained an Episcopal priest. Mollie had been raised Presbyterian, and was a graduate of the General Theological Seminary. For a decade she ministered at the Church of St. Luke in the Fields in New York's Greenwich Village. Through the AIDS epidemic, she became recognized with sincere and grateful affection by the epidemic's victims as Mother Mollie or Mother McGreevy.[36]

Rev. Mollie Paine-
McGreevy

*Wife of Thomas James
McGreevy*

Later, Mollie associated herself with the St. Francis Episcopal Church in Stanford, Connecticut. She signed the *Declamation for Marriage Equality*, supporting lesbian, gay, bisexual, and transgender equality. When she married again in 1976, Mollie took actor Earl Hindman as her husband. Hindman was famous in his the role as the never-seen character, Wilson, in the hit television show *Home Improvement*.

Before parting ways, Thomas James McGreevy and Mollie Paine had three daughters, Pamela Paine, Jessica James, and Barbara Helen McGreevy. Pam graduated Bryn Mawr College, and later obtained an MBA degree from Columbia. Her mother likened her to a character out of a Jane Austin novel: *"bright eyed, alabaster skinned, smart and sensible."* Mollie thought of Pam not at all like she thought of herself. *"She's more reserved, more cautious and more ladylike."*

After attending Columbia, Pam worked in Rochester, New York, as a senior product manager for Bausch & Lomb. On a blind date in the middle of a Rochester blizzard, Pam met her future husband, Jeffrey Daniel Newman, a research scientist at Eastman Kodak. The following Fourth of July, Pam invited Dan to her mother's family compound on Lake Champlain, where "the kitchen table is always packed with aunts, uncles and cousins and the motto is 'Survival of the Loudest'." The Paine family agreed Dan belonged.

Pamela McGreevy

Daughter of Thomas James
& Mollie Paine McGreevy

Mollie said of him, "Dan is a very good listener and very sweet. He isn't somebody who has to make his presence felt. He's not afraid of silence. Sometimes, I'm talking to him on the phone, and there will be a long pause, and I'll say, 'Operator, operator!' And he'll say: 'I'm still here. I'm just thinking'." In the world of Pam's father, silence was a welcome thing. Not so much, though, among her mother's family.

On May 18, 1997, the family returned to the Episcopal Church of St. Luke in New York City. There, Rev. Molly Paine McGreevy officiated with Rabbi Joseph H. Gelberman to wed her daughter Pam to Dan Newman. In her homily, Mother Molly advised the wedded couple that marriage was like a gazebo with a sewage plant beneath. She also advised that passion should never substitute for love, and that the couple should never forget to telephone their mother. Not so curiously, the bride and bridegroom did not move in together immediately. Not because Dan was thinking about it. But Pam was. Pam excused the arrangement. "We live apart now, mostly because I've got a cat, and he's allergic to cats," Pam added, "I've known the cat longer than I've known Dan, so I just hope I don't have to choose."[37]

Following his marriage to Molly, Thomas James McGreevy was married Susan Colby Brown, a graduate of Mount Holyoke College in Massachusetts. Susan's summers were spent at her grandparents' home in northern Wisconsin. There her Aunt Micky, an enthusiastic lover of nature,

Susan Colby Brown-McGreevy

Second wife of
Thomas James McGreevy

became Susan's inspiration, leading Susan eventually to becoming a distinguished trustee of The Nature Conservancy of New Mexico, and a board member with Audubon New Mexico.

Susan was more in tune with the family heritage of Thomas James McGreevy than his first wife Molly Paine. Susan had been a teacher with the Renesan Institute for Lifelong Learning. Her specialty was southwest studies. She became a curator of exhibits, conducted research, gave lectures, and published two books. One book she wrote about Native American culture.[38] Her second book was about Navajo basketry.[39] Her biography with the Santa Fe Conservation Trust in 2008, that preserves and protects open space on New Mexico, stated, "Susan McGreevy's professional life has focused on Southwest Indian arts and culture since 1970, when anthropology field work took her to the Navajo Nation. She served as Curator of North American Ethnology at the Kansas City Museum of History, and later as Science Director of the Wheelwright Museum of the American Indian in Santa Fe. Susan currently is a research associate at the Wheelwright, the School of Advanced Research, the Museum of Indian Arts and Culture, and the Museum of International Folk Art." Of her work at the Wheelright Museum in repatriating historical artifacts, Susan said, "We invite Indian elders to identify religious materials and ask them what should be done with those materials. Very often they tell us just to keep them." Unequivically,

Susan was of the belief that "ceremonial objects do not belong in a museum," adding that objects made for a functional use "should be allowed to self destruct in the normal order of things."[40] Such belief eased her loss when Thomas James McGreevy perished beneath the ocean.

THE ANONYMITY MAINTAINED ABOUT THE JAMES FAMILY'S RELATIONSHIP TO THEIR POST-CIVIL WAR OUTLAWS passed successfully from T. M. through his children, and from Vassie James to the generations succeeding her. So, too, did the family penchant for education, and the advancement of social justice. Considerable wealth had been built up in these family lines. The teacher from Kentucky turned merchant millionaire of Kansas City, had established more than enough wealth to be inherited by his descendants. His riches insured future generations a tradition of elite education. Typical of the James, the family's dedication to high standards for education and to T.M.'s mandate for quality, matched with social responsibility, remained steadfast. Outlaws did not fit into the family picture Thomas Martin James envisioned. This particularly had been stated repeatedly by T. M.'s wife, Sarah. She, like other in-law relatives of the James, made it clear that she did not wish her family to be associated with her husband's relatives.[41]

With the mandate secured and sternly intact, virtue was established. That virtue forged stature which was measurable, respected, and admired. There was no hauteur, loftiness, or aspirations to greatness about this James family imperative. Instead, among the family was nurtured a quiet sense for decorum, decency, and yet also, for personal achievement and distinction. Better, not to speak of outlaws. Best, to concentrate on building a constructive future. Best to let the notorious history of Frank and Jesse James atrophy and die in its legend and mythology.

As their invaluable reputation progressed into the 21st century, descendants of the James family continue in such fashion, reluctant to recognize any relationship between them and their infamous cousins. By contrast, the descendants in the line of Jesse and Frank James felt more isolated than ever. Among the James bouquet of lushly blossoming flowers, the broken stemmed carnation forever slumps. Feeling more like Frank James' son Bob, the family at James Farm seemed less than immediate kin of the complete James family, and more like shirt tail cousins.[42]

Kansas City Journal-Post, December 31, 1929

IN 1865   TODAY   IN 1895

THE OLDEST STORE IN KANSAS CITY

Discriminating hostesses of four generations have chosen china and glass at this store, operated continuously by the same family for 67 years. We are proud of the fact that James' china has become an established tradition in Kansas City. Tomorrow 75,000 families will be seated at New Year's dinner tables graced with china from T. M. James & Sons. We wish them all a Happy and Prosperous New Year.

Our sincere desire is that we may serve coming generations in the same manner, with a business policy built and maintained on the same high principles of honor and integrity. It is an honor to have grown up with Kansas City—to have witnessed its infancy, its adolescence and to see it emerge as a fair, full-grown metropolis, worthy of a place among the most beautiful home cities of America.

T. M. JAMES & SONS CHINA CO.
Specialists in China and Glass Since 1863
1114-1116 GRAND AVE.

Forever afterward for the James family and their descendants, cautious forethought of consequences became both a prelude and requirement to action. Those who breached the precept or violated the principle - as did Daniel Lewis James Jr. - would suffer dearly as nailheads for society's hammer.

Daniel Lewis & Lilith Standward James Jr.

Chapter Nine

All for the Underdog

One great grandson of T. M. James was driven to self-imposed anonymity in the extreme. His personal identity was destroyed, redefined, but ultimately erased by the pseudonym he created to distance himself from his own identity. If Rev. Joseph Martin James made of his life something "talented, but erratic" through a lack of self-discipline, this James exercised abundant self-discipline to what appeared to become the same effect. Despite a meaningful social and literary contribution, destiny did not relinquish the name of Daniel Lewis James Jr. from derision, retribution, and - like his cousin Jesse James - fame.

Dan James was sent to the Massachusetts boarding school Andover Academy. He had graduated Vassie James' Pembroke Hill School at age fifteen. His family did not think he was ready to attend Yale until he was suitably prepared by a year at Andover. Among those in his term at Yale was Despina Plakias Messinesi who became fashion editor of *Vogue* magazine, Gerard Piel who became publisher of *Scientific American* magazine, and William Davis Taylor who became publisher and chairman of the board of the *Boston Globe* newspaper. In 1933, Daniel Lewis James Jr.

graduated Yale University in the company of future Supreme Court Justice Abe Fortas. Soon to graduate were the famous architect Eero Saarinen, the architectural writer Brendan Gill, and the notorious political activist from the Vietnam era, David Dellinger of the Chicago Seven.[1] Among all these *literati* and notables with whom he was educated, Dan James was the only one to major in classical Greek.[2]

His father Daniel Lewis James Sr. was described as a "business aesthete...who painted." He preferred being addressed solely as " D. L." Thelma Duncan Barr, the wife of Jesse James' grandson Lawrence Barr, wrote that she met D. L. once, but didn't like him. He appeared "too aloof" for her country taste. Even inside his own family, D. L. was regarded somewhat as a snob. But D. L. James was not without dash. He was a Kansas City tennis champion. He took on Bill Tilden, the world's number one tennis player for seven years. D. L. could do a no-hands fl ip; and he often dressed in white tie and tails.

Barbara James
Daughter of Daniel Lewis & Lilith James Jr.

D. L.'s granddaughter, Barbara James, recalled him from her childhood. "D. L. and [his wife] Lillie visited us in Hollywood, staying at the Garden of Allah, which was diagonally across Havenhurst St. from our house. I was playing on the steps of the hotel's famous kidney-shaped pool. For some reason I decided to walk down to the bottom of the steps, which was over my head, and proceeded to drown. D. L. was coming out of their room to go to dinner as I disappeared. Without hesitation, he jumped into the deep end of the pool, struggled to the shallow end, and pulled me out. He was in full white tie and tails, and he couldn't swim."

On another occasion, D. L. and Lillie were dining at the Coconut Grove in Los Angeles with Barbara's parents Dan and Lilith, at the height of Frank Sinatra's bobby-sox era. As Barbara recalled, "my mother noticed Sinatra and entourage at a nearby table. She remarked she would be able to get our high school neighbor to babysit me forever, if she could only get an autograph from Frank Sinatra. My father was embarrassed, and tried to get the matter dropped. But D. L. jumped up and insisted that he would go and get the autograph for her. So he walked over to the hottest group of celebrities in Hollywood, and said, 'Excuse me, which one of you gentleman is Frank Sinatra?' Sinatra was charmed, and bought him a drink."

D. L.'s social coterie in California were more accepting, being D. L. was a creative type, trapped in a business suit. Having graduated Yale like his son, D. L. worked at T. M. James & Sons throughout his life. During summer vacations, D. L. wrote plays and mounted stock theatrical productions in the artist retreat of Carmel-By-The-Sea in California.

Preparing for retirement, D. L. commissioned a summer home in 1917 to be built in the Carmel Highlands, overlooking the ocean. The money for the expensive construction came from an inheritance of his wife Lillie Snider.[3] D. L. selected Charles Sumner Greene, of Greene & Greene in Pasadena, not yet famous for defining the craftsman style of architecture. Greene was living in Carmel, and had visited Tintagel Castle on the Cornwall coast in England in 1909. As an artist descended from kings, D. L. was charmed by Tintagel's legend as the birthplace of King Arthur. Greene's conceit of a raw architectural adventure combining California mission and English manor style embedded upon a bedrock promontory, looking out to sea like an ageless castle, charmed D. L. equally as it did Greene. D. L. ordered its construction.

The home was strong, entirely constructed by hand, of randomly coursed stone, quarried from Malpaso Canyon nearby. Redwood framing, resting on thick walls of solid stone, supported a naturally baked red tile roof. Its interior walls were roughly plastered. The aesthete and the architect clashed over overage costs. Construction dragged on past three years. Finally D. L. put a halt to construction. Before dying, D. L. employed Greene again to build a library addition, which his son Dan then terminated upon his

Seaward

father's death. D. L. intended the rock manor both sanctuary and defense, where his family and friends could harmonize in sublimity with nature. D. L. christened his retreat, Seaward.

The Kansas City family spent their summers basking in the peace and composure of the Pacific Ocean. The stir of excitement was found in the company of local writers Lincoln Steffens and John Steinbeck, who were frequent visitors to the James home.

A good friend and visitor of D. L. was the artist Theodore Morrow Criley, who had been born in Lawrence, Kansas, and who knew of D. L.'s infamous cousins. Criley began his studies at the Art Institute of Chicago, and later attended the Academie Julian in Paris. Criley also owned hotels in Chicago and Kansas City, arising out of a hotel his family once owned in Lawrence, Kansas, that was robbed by the James brothers. Whenever the check arrived after dinner and Criley won the privilege for its payment over the lordly D. L., Criley routinely joked, "That's why the James are so rich, and the Crileys so poor." Unto today, five generations of the Criley family have remained close friends with the James, continually barbing the same private joke whenever they gather.

Criley's identification with Frank and Jesse was amusing to D. L., particularly since he could recall as a young man arriving at T. M. James & Company in the early morning on several occasions with his older brother, Thomas Martin James II, only to find Frank James sitting on the steps, after being released from jail. Frank was waiting for T. M.'s arrival and the opportunity to ask T. M. for financial assistance. When paid, Frank disappeared around the back of the store, not to be seen again until the next time he needed help.

At Seaward, D. L. wrote a play in five acts, patterned after Shakespeare's plays, about his notorious cousin Jesse James. D. L. had written numerous plays, including one on Arctic exploration. None ever was completed. Family critics thought him improper to dramatize the outlaw in any heroic perspective, let alone to write about him at all. Ever thoughtful, D. L. was undeterred. He never did resolve if his protagonist was a sinner, or sinned against. To his family's relief, D. L. never completed his play.

What drove D. L. to write cumpulsively about the notoriety of his cousins was for the most part incomprehensible to his family. D. L. perceived his cousin Jesse reflected the same issues voiced by D. L.'s friends in Missouri and Carmel. Those were the artist Thomas Hart Benton, an activist in leftist politics; the novelist Sinclair Lewis, who wrote about individuality being erased by conformist values; and the psychiatrist Karl Menninger, who observed that what distinguishes people, is not the events in their lives but the manner in which they react to the events.

In so much as Jesse was D. L.'s blood kin, to study Jesse James was to reflect on D. L.'s own existence. The thinking of Menninger and all of D. L.'s friends became thematic grist, transferred to his son, Dan James Jr. The identical themes not only recurred in Dan Jr.'s writing, they veritably exploded upon the larger stage of his life, arising to operatic scale, proportional to the classical Greek tragedy he studied at Yale.

FRESH FROM GRADUATION, DAN JAMES JR. CLERKED BRIEFLY IN T. M. JAMES & SONS. But beyond the door of the family store, social reform summoned him. The era of the post-Depression was a turbulent and violent one. Workers were losing jobs. Families were losing homes. People were starving. Dan read Marxist writings. In Texas and Oklahoma, Dan organized field workers, while working the oil fields, hauling truckloads of number six pipe. By the mid-1930s, he joined the Young Marxist League. Participating in a public demonstration in Kansas City sponsored by the League landed him in jail, about the same time his cousin Barbara James-McGreevy was jailed for demonstrating on behalf of birth control.

Bailing out Dan from jail, D. L. suggested Dan commit his politics to paper. Father and son collaborated on a play, titled *Pier 19*, about the General Strike of San Francisco in 1934, known as "Bloody Thursday." Dan had worked with the longshoremen's organizer, Harry Bridges, as an errand gopher. Shortly thereafter, Dan realized, "I was not supporting myself, and it was time to join my comrades in the working class."[4]

Charlie Chaplin 1889 - 1997

Finding himself with Charlie Chaplin, who was a neighbor on Fountain Avenue in Hollywood and occasionally a guest at Seaward, Dan James and Chaplin authored the movie *The Great Dictator*.[5] Dan observed the improvisations of the British mime upon a draft outline, taking detailed notes at every turn.[6] The two collaborated on the story. More important were the themes of the story. The process was repeated until Chaplin was satisfied his story and message was captured on celluloid.

In Chaplin's new talkie, Dan provided distinctly American verbiage that the British born Chaplin could not. Dan embedded his own themes. The film opens in Dan James' words, *"This is the story of the period between two world wars, an interim during which insanity cut loose, liberty took a nose dive, and humanity was kicked around somewhat."*

Giving voice to America's most beloved mime, Dan James broke his family heritage of silence to openly challenge governmental authority once more in the name of liberty. Just as his cousin Jesse had done. Just as his great grandfather's band of rebel preachers had done. Dan James challenged no less than the tyrannical governments of Germany's Hitler and Italy's Mussolini.

The collaborative relationship between Chaplin and Dan James was close. In Chaplin, Dan James found his mentor. He called Chaplin his surrogate father.[7] At extended lunches between filming, the two argued strenuously over social issues.

Chaplin in *The Great Dictator*

At night, the Communist Party provided Dan a social life, filled with fund raising events for numerous social causes. Chaplin has been regarded historically as being a member of the Communist Party, although Dan's daughter Barbara states Dan never saw him at meetings. "He did not know whether Chaplin was a Communist, but from working with him closely for four years and some odd [months], he doubted it very much. He thought Charlie was too sensitive to oppressive institutions to be fooled into joining the Communist Party."[8]

During this period, young Barbara James received a family lesson in public politics versus a private citizen's ideological belief. "Pop and Mama never actually told me they were members until the subpoena came. I knew that we did not believe that American Communists were the dupes of Stalin, or that Russians and Stalin in particular were evil. We believed the Russians were our allies, and that they were building an egalitarian and just society. We also believed fervently in equal rights for everybody, including for women, which was very unusual at that time, even among Communists...

"When I was about 8 or 9, (1946 or '47) the horrid little snobby girl next door informed me that Stalin was a dictator. I denied it stoutly. Given that Pop had convinced me of the evils of dictators very young, while he was working with Charlie Chaplin on *The Great Dictator*. I went down to his room to find out why anyone would tell me anything so stupid, and he handed me some sort of garbage about 'Well, it's a question of dictatorship for what purpose.' I was totally shocked - the font of all rational thought and critical thinking believed a piece of obvious bullshit as a deliberate act of will. It hadn't occurred to me that was possible. But he had convinced himself that relying on his own reason amounted to undisciplined hubris. If everyone did it, there would be no solidarity. Solidarity was the vital weapon in the struggle against capitalist injustice... WHAT a crock!"[9]

In Barbara, another generation of the James came to grasp the struggle between government and oppression. "Later in the 40's, the Party determined that a writer named Albert Maltz had transgressed unforgivably by publishing an article making the argument that artistic work should not be judged solely on its political content, but that its artistic merit should also count. For this, he was forced to recant, publicly and humiliatingly several times, one of which occurred in our living room. The orders to do this actually came through the Party structure from Moscow. Pop continued to attempt to discipline his personal ego and talent to reflect the Party line, but Mama said that after that she took her knitting to meetings."

Ideology, Barbara learned, was stoked by injustice. "Also in the 40's, Los Angeles was rocked by the Sleepy Lagoon murders, attributed (on very trumped up evidence) to a group of young Chicanos. Police brutality towards Mexican immigrants flourished like the green bay tree, and many perfectly innocent Mexican and Mexican-American young men were beaten, killed, and/or hustled into prison without fair trials. Gangs of sailors cruised east L. A. looking for guys in zoot suits to beat up. Then the police arrested

Albert Maltz
1908 – 1985

Norma Barzman
1910 - 1989

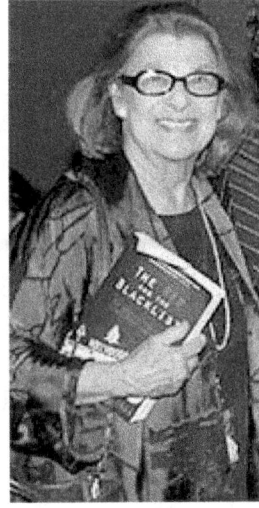

the victims. Papa and Mama, and some other friends like Norma Barzman and Louise Losey, wanted the Party to intervene and try to help, but the Party agenda did not include being distracted by actual, rather than theoretical, injustice."[10] Action, Barbara also learned, was the James family's imperative response to injustice. Help would not come from politics, unless ideology required it.

After the bombing of Pearl Harbor, Dan was declared 4-F. He was prevented from serving his country due to tuberculosis he had suffered. Between his senior and junior year at Yale, Dan had spent a year in a sanatorium.

In lieu of military service, Dan wrote a play called *Winter Soldiers*. The title he gleaned from a pamphlet published in 1776 by Thomas Paine. *These are the times that try men's souls. The summer soldier and the sunshine patriot will, in this crisis, shrink from the service of their country; but he that stands it now, deserves the love and thanks of man and woman. Tyranny, like hell, is not easily conquered; yet we have this consolation with us, that the harder the conflict, the more glorious the triumph.* The script for *Winter Soldiers* won the Sidney Howard Memorial Award, and also $1,500 from The Playwrights Company, enough to mount a production with unpaid actors at the New School for Social Research in New York.[11] The play was additionally honored when compiled in a book of best plays.[12]

Closing the play after 25 performances, Dan returned to Los Angeles to write a screenplay of the piece. But the project stalled. Dan's wife, Lilith Stanward, a Hollywood native and former ballerina, one night attended a Communist Party workshop on women's rights. Lilith returned home with an idea for adapting Dan's story to highlight the emancipation of women, as a heroine goes from hoop skirts to bloomers.

Written against the backdrop of World War II, when blacks were moving out of the South into an industrial work force, and women also were moving out of the home into the workplace, *Bloomer Girl* is set in the pre- Civil War era, interweaving themes of black and female equality, war and peace, and politics. The play's principal character, Dolly, is based upon the inventor of the bloomer, Amelia Bloomer, a contemporary Susan B. Anthony who was an acquaintance of Vassie James. As a fighter in the suffragette movement for women's rights, Bloomer advocated, "Get rid of those heavy hoop skirts; wear bloomers like men; let's get pants; let's be their equal." In the play, Dolly politicks for gender equality, as her rebellious niece Evelina politicks her suitor, a Southern slaveholding aristocrat, for racial equality. As the play's librettist, Yip Harburg, stated, *Bloomer Girl* was about *"the indivisibility of human freedom."* [13]

BLOOMER GIRL

THE PLAYBILL
For the Sam S. Shubert Theatre

Yip Harburg 1896 1981

Song lyricist whose repertoire includes
Brother, Can Your Spare a Dime.
April in Paris,
Over the Rainbow,
& all songs from the film
The Wizard of Oz.

Member of the Hollywood Blacklist

Bloomer Girl opened on Broadway October 5, 1944. Dan insisted Lilith's name come first in the show's credits.[14] The play was an instant hit, lasting 654 performances.[15] Dan remained modest about the show's success, considering his contribution a failure. "...I seem not to have given full credit to my collaborators on the 1944 musical comedy *Bloomer Girl*...The facts in brief are as follows: the originator of the story idea from which the musical grew was my wife, Lilith James, who charmingly chose the perversities of Fashion to dramatize the early struggles of the Women's Rights Movement. She also developed the principal characters. I joined her in writing a first draft of the libretto. It failed to satisfy our lyricist, E. Y. Harburg, and Harold Arlen, the composer. It also failed to satisfy us. An impasse developed at which point all agreed to call in the team of Sig Herzig and Fred Saidy who were experienced writers in the field of musical comedy. They reworked the material to the satisfaction of everyone but Lilith and myself, who had hoped to invade Gilbert & Sullivan territory, with what we thought was a light-hearted paradoxical look at history. What I took for a personal artistic failure for which I blamed first of all myself, went on to become a lavish entertainment which played on Broadway for eighteen months and has since often been revived in summer theater. If I was not delighted, audiences certainly were and full credit for this should be given to Sig Herzig and Fred Saidy (now deceased) without whom the production would never have taken place..."[16]

DAN'S ENTHUSIASM FOR THE COMMUNIST PARTY WANED. HE FEARED WHAT MIGHT YET COME OF IT. The party, he believed, was anachronistic. He stopped attending meetings. He worked on a novel about Kansas City, but never considered it worthy of publication. Dan never imagined it would be his daughter to bring him the bad news.

"One fine hot July morning," Barbara wrote, "I opened the front door and there were two guys in snap brim hats, dark suits and incredibly shiny shoes, asking for my parents. At 10:00 a.m. in Los Angeles, this is not usual attire. Remember, the parents had never told me that they actually belonged to the Party. Mama was washing dishes, and she turned pale. Pop was down on the tennis court and she told me to run and get him. He came up sweaty and puffing and they handed him the subpoena. I didn't realize it at the time, but he was trying to sell the producer he was playing tennis with on a story idea. The subpoena put the kibosh on that...the rest is Congressional Record...

"The House Un-American Activities Committee [HUAC] had commenced its investigations into Communism in the entertainment community, and wreaked havoc with our whole world. The studios helped with their patriotic duty to expose Communist propaganda by refusing to hire anyone who did not cooperate with the Committee. This was the famous 'Blacklist.' People often think of the Blacklist as something the government did, but it was the 'patriotic' studio heads who instituted it. The government just forced people into the position where they had to deal with it. Cooperation meant recanting your communism and naming all the people that you knew were (or had been) in the Party. The catch 22 was that you couldn't tell the truth about yourself without being a stool pigeon. At the outset, there was no clear way to address the problem without going to jail or ratting. That was when the Hollywood Ten went to prison. They were our friends and acquaintances."[17]

Barbara witnessed the disintegration of her father's career, and the end of her family's way of life. Both wrenched by the muscle of government. "What was happening to our world was dreadful. We had friends in prison. We had friends whose breadwinners were in prison. Many of our friends went to Europe and continued their careers. But they left a big gap behind. Mama's best friend, Fran Bercovici, committed suicide. And, of course, the ones who ratted were no longer your friends."

The House Un-American Activities Committee - HUAC
Second from right sits the future U. S. President Richard M. Nixon

Who betrayed her family registered clearly with Barbara. "Pop and Mama were named by our dear friend Leo Townsend, who we used to go on trips with and sail with. They were also named by Dick Collins, our neighbor with the model trains in his attic, whose beach house we used to go to, and whose children I baby sat...These are the rats." Screenwriter Richard Collins had revealed Dan's membership. Collins suggested Dan might prove a cooperative witness. "These people got off free; they continued to work, and they have had to live with themselves...Many of them seem to have dealt with the guilt by believing things that aren't true. Both Leo and Dick claimed afterward that they only named people that had already been named by someone else. The record shows this not to be true, and Pop and Mama were two of the ones that these guys named for the first time."[18]

Richard Collins was, in fact, a Communist Party member for nine years. He attended meetings twice a week and was a treasurer.[19] At the same time, he was reporting to the FBI.[20] Collins and his wife to be, Dorothy Comingore, had been Dan and Lilith's guests at Seaward with Chaplin. The film star was a notorious womanizer and was attracted to Comingore. When the relationship turned sticky, Chaplin's solution was to hire Comingore as an actress. Comingore and Collins later married, had children, but soon divorced. Under questioning on October 6, 1952, Comingore invoked her

Fifth Amendment right before HUAC. She soon was accused of being an unfit mother because of alcoholism and her Communist sympathies. A year and a half after the hearings, Collins was involved in a nasty custody battle for the couple's children.[21]

Dorothy Comingore
1913 – 1971

*In a scene from
Citizen Kane*

Dan never talked with Collins again. Barbara commented on the silence, "the idea that Pop never forgave the people who named names, like a true grudge holding James, this is a shocking misunderstanding of my father. He was a man who perpetually reviewed his inner man to be sure he was not being unfair to anyone. When the blacklist came and I was angry with our ex-friends who were naming our friends and sending them to jail or to Europe, he gave me a lecture I never forgot, about how people like us, who had enough that we could afford not to work, never had any right to judge anyone that had to make a harder decision than we had. And he lived it, too. I never heard him say anything harsh about the people who kept their jobs by turning in their friends. He truly didn't believe that you have the right to condemn forced choices like that because you don't know what that pressure is for the person who is cracking under it. I have never known anyone less likely to hold a grudge, or more likely to condemn the misuse of power that forces people to make choices like that."

Under investigation in the HUAC hearings, Barbara perceived that "Pop and Mama and other ex-Commies in the same boat, got given three basic choices.

"Tell the Committee that you have a right to free association under the First

Amendment, and your political beliefs are protected from government interference. People who did this went to jail for the rest of the term of the Congress in session, which was generally about 10 months.

"Tell the Committee that you are not a Communist, and that you will not tell them whether you have ever been a Communist. After the Smith Act became law, the Party was an illegal organization, so you could refuse to answer questions about people who were in the Party by citing the Fifth Amendment prohibition against self-incrimination. You didn't go to jail, but the studios blacklisted you and you could not get work. You may wonder why the Studios invented and used the Blacklist. In one word - union busting. It was a great way to break the Screen Writers' and Screen Actors' Guilds, as well as to get cited as patriots.

"Tell the Committee you were a Communist; you are ever so sorry, and name everybody you know who was in the Party with you, including your closest friends. You may also wonder why the Congressmen on the HUAC were so adamant about 'naming names.' Politicians need publicity, and any time they could get someone to name a celebrity, they would get big media coverage. Pop was a very small fish, but I think their main object in grilling him was the hope that he would name Chaplin. They had the wrong small fish."[22]

The hearing was early in September, 1951. "I was 13," Barbara recalled, "and just starting my second semester at Hollywood High School. It was a three year high school, and I was in the 10th grade, part 2, because I started in January. The rest of the kids were two years older than I was, but I was the second-tallest girl in the class. To be kind about it, I didn't fit in very well, but my grades were excellent...

"All the hearings were on the radio, and people listened to them. I tried to be inconspicuous. Ruth Halliday (a teacher) made excuses for me to have lunch in her classroom, 'helping' her instead of having to eat with the other kids while it went on. She had taught Mother before me, and she remained my beloved friend for years afterward, until she died in Carmel. I heard the hearing that evening on the radio.

"Mama was very scared, and being very brave about it, but she made a great effort to wear just the right thing. That was the period of the Dior 'New Look' in fashion. After the short skirted businesslike fashions people wore during the War, everyone swanned about in high heels, long bell-shaped skirts, and tiny corseted waists. Mother had a black silk organza shirt-dress of the Dior kind, with elbow sleeves with cuffs and a wide patent leather belt. She used to make a lot of silly hats, and the one she made for the hearing was a small black organza...with French silk old-fashioned roses on the brim that made it dip in the front. To my knowledge, she never wore or made herself another silly hat, ever. It was a shame, I thought. I loved her silly hats. She was gorgeous, with her huge brown eyes and her ballet dancer's carriage...

"Pop, of course, wanted to educate the Committee to the mistake it was making...He was going for a lecture on intellectual freedom and the American Way."[23]

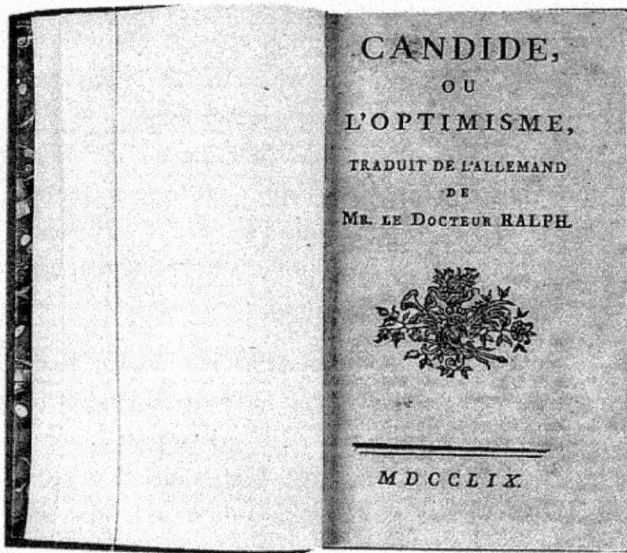

CANDIDE,

OU

L'OPTIMISME,

TRADUIT DE L'ALLEMAND

DE

MR. LE DOCTEUR RALPH.

MDCCLIX.

Dan James had hoped to produce his father's first edition of the book *Candide*. Voltaire, the author, had published the book under the pseudonym, Monsieur Le Docteur Ralph. With visual aid in hand, Dan intended to confront HUAC. If HUAC continued to prevail in their ruthlessness, if Congress continued to deprive one's freedom of association, and if the United States government continued to despoil freedom of expression, all writers would be forced to disguise their identities like Voltaire. Dan was cut off.[24] As Barbara said, "He got run over by a well-oiled train. They didn't let him get his book out of his pocket, and he was only allowed to say that he refused to incriminate himself." Dan James was blacklisted as a Hollywood screenwriter. In effect, his own federal government had exiled him. Just as Dan James predicted, his identity as a writer was forced underground.

One James down was not enough for HUAC. "Then they started in on Mama," said Barbara, "making the bad mistake of patronizing her and assuming she was a piece of fluff. They wanted to know if 'there was any little James at home.' She allowed as how she had two daughters...She gave them a significant earful of what she considered her patriotic duty, and how she expected her daughters to do the same...they couldn't cut her off, until she had gotten in several body blows about the sort of respect that she didn't have for the Committee and its proceedings. She had survived several gavel bangs, and an admonishment." Lilith Stanward-James taught young Barbara another James family lesson in political resistance, leaving Barbara with sufficient appreciation to exclaim more than five decades later, "YAY, MAMA! WAY TO GO!"

"So they didn't go to jail, and they did get blacklisted," noted Barbara. "It hurt, too, because just before he got the subpoena, Pop had sent out a play about East Los Angeles to several possible producers and had gotten a letter back from Jose Ferrer, saying he wanted to do it. But, of course, he couldn't do a blacklisted guy's play, being a liberal and somewhat in the sights of the Committee. And Pop couldn't put a false name on the play and send it out again, because it was already known to be his. Bad luck all around. And the parties pretty much stopped. The circle of friends dwindled to old non-Communist friends, and dear family connections that weren't in show business, and the new neighbors in East Los Angeles.

"Pop did guilt a lot, and he worried about the fact that he didn't suffer as much as people who had to sell their work to support their families. Mama didn't talk about it, but as she aged she became more and more convinced that the bad times were coming back...Pop also was able to forgive the rats. He believed that nobody had the right to judge other people in extreme situations that were unique to them. Certainly, he didn't think he had that right."

As D. L. James, and others among the James family, had been left to sort the residue of their cousin Jesse's conflict with government, Barbara James was left to absorb how her parents' conflict with government had strained their family in modern time. "When I was in the 11th grade, I became friends with Annie and Susie Levy, who were also children of the

Blacklist. Their parents, Peg and Mel were very hospitable and ran sort of a *soiree* for young persons with intellectual pretensions and a fondness for folk music. I was allowed to go with my friends, and I had a very good time. Peg was a warm, hospitable woman and a good cook ...I knew Mel had ratted, but his daughters gave me a story about how he had to protect somebody or other, all very mysterious. Mel was an intellectual bully and enjoyed teaching intellectually ambitious young people how callow and undereducated they were. The way he treated his womenfolk also made me uneasy, but I did love Annie and Susie and all the socializing...One evening when Mel was holding forth as usual, the doorbell rang. I could see his face when he opened the door. It actually turned green, and he suddenly looked much smaller. It was a very strange phenomenon. Outside the screen door was Pop. Mel even looked like a rat just then. He didn't know what to do or expect. And Pop was SUPERB. 'Hi Mel,' he said, holding out his hand, 'can I have Barbara back?' On the way home I told him how proud I was of him, and he told me about it not being his job to judge.[25]

Lester Cole
1904 - 1985

"I know something now that I didn't know then, and I'm sure Pop didn't know. When our dear friend Lester Cole went to prison as one of the 'Hollywood Ten,' he made a deal with Mel that Mel would pass off as his own a script that Lester had written but couldn't sell under his own name. They were to split the proceeds in half and Mel would give Lester's half to Lester's wife Johnnie. The Coles had two kids and they really needed the money. Mel sold the script and kept it all. Johnnie never saw any of it. I think Pop might have behaved differently if he had known that. He was very fond of Johnnie and the boys.[26]

"Mother was not so forgiving. When she was staying with us in Wisconsin, she was starting to lose her memory and her speech. There was a blacklist special on the TV and they were going to interview Dick Collins. I asked her if she would be curious to see what he was like now, more than 40 years later. She pulled herself up straight, looked me in the eye and said, 'He's a JERK!' Then she went upstairs."[27]

DAN JAMES WATCHED AS HIS SCREEN WRITING CAREER EXPIRED IN SLOW MOTION. He complained that A-list writers rarely joined the Communist Party. The Communist Party was mostly B-list talent. Dan was forced into their B-list ranks. For the British market, Dan scripted a film with Eugene Lourie in the late 1950s. Lourie was former art director for the films of Jean Renoir. In the credits Dan James appeared as Daniel Hyatt. The film *The Giant Behemoth*, released in 1959, shows a biologist who warns of the effects of nuclear radiation. A sea monster, dying of radiation, invades London. Nature strikes back against mankind's destruction of the environment.[28] A couple of years later Dan re-scripted the film for Lourie to direct. Dan didn't appear at all in the credits for this film. *Gorgo*, released in 1961, finds another sea monster, destroying London while trying to save her baby from unsympathetic humans.[29] The film ends with the two monsters returning to nature and to the sea, triumphant over human civilization. At Seaward, Dan James retreated from a hostile world to the comfort of his own sea, bringing home an imagined sense of artful retribution. More than two decades later, the full manifestation surrounding his decline resurrected him as a classic American writer of meaningful merit and substance.

Chaplin returned to his native England. Dan James exiled himself with Lilith to the *barrios* of East Los Angeles, where he wrote a Christmas pageant at the request of a friend. Barbara explained, "they started working in East L. A. when they quit the Party, before they were blacklisted, after the Zoot Suit Riots. And the church association was being asked to help a group of liberal religious entities that called themselves the 'Church Federation.' The Federation did nondenominational secular good works with at-risk youth in the slums. My parents never belonged to any church and were atheists. There was nothing spiritual about them. They were asked by a nice woman

Movies posters for *The Giant Behemoth*
The poster above appeared in the UK
The poster below was for the U.S. market

named Ruth Hughes to write a Christmas pageant for neighborhood kids to put on. My parents liked it so much that they stayed and made it their social neighborhood. The *posadas* were a smash hit, and we did them every year thereafter on the little street where they worked."

In the Lincoln Heights neighborhood east of downtown Los Angeles, Connie Rios recalled, "so it just happened that one day here comes this blue convertible two door, and here they come. Naturally we wondered what are they doing here. We didn't know. So they watched us and we played baseball, and finally they approached us and said, 'Would you kids like to organize a club?'."[30]

Dan and Lilith organized the Hep-Kitties, a youth club. They took young people of the *barrios* to the beach and to museums. They hosted them in their Hollywood home and at Seaward, introducing them to celebrities. They got jobs for family members in the film industry trades. They put their kids through college. And they drank together in their *cantinas*. Barbara added, "they expanded into all kinds of relationship-building, education, health, and consciousness rising; they provided necessary refuge or bail, or the occasional abortion, for a large number of what used to be called underprivileged youth." Dan and Lilith James became godparents to succeeding generations of Hep-Kitties.

Bobby Verdugo later recalled, "He brought over the rough draft, because he wanted us to help... We were going 'Wow! This is neat. This is a trip.' Why couldn't I have done something like this? Here was this man, at the time 71, I guess, and he's writing as a teenager and he's doing it believable."[31]

From experiences in the *barrios*, Dan James wrote a novel, titled *Famous All Over Town*.[32] His 14-year-old Chicano protagonist, Chato Medina, in the metaphor a mid-century hipster, is a cat from the old inner city. Chato's themes reflected Dan James, his family, and their social conflicts. Chato comes from a traditional family. His family has problems. It keeps secrets. As if Chato was Jesse James, when the Southern Pacific Railroad demolishes Chato's neighborhood, the youth protests the destruction by chalking his name everywhere, in the process becoming "famous all over town." Chato is jailed for his crime. He writes about his plight and the plight of his family. Chato suffers discrimination because of his family ancestry. He also suffers the isolation and aloneness that result. He feels the need to connect and to feel important. He intends to be a victor over his circumstances.

Sensitive not to attract attention to his past for fear his book would not be published, Dan James produced a pseudonym like Voltaire's Monsieur Le Docteur Ralph. Like Joseph McJames, Dan altered his identity. Not altered so to be misleading, but altered cleverly enough to remain true to who he was within his disguise. For his Christian name Daniel, he substituted the pen name Danny. His surname of James, he replaced with the surname Santiago, derived from the Hebrew Ya'aqob. When translated into Spanish, Santiago becomes Santo Jacobo - translated into English as Saint James, the very name with which Joseph McJames christened the hotels he built. Hence, the martyred Daniel Lewis James Jr. creatively transformed himself into the near saintly protagonist, Danny Santiago.

Danny Santiago became Dan James' nemesis. All might have been fine had Dan's book not attracted such strong critical acclaim. His publisher, Simon & Schuster, wanted to submit the work for a Pulitzer Prize. The submission, however, would require a photograph of the author to accompany it. His nomination did not provide a photo. Soon his book won the Richard and Hilda Rosenthal Foundation Award, accompanied by a

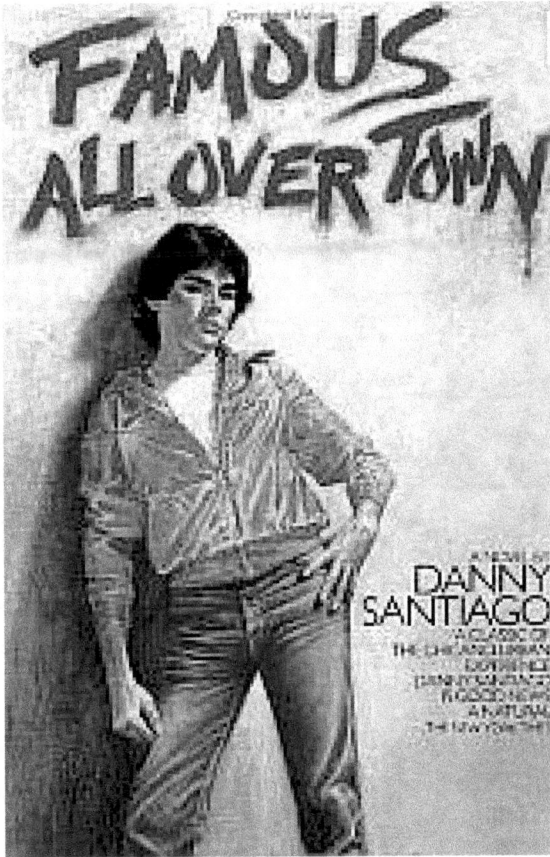

$5,000 prize.[33] When the American Academy & Institute of Arts & Letters set up a luncheon to recognize Danny Santiago and give him his award, the author failed to appear. An investigation ensued. Soon Danny Santiago was discovered to be the Daniel Lewis James of Hollywood's Black List. Having once been subject to an inquisition in 1951, on January 26, 1985 Dan James was summoned again to a second inquisition. This time Dan declined.

Assembled by "a kangaroo court of intellectuals" as one writer called the Hispanic elites who gathered, the inquisition posed the question, "Danny Santiago: Art or Fraud?" Ishmael Reed, himself a non-Hispanic, incited the *Before Columbus Foundation* of Berkeley, California to conduct the inquiry, held at the Modern Times Bookstore in San Francisco. Many established Hispanic writers represented the Foundation as peers. The panelists were

Ishamel Reed
Rudolfo Anaya

Juan Felipe Hererra
Gary Soto

"kangaroo court of intellectuals"

Gary Soto, Rudolfo Anaya, Thomas Ibarra, Myrta Chaban, and Juan Felipe Herrera. About 120 guests attended. Dan James was branded a fraud.[34] Black listed first by Hollywood, Dan James was brown listed now by the Hispanic community he faithfully and quietly had served.

Since his condemnations, *The Great Dictator* has proved itself a film classic. The Writer's Guild of America, also since, has corrected the record of film credits for Dan's films *Gorgo* and *The Giant Behemoth*.[35] Since being brown listed, Dan James' book has been used as a study book of Chicano culture from high schools to college universities. On October 8, 1988 in the Lincoln Height community of Los Angeles, the *800 Latinos* whose group appeared in Dan's book as the "Clover Street Club" eulogized Dan James. Councilwoman Gloria Molina presented Lilith with a resolution from the Los Angeles City Council, confirming the contributions of Dan James to East Los Angeles *barrio* life. Several generations of those whose lives were affected by Dan James one after another eloquently affirmed his vindication.[36]

The vindication of Dan James has continued since. In 2001, the historian Patricia Nelson Limerick addressed the layer upon layer of history existing in the West, which she defines as literally "something of the soil."[37] Of Dan James, Limerick wrote, "when we confront the fact that Dan James could write as Danny and could *not* write as his Anglo-Kansas City, elite, post-Communist Party, Dan James self, we are on the turf of cultural politics, but we are also on the turf that lies close to the soul. Whatever the maddening term 'authenticity' might mean, there was authenticity and meaning in Dan James's search for a set of relationships more trustworthy than the company of the informers and ideologues of Cold War Hollywood. If we describe James' relationship to Mexican American ethnicity purely in terms of trendy anti-modernism, romantic racialism, or even kinder, gentler cultural imperialism, we give a deep story a shallow meaning. What is, to me, most terrifying about the present state of American race relations is the evidence that many white Americans are indifferent to, ignorant of, or even bored by the dilemmas faced by nonwhites. Whatever else Dan James signifies, he signifies a response to ethnicity that is radically different than that chilling lack of empathy."

DAN JAMES LOST HIS FAMILY'S LIFETIME FRIEND, MISSOURI ARTIST THOMAS HART BENTON, in January of 1975. Dan and Tom had shared kinships that were spiritual, professional, and familial. Tom was a distant cousin to all of Dan's cousins who descended from Jesse James Jr. and his wife Stella McGowan. Their mutual relative was the Kentucky explorer Daniel Boone, Stella's 3rd great grandfather and Tom's ancestral first cousin.[38]

Thomas Hart Benton 1889 - 1975

Like Dan James, Tom Benton came from a political ancestry. His father Maecenas Eason Benton served the Confederacy in the Civil War, afterwards becoming U. S. District Attorney for the Western District of Missouri. He was called Col. M. E., "after the southern fashion of the day" as Tom put it. T. M., J. C., and D. L. James were addressed the same. Col. M. E. Benton never achieved the military rank. Tom said, "Dad belonged to a race of men who, with Andrew Jackson, could brawl all over the racetracks and barrooms of Tennessee, shooting, stabbing, and cussing each other, and yet who were capable of maintaining to the death their good breeding and their assumptions about democracy. With the first families of the West,

Sen. Thomas Hart Benton 1772 – 1858
Col. Maecenas Eason "M. E." Benton 1848 - 1924

gentility was not so much a matter of actual conduct as of attitude."[39] As a Democrat, Col. M. E. Benton was elected to the U.S. House of Representatives, where he served in the fifty-sixth Congress through the fifty-eighth.

Tom's namesake was his great granduncle, Senator Thomas Hart Benton, born in 1772. As an aide-de-camp to Gen. Andrew Jackson in the War of 1812, Sen. Benton became an activist for Jackson's vision of Manifest Destiny, but not without alienating Jackson first. Hearing that Jackson had insulted his brother Jesse Benton personally and repeatedly, Benton assaulted Jackson. The General was shot in the shoulder, and the two became bitter enemies. Benton left Tennessee for Missouri, where he embarked on a law career, and edited the *Missouri Enquirer* newspaper. When the Missouri territory became a state, Benton was elected a Senator. His differences with Jackson were sidelined. When Jackson lost the presidency to John Quincy Adams, Benton became Jackson's senatorial leader to abolish the Bank of the United States. Benton advocated for a currency that was hard money, backed by gold. He introduced a bill requiring the purchase of federal land in hard money. The bill was defeated. For the vigor of his effort, Benton was dubbed "Old Bullion." When Jackson became president, Jackson instituted Benton's bill by executive order in his *Specie Circular.* When Jackson was censured by the Senate for cancelling the charter for the Bank of the United States, Benton lead a campaign to expunge the motion from the official record. Under Jackson, and later under President Millard Fillmore, Benton advocated numerous causes: westward expansion, Indian removal, the annexation of Texas, the war against Mexico, securing the Oregon territory and border with Canada, and the California explorations of his son-in-law John C. Fremont. With the election of James Knox Polk as president, Benton's power took a downturn. So did his advocacy of slavery. Having been a lifelong slave holder, Benton declared himself in opposition to the institution. Benton had placed himself in opposition to his party and his state. In 1852, he was defeated for re-election. He ran for Governor in 1854, but lost to Trustin Polk. Before dying in that same year, he published his autobiography, *Thirty Years View.*

Tom Benton eschewed the politics of his namesake, as well as those of his father. Instead, like Dan James, Benton created a politically charged and embattled persona of his own. Equally like Dan James, Tom Benton could not escape becoming political in what he did. Living in both Missouri and Washington D.C., Col. M. E. Benton groomed his son for a career in politics. Instead, Tom chose a direction of his own. In the summer of his seventeenth year, Tom approached the *American* newspaper in Joplin. "Do you need an artist on this newspaper?" he asked. "Yes, we need an artist, but a good one." "I'm your man," Tom said. Soon he was drawing for the *St. Louis News Dispatch.* In a span of summer months, "I was a man of the world, and no damned schoolboy." For discipline, Col. M. E. enrolled Tom at a military academy in Alton, Illinois. Tom recounted, "the place was a bore to me. I couldn't stand it."[40] In the New Year, Tom enrolled himself at the Art Institute of Chicago. He proceeded to study at the Academie Julien in Paris, where he met the Mexican artist Diego Rivera, who later became a Communist and a famous social muralist. After serving as a draftsman in the U.S. Navy, Tom taught at the Art Students League. He was active in leftist politics.

As politics earned Dan James anonymity as a writer, politics earned Tom Benton fame as an artist. Tom's *Indiana Murals* for the 1933 Century of Progress Exhibition in Chicago drew controversy for his depiction of the Ku Klux Klan. The drawings needed to be approved by Col. Richard Lieber, the director of the Indiana Department of Conservation. Lieber objected to the Ku Klux Klan representation. Tom insisted the Klan was an undeniable political reality. As evidence, Tom invited legislators from the Democratic Party to discuss the Klan's influence upon their predecessors in the Republican Party. The politicians reveled in the sins of their political rivals, and Col. Lieber acquiesced. The Klan remained in Thomas Hart Benton's murals, ever controversial to present day.[41]

Indiana Mural
by Thomas Hart Benton

In Paris, France, Tom resented the dominion the Paris school held over New York. Dan James commented, "...the New York School was suddenly doing what Tom Benton wanted to do himself. They were chasing Paris out of this country, you know, becoming the world's center."[42] Much like the Virginian ancestors of Dan James who viewed Danville and Lexington, Kentucky, as the "Athens of the West," Tom began to conceive of Kansas City as the true Athens of America. He retired to a teaching position at the Kansas City Art Institute. "When he moved to the Left, apparently, in the 1920s it was as against the bourgeoisie. Then, in the Left, he found it stifling and inhospitable, so he fights them, too; and he is fighting constant battles between Right and Left, finding, charting his own course for his Middle American Athens that he dreamed of," said Dan James. "It must have been damn disappointing not to have had that happen." [43]

Dan James stance in Benton's portrait of Jesse James also is evident in the stance below of Jesse James' great grandson, James R. Ross, when the James family visited Hearst Castle in 2002.

Newspaper publisher William Randolph Hearst had replanted trees at Hearst Castle that were removed from the home of Jesse James' uncle Drury Woodson James in Paso Robles.

Tom's painting of the Heartland he knew was identified as "regionalism." Benton's and Rivera's murals would come to share as much in painting technique as in political messages. The late 20th century art critic Robert Hughes described Tom and his work. "No American artist until Andy Warhol understood the art of publicity better; a cantankerous loudmouth brimful of vitality, Benton had an unerring eye for the jugular of the media. He was a dreadful artist most of the time. His work was genuinely popular in part because of his ability to attract controversy, but mainly because it was bad in the way that popular art can sometimes be, not vulgar in the tasteful, closeted, Puritan-wistful way of an Andrew Wyeth, but 'life-enhancing.' It was flat out, lapel grabbing vulgar, unable to touch a pictorial sensation without pumping it up."

In 1936 Tom Benton did a mural of Dan James' outlaw cousin Jesse James, characteristic of Hughes analysis. Dan James claimed the man in the painting stopping the train was him.[44] Dan's daughter Barbara states, "there is no question but that Pop modeled for Jesse in the Benton Caucus Room mural. If you buy a museum postcard of it at the guest counter, it says so. Also, the stance is unmistakable. For accuracy's sake, of course Jesse wouldn't have looked like that from the back because he was a much shorter man."

In Hughes' critique, "Benton assembled a kind of 'kinetic' composition in which nothing is at rest, everything strains and heaves against everything else...his human figures look strangely over-determined." When Tom placed Jesse James in a wall decoration for the House Lounge in the Missouri State Capitol, Hughes remarked of the installation, "...as one aggrieved legislator complained, you couldn't settle down to the quiet games of cards without Jesse James about to jump off the wall onto your back."[45] Dan James identified with Tom Benton. "I think he was looking for the Chaplin audience," Dan said of Benton. "He felt that he could...set certain strings vibrating in America, among the American people, that would...give art an immediacy that perhaps it had in the Renaissance, where...it became a fighting thing, you know, when somebody finished something, the whole damned population would turn out to see it."[46]

Tom Benton summarily proved Dan James' analysis when Tom was dismissed from the Kansas City Art Institute, after disparaging the Institute as "a graveyard run by a pretty boy with delicate wrists and a swing in his gait."[47]

Dan James excused Tom Benton. "He felt they had a bunch of fakes there. He was very harsh on what he called the 'limp wrist crowd.' And actually made it rather tough for them. Some of them were a bit lacking in talent, but others were very, very important and excellent curators, it turned out. It wasn't the best aspect of Tom that he wanted to take out after that."[48]

THE LIFE OF DAN JAMES WAS COMING TO ITS END. Appearing in the Ken Burns' television documentary *Thomas Hart Benton* for the Public Broadcasting System, Dan offered a summation of his longtime friend, a kind of elegy expected for America's mythic heroes of the West. "Tom Benton was a small man with vivacity and a pugnaciousness of a bantam rooster. He made great use of that wonderful mustache of his. Very sparkling eyes. Never saw him at a loss for a word. He had a great persona of a hard drinking, tough guy, who happened to be an artist, you know. His pride was to be able to drink with anybody, and fight with anybody, and fuck with anybody, and so forth. A real he-man!"

By contrast, Barbara James offered a summation of her father. "Benton was a bantam cock of a man. Pop was more of a great dane. He was not a dynamo. He did not fight, or hustle. He wrote lying down. He moved slowly, but with a peculiar awkward grace. Remember, he was nearly a foot taller than his father...He was the epitome of grace...Growing up to be 6', 6" in the twenties was a painful process. Pop eventually became a good tennis player (like his father), using his reach rather than speed, but his father regularly beat him. He also fenced, which was approved of, and allowed his reach to work for him, and for obvious reasons played basketball. He also was a very strong swimmer."

For Dan who confronted the social issues of his day on every level, Barbara had an additional evaluation. "He was a brilliantly critical thinker, and teacher of critical thinking...he subjected himself to the same relentless critical evaluation that he used on the world in general. He had a lot of personal discipline. He was capable of being angry, but he didn't make a career of it." In Barbara's summation, "everything he did was big. The attention he paid to other people was extraordinary. Think BIG, when you think of him. Nothing was small, least of all his generosity."

Before he died in 1988, Dan was pestered by the *Los Angeles Times* newspaper to write something about his curious predicament of fame and anonymity. On August 15, 1984, the *Los Angeles Times* published "Danny Santiago Makes a Call on Daniel James." Santiago started his report with an observation, "James is all for the underdog." He then quoted Dan James at Seaward. "My father designed this extraordinary room, hoping it might lead him to the masterpiece which eluded him all his life. He died before it was finished. His unproduced plays fill those bottom drawers over there. And for 20 years I faithfully followed in his footsteps, except that I consigned my masterpieces to the city dump. Two generations of literary failure. And now, suddenly, unbelievably...this...Instant fame!" Danny Santiago then confronted Dan James about his purloined use of Danny's name. James smartly parried Santiago's thrust, sidestepping the duel. As Danny Santiago departed, he left Dan James to answer the busy telephone ringing, calling for his celebrity. Piqued by Dan's elusiveness, Santiago stole Dan's Hermes typewriter in Dan's very presence, "and left him to the enjoyment of his ill-gotten fame."

Daniel Lewis James Jr. wrote professionally no more. Like Jesse James, Dan James had been defeated by none less than his own United States Federal Government, its politicians, and society. He was betrayed by his own profession and by his friends, but he was famous all over town.

In his anonymity, Daniel Lewis James Jr. acquired fame like Jesse James. Only to one, it was claimed, had Dan ever confided his true identity. On January 14, 1988, Dan wrote to Fr. Alberto Huerta, to comment on an article the Jesuit priest had written about Joaquin Murrieta, the notorious bandito outlaw of the California coast.

> *Dear Alberto,*
> *Viva Joaquin and Tiburcio and Gregano.*
> *Likewise Jesse James and Robin Hood.*
> *All it takes apparently is a lost war,*
> *hated victors, Normans, Gringos, Yankees,*
> *and sympathetic paisanos.*
>
> *Love, Danny* [49]

Nellie Willard Werger

Martha Willard Diehl

Granddaughters of Daniel Lewis & Lillith Standward James Jr.

Dan's statement to Fr. Huerta of a "first All-together" befitted a purposeful life that began with a study of classical Greek. As Barbara explained, "Dan was given to hyperbole. If it wasn't cosmic - grief, alienation, uproar, celebration - it wasn't worth commenting on." She also added, "Father Huerta was not the only person who knew Danny's identity. Many people thought they were the only person who knew. It pleased them and harmed no one, and Pop was a genius at focusing his extraordinary attention on the person at hand, and convincing them they were the only two people in the world who understood each other."

With only months remaining, Dan added, "we had the whole entire family here for Christmas - our first All-together in history." Dan had forgone his class reunion at Yale to gather with his family. Throughout a lifetime of adversity, Dan always recaptured himself in the embrace of his family. "We got together a lot, for people who lived in different places," said Barbara. "Two of our numbers were in the Merchant Marine, for example. The April after this Christmas we rented a house in Kauai, and all of us spent two happy weeks there. He died in May."

Beyond the family of Daniel Lewis James Jr., the wall that his grandfather T. M. James erected remained as resolute as Seaward, Dan's fortress and retreat. In recent years, when one of his family was asked to discuss Dan and his James family as a whole, the request was denied. Contact was broken off. The only response was a brief, chilling question, drenched in suspicion, "why are you doing this?" Then, once more for the outside world, fell the silence of the James.

James Burns Malley, Esq.

Chapter Ten

Useful to the Lord

On the distant coast of Massachusetts, far from Kentucky, Missouri, Texas, and most places where the James family lived, Joan Beamis challenged the James family's code of silence. While she did, her brother James Malley took the soul of their James family ancestry to another continent.

Rev. James Burns Malley S.J. led a life that fulfilled the spiritual destiny of the James family. Jim's ministerial work could have offered his sister Joan an abundance of family history of the kind she sought. More specifically Fr. Jim's work would have provided Joan knowledge of her family's endemic James character, could Joan only have recognized the signs at the time. Many of the actions of Fr. Jim's ministerial life were reflective of James family traditions.

Jim Malley took the long road toward his family's profession of ministry. Jim had a boyhood love for the Navy. He hoped to attend the U.S. Naval Academy. To prepare, he attended the Admiral Farragut Academy. Graduating in 1939, Jim was disappointed he did not command the math and science skills required for a naval career. Alternatively, Jim attended

Dartmouth and pursued a study of history, "amounting almost to an instinct," he later claimed. His senior thesis won the Jones History Prize. Despite the fact that Jim, like Joan, knew absolutely nothing about the history hidden within their family, Jim Malley graduated in 1942, commended with "Highest Distinction in History."

Between 1943 and 1946 Jim Malley found himself in the United States Navy as a line officer, serving on an amphibious ship in the Pacific. First he was its executive officer, then later its commanding officer. Leaving active duty, Jim attended Harvard Law School. Graduating in 1949, Jim accepted a position with a Boston law firm. Later that year, Jim was recalled to active duty. This time Jim was assigned to an Admiral's staff as an intelligence officer. Three years later he was back in the law profession in Manchester, New Hampshire, as a tax and estate attorney.

"With wonderful law partners and interesting work, I had everything out of law that I ever wanted, but it was not enough." In September of 1957 at age thirty-five, Jim relinquished his law career and began eight years of theological studies, culminating in his ordination as a Jesuit priest in the Roman Catholic faith in 1964. Over centuries, the Jesuit order has been recognized for its dedication to education and for nurturing a savvy, street smart, political activism.

Fr. Malley requested a missionary assignment to Brazil, and was sent to the town of Bahia. "I felt drawn there for a number of reasons. My mother's family went back to Spanish-speaking days in California.[1] There was a strong appeal in the Catholic Church to help Latin America."

During six years in Brazil, Fr. Malley observed that, "especially in cities, where many of the people were removed from their rural roots, many were not regular churchgoers for a variety of historical and social reasons.[2] However, many of the 'unchurched' were deeply religious in their outlook and philosophy. It's a spiritual reality in the way God is active in their lives. The Catholic Church had not always been on the side of the poor in Brazil, but in the wake of the Second Vatican Council, the National Council of Brazilian Bishops became very committed to social change as a mandate in its religious message. This change caused some problems with some of the clergy and with powerful laymen, especially the very wealthy and the military."

Jim became dismayed when he saw "the United States all too often fearfully backing the status quo." In Brazil, Jim worked with the Peace Corps, Protestants, Catholics, and Marxists. In one project that he remembered with grateful fondness, "Together we'd get the pipes laid and running water to the people who had never had it before...my heart was too much in it to be choosy among those seeking help."

As his term of ministry progressed, Fr. Malley and other priests in Brazil who were socially active became political targets. "We were spied on. Often we were called Communist priests by the military and the Conservative right. We were concerned that, among the Brazilians poor whom we served, friendship and cooperation with us could hurt them. They were highly vulnerable." Fr. Malley's own vulnerability came into focus, too. "The militant Right saw us as Communists, even though I celebrated mass every night in the little shacks in which our people lived. It was ironic, too, that simultaneously I also was accused by university students from the militant Left. Because I gave food to hungry women to feed their families, they said I was 'delaying the revolution'."

"I left Brazil for rather humble reasons. We had gone to Brazil, innocently enough, with a very superficial grasp of the reality and a bit of a 'savior complex' in the context of Vatican II and the Alliance for Progress. After some years of experience making friends with many Brazilians, I became convinced that changes of a very profound nature were indeed needed in the political, economic, cultural and ecclesiastical sectors of Brazilian society. But I also became sensitive to the fact that Brazilians - who sought reform more than I - resented my observations on the need for reform because I was a foreigner with a very imperfect and incomplete understanding of their history and the problems of their country and culture...The foreign clergy in Brazil were accused, with considerable justification, of being 'ecclesiastical imperialists' - trying to make over the Brazilian Church in a North American image. Little did we suspect what lay ahead of the North American Church. If there were to be profound reforms in Brazil - for which I still pray - they would have to come from Brazilians, as their President is trying to achieve now. It seemed to me at the time that foreign clergy was part of the problem, and had been for more than two centuries. Believing that way, I felt I had to leave and I hoped to continue working for Faith and Justice in my own country - where we had, and have an abundance of problems. Not many agreed with me at the time. But I had to live with my own conscience."

Fr. James Malley requested reassignment to ministries in the United States. In Washington, D.C., he joined the campus ministry at the Georgetown University Law Center in 1973. Later Fr. Malley worked in the campus ministry at Boston College Law School. At both schools, his ministry was a "free floating" and somewhat informal one, practiced principally among law students, faculty, and staff. His work at Georgetown and later at Boston College he found carried many analogies to his work in Brazil. Fr. Malley still served "the impoverished," only this time his "parishioners" were hassled students in the stress-filled context of a national American law school. In addition to the usual religious ministries, he taught, administrated, and personally counseled with persons of every religious faith.[3]

On its surface, the life of Rev. James Malley may appear an ordinary life, accented by special events and circumstances. "I have tried to be useful to the Lord in the Society of Jesus [i.e. Jesuits] by practical utilization of my theological and legal training and background, initially among the poor in Brazil, but now mainly among law students of every religious calling who were seeking to grapple with the many personal and professional challenges of a demanding law school environment. I was never a 'scholar,' but rather one who tried to work in a Christian way with people in the practical problems of their lives. I have been blessed with God's abundant help and have tried to be a good Christian and a compassionate friend to all."

In reality, the life of Rev. James Malley came to him by a genetic evolution that could be described as divine, despite whatever individual authority he personally exercised over his life's daily execution. The same might be said of his sister Joan Malley Beamis and her work to define the James family's history.

No manifest or clandestine spirituality, though, could be attached to one great grandson of Jesse James, James Randall Ross, who was conspicuously vocal in his pride that he descended from an outlaw. The James spirituality for social justice nonetheless lay subverted in his work, as it did for Fr. James Malley and his sister Joan Beamis.

Rev. James Burns Malley, S .J.

Judge James Randall Ross 1926 – 2007

Great Grandson of Jesse Woodson James

Chapter Eleven

No One in Our Family Backs Down

Like T. M. James and many children in the James family, James Randall Ross grew up deprived of the association and influence of his biological father. Ronald Munro Ross abandoned Jim and his mother Jo Frances James shortly after Jim was born. Jesse Edwards James Jr. took in his daughter and grandson. Jim grew up with Jesse James Jr. as his surrogate father. From childhood on, Jim was privy to a lifetime of confidences, known only to the outlaw's closest and most intimate family.

Among the great grandchildren of Jesse James, only Jim Ross knew from childhood that he was a direct descendant of the outlaw Jesse James. Because of that intimate relationship, Jim never was introduced to his many cousins. Jim never met the screenwriter Daniel Lewis James, or the genealogist Joan Beamis, or numerous other cousins of his own third generation.

While his cousins hid from the shame of their family stigma, Jim Ross did not. Growing up proudly with Jesse James Jr. as his *de facto* father, Jim viewed his special kinship to the outlaw as quirky, peculiar, and even funny. Jim reveled in his inheritance with gusto, despite the fact that doing so would guarantee and secure his undoing.

ONE TOPIC ALONE WAS FORBIDDEN IN THE HOME OF JESSE JAMES JR. Jim Ross learned much about his infamous great grandfather from Jesse Jr. Casual references to the outlaw were too numerous not to be overheard. The outlaw was a daily specter, who couldn't be kept hidden. Jesse Jr. didn't even try. He just held his daughters and grandson close. Jim's father, Ronald Munro Ross, was another matter, however. Jesse Jr. insured the abusive husband and errant father the total silence and complete ostracism from his clan. Jim never learned anything at all about his biological father. Once gone, the subject of Ronald Munro Ross was avoided forever by the family of Jesse James Jr.

Jesse Edwards James Jr.
1875 – 1951

Son of Jesse Woodson James

Jim had little recall of his natural father. In a memoir Jim provided to his immediate family shortly before he died, Jim wrote briefly of the man who abandoned him.

"Genetically speaking, you receive the genes. Mine were those of Jo James and Ronald Ross. Although I remember seeing my father only three times, his

failing was liquor, and that was the reason behind the separation and divorce, along with the fact that he got mad at my mother while [she was] *pregnant with me and knocked her down a flight of stairs. For a long time I did not like him for he did not pay child support, and* [for] *what he did to cause the divorce. After his death in the 1950s, and as I matured, I realized that drinking is a sickness, and I forgave him."* [1]

Jim's father merited the silence of the James family for more than his alcoholism and for more than what Jim Ross knew. Beyond being an unsavory and violent wife beater, Ronald Munro Ross was a lawbreaker.

RONALD MUNRO ROSS AND JOE FRANCES JAMES WERE MARRIED on September 21, 1925, in Independence, Missouri. Jim was born July 6th of the following year. From the start, the relationship was abusive. After a few years of separation, during which Ron Ross lived with his brother Francis Dundas Ross III at 423 Maple St. in Kansas City, the couple finally divorced on August 23, 1930.

Newspapers reported Joie received custody of the couple's four year old son, "Ronald M. Ross Jr."[2] In Jim's own memory, he never recalled having been named his father's junior. "The first three years of my life, between 1926 and 1929, I do not remember. But I believe they were formative for my entire life."[3] In his memory, he always had been called Jim, and his full name always had been James Randall Ross. If his birth name had been changed, Jim never said so. When asked what was the source of his middle name Randall, Jim responded with a shrug of his shoulders, saying, "That's the name I was given."

As if he was an adopted orphan in fact, Jim recognized Jesse Jr. as his sole father. Jim always referred to Jesse Jr. as Daddy, and to Jesse's wife, Stella Frances McGowan, as Mom. At home, Jim called his natural mother by the name her Daddy and Mom called her - Joie. On rare occasions, however, Jim did refer to Joie as Mother in public, but only if he believed strangers might be confused if he addressed her by name.

In his boyhood, Jim told Jesse Jr. that he wanted to be an attorney, just like his Daddy. Jim said Jesse Jr. imposed only one condition - that Jim not practice criminal law. Jim sealed the bargain with his promise.

Before Jim could pursue his study of law at Penn State University, or obtain his law degree from Southwestern School of Law in Los Angeles, World War II intervened. Jim found himself in the U.S. Coast Guard, patrolling the California coast line in a submarine. "It was not at all a boring job," as Jim said. "We had several encounters that were frightening." Jim stated his submarine had encountered German U-boats off the California coast on at least two occasions.

After the war, Jim Ross became an attorney. He built up a substantial personal injury law firm in the San Fernando Valley of Los Angeles. Jim later was a founder of Independence Bank in California. As his professional success drew recognition, Jim was appointed a Superior Court judge in Orange County by a former Jesuit, Gov. Jerry Brown. In his spare time, Jim also wrote a book, titled *I, Jesse James*, recounting the stories Jim heard while growing up in the household of Jesse James Jr.

In 1969 Jim was elected president of the Los Angeles Trial Lawyers Association. He subsequently served as vice-president of the California Trial Lawyers Association. When Jim ran for president of the state association, he was defeated when his opponent misrepresented Jim's professional experience. Jim's campaign announced he had tried 350 cases to a verdict. His opponent claimed Jim's statement could not be true statistically. His opponent did not prove the counter-claim. Jim's mathematics was verifiable fact. Jim's prodigious production was under-estimated. Jim lost the election as voters foolishly fell for a political fabrication at Jim's expense.

"Although I was defeated, I was not a quitter and remained active in the organization. At one seminar I agreed to talk on slip and fall, and ended up following Melvin Belli, 'The King of Torts,' whom I revered for a long time. When Mel finished his presentation, a lot of attendees got up to leave. The program chairperson took the microphone to announce; 'You've now heard the King of Torts, the next speaker is Jim Ross, the King of Slip and Fall.' ...Mel left the podium, took his seat in the front row and took notes on my presentation. Imagine the great Melvin Belli was taking notes on my presentation. My ego was expanded, and forever after I was known as the King of Slip and Fall." [4]

The moniker would prove prophetic. A single case eclipsed the entire judicial career of Judge James R. Ross, costing him his due respect and ultimately his judicial career.

POLITICAL ENEMIES TARGETED JUDGE JAMES R. ROSS FOR REMOVAL FROM HIS JUDICIAL OFFICE.

"The biggest high profile civil trial over which I presided was a case in which two gays wanted to dance together at Disneyland, and were not allowed to dance together, and were thrown out of Disneyland."

On September 13, 1980, Andrew Exler and Sha wn Elliott, both in their late teens, were dancing with each other at the Tomorrow Land Terrace when they were physically removed by five security officers. The pair was interrogated at Disneyland's security office, and then physically ousted from the premises.

"When the case began, the Disney attorneys presented a ten-page brief that stated Disney was entitled to an advisory jury."

Knowing he held court in Orange County, California in a seabed of ultra right-wing political conservatism which Disney attorneys were counting upon for victory, Judge Ross empaneled an advisory jury to assist in overhearing the case. The judge was not unmindful he was up for reelection in 1984. The jury's decision was non-binding. But if he wished, Judge Ross could render the jury's verdict as his own. In Jim's personal estimation, the jury's decision could go either way.

The case was heard. The jury verdict came in short order by a vote of 10 to 1. The jury soundly affirmed Disneyland had violated the civil rights of the gay couple.

"I upheld the jury and granted a permanent injunction restraining Disneyland from barring the two gentlemen from dancing together at Disneyland."

Reaction to Judge Ross' decision was swift and immediate.

"The case was in all the media from coast to coast. Not only did the press in Orange County and elsewhere castigate me, I received a lot of letters doing the same, with the best one addressing me as 'Dear Queer'." [5]

After serving twelve years on the bench with never a problem or complaint, the political fallout of his decision caused Judge Ross to retire early from his court in 1995. Early retirement still allowed Judge Ross to accept the occasional judicial assignment, while retaining his pension. However, the political pressure to separate Judge Ross from all judicial assignments was relentless.

In 1998, the California Commission on Judicial Performance held a hearing regarding new charges brought against Judge Ross that he had intimidated attorneys, told an off-color joke during a sexual abuse case, dozed off during a trial, and sold his book *I, Jesse James* from the bench. The panel recognized "that willful misconduct does not compel removal from office…that a lesser sanction may be appropriate for a judge 'who showed himself ready, willing, and able to reform under a less severe sanction'."

Wishing to expedite the complaint, the Commission wrote to Judge Ross, offering to drop the charges if the Judge would simply stipulate to showing an angry demeanor toward the offended attorney. Judge Ross refused their offer of settlement, responding in writing...

"I will not back down. As a direct descendant of Jesse James, no one in our family backs down."

The panel misjudged Judge Ross. The panel only wanted evidence of some rectitude to quiet the complaint. Judge Ross persisted in denying any and all acts of misconduct. He offered no contrition.

The panel switched gears expeditiously "to protect the public and the reputation of the judiciary." Noting Judge Ross already had resigned his office, the panel slammed Judge Ross with a censure, barring him from taking any further assignments from any California court.[6]

Judge Ross denied he had been a target of any reprisal. A short list of interviews, however, with a retired Orange County judge and also a former president of the Orange County Bar Association, revealed the cause to remove Judge Ross related more to his controversial finding in the Disneyland case than it did to his judicial conduct, or to any of the specific charges brought against him.

One of the plaintiffs in the controversial case, Andrew Exler, reappeared in 2001 wanting to express his sincere gratitude to Judge Ross. His day in Judge Ross' court had changed Exler's life. Exler had changed his name legally to the mono name "Crusader" in July of 1995. "I was called a crusader anyway," he said, "a crusader for civil rights."[7] Crusader was living in Palm Springs since 1987. He became a paralegal, and was self-employed as a proofreader of court transcripts and depositions.

A generation after Judge Ross had affirmed his decision for civil rights, reporter Frank Ahrens made an announcement in the *Washington Post* in

Andrew Exler
aka Crusader

At Disneyland

April of 2007 with his tongue in cheek, "Same-sex weddings are coming out at Disneyland." Ahrens reported the Walt Disney Company had announced a change of policy. Affirming that Disney already allowed the use of facilities to same-sex couples, the company stated it further would allow couples to exchange vows in commitment ceremonies at Disney theme parks and cruise ships, starting at a mere $4,000 and ranging up to tens of thousands of dollars per event.

This time, Disney wisely sidelined its attorneys. Instead, Disney imagineers fashioned an artful and creative approach, consistent with Disney corporate character for fanciful invention. Since actual same sex marriages were outlawed in California and Florida where the Disney flagship parks were located, cheeky Disney offered same-sex couples "The Fairy Tale Wedding." A Disney spokesman ironically stated, "We believe this change is consistent with Disney's long-standing policy of welcoming all guests in an inclusive environment."

The public was mute about the policy change. But censure from the Baptist community was prompt. Rev. Steve Smith of the First Baptist Church in Orlando, Florida, criticized Disney. "At the end of the day, they're in business to make money. This is an untapped market for them, obviously. I'm not entirely surprised that Disney would make a fiduciary decision over a moral one."

Disney had learned a lesson in social tolerance in Judge Ross' court; albeit Disney twisted the lesson to its profitable benefit. Like his great grandfather, Judge Ross subtly instructed America that no morality could be expected from a corporation upon which politicians and the economy of a nation banked.

Reviewing his career, Judge Ross was proud justice was served by his court, and the cause for justice had been advanced. He revealed no selfish personal regard in the retaliation he suffered. The Disney case made history. Protective legislation in civil rights followed. In the Judge's estimation, personal liberty was protected and expanded. An individual's freedom would not be diminished by corporate prejudice or dictate.[8]

Noting the demise of Judge Ross just days before the Disneyland announcement, the *Orange County Weekly* acknowledged on March 8, 2007, "James Randall Ross was not a typical judge." Regarding his Disneyland decision, the Associated Press reported, "...with that one ruling, Ross proved himself a far better man than his famous ancestor."

Despite all the efforts directed to establish social retribution in the violent days of Jesse James, in the modern era social retribution was achieved non-violently by the outlaw's great grandson through his court. For the James family, however, the engineering still came with a price.

WOULD THE DESTINY OF JAMES RANDALL ROSS BEEN ANY DIFFERENT DID HE NOT IDENTIFY HIMSELF WITH HIS INFAMOUS GREAT GRANDFATHER JESSE JAMES? Would Jim Ross have been so emboldened otherwise? Would he have been mollified, instead, to ride a safer current, avoiding the riptides of destiny and the tsunami of his great grandfather's history? Might he have withered instead before the expedient bargain offered by the judicial commission? Had Jim Ross known the history of his natural father Ronald Munro Ross, would his behavior have been any different?

Periodically, Judge Ross made attempts to learn more about his father Ron Ross. Jim had a vague recollection of him speaking in a Scottish accent. He thought he was possibly an immigrant from Scotland. Jim sometimes thought Ron Ross had returned to Scotland.

If his father was the alcoholic Jim heard him to be, was his father's life cut short by it? Might there be health implications for Jim, for Jim's children, or grandchildren? Jim was not a drinker, except for his love of good wine. Jim's wife, Rosemary, once had been a *sommelier* for the Lawry's restaurant chain in Los Angeles. Jim could drink wine like water. If Ron Ross lived a short or lengthy life, what became of him?

Jim often recalled Jesse James never knew his natural father, either. Rev. Robert Sallee James died on a mission to the Gold Rush when Jesse wasn't even three, the same age as Jim when Ron Ross abandoned him and his mother. Jim's Daddy never truly knew his father, too. Jesse Jr. was only seven when he watched his father be killed. How are lives affected, when children never know their fathers? Can such a circumstance, repeated over and over in a family, be genetic?

Jim pondered his identity, and how it might have evolved if he had only the slimmest knowledge of his biological father. Like any orphan, fear and doubt periodically neutralized Jim's motivation to investigate further into what happened to Ronald Munro Ross. No enlightenment ever materialized for Judge Ross. The re-discovery of Ronald Munro Ross came only after Judge Ross died.

RONALD MUNRO ROSS WAS NOT AN IMMIGRANT FROM SCOTLAND, AS JIM ROSS BELIEVED. In fact, Jim's father was born in St. Louis, Missouri, on December 13, 1909. But he was in fact the son of an immigrant. Jim's immigrant grandfather was Col. Francis D. Ross Jr., born in Devonshire, England on January 3, 1870. Jim Ross' great grandfather, Francis Ross Sr., came from Rosshire, Scotland, the seat of clan Ross for countless, ancient generations.

Like the Welsh side of his James ancestry, the Scottish side of Jim Ross also reached back far into antiquity. The warrior Ross clan participated in every war between Scotland and England for eight hundred years. Across the globe, the Ross made a name for itself. An uncle of Jim Ross, Capt. George Ross, was killed in the British invasion of Tibet recently in the early 20th century. If Jim Ross had wanted to know about his paternal ancestry, the judge need only have gone to a library. The history of his Ross grandfather was published since 1908.[9]

With a scholarship in hand, Col. Francis D. Ross was educated at Blundell's, a prep school for Oxford and Cambridge, where boys were taught Latin and Greek in the old style, governed by the swish of a birch. Founded in 1604 in Tivorton, England, to educate the sons of local merchants, Blundell's produced numerous clergy and gentry who took England to Civil War and the Glorious Rebellion to preserve their Protestant faith. Ross entered Blundell's in 1880, just as the school expanded to Hoverton. Three years at Blundell's merited Francis D. Ross his scholarship to Oxford, but the young man never attended.

At the age of fifteen, Francis D. Ross turned his back on higher education, and on his own father and family, to self-educate himself in America. Having grown up in the coastal town of Devonshire, Ross easily secured employment as a sailor on America's Great Lakes. Within a year, he was working in the office of a meat packing house in Chicago. A couple months later, he worked in a railroad office. Less than a year on the job, Ross boarded a train and headed west. Across Indian Territory, New Mexico, Arizona, Oregon, and California, Ross roamed from ranch to ranch. Wherever he could find the opportunity, he managed the ranch. Eventually he owned some. With a small amount of capital, Ross opened a mercantile business in Kansas City. It lasted only two years before the ambitious young man advanced to new opportunities.

On April 10, 1895, Ross married Christine Amelia de Rhett, who also had come to America from England. A family of five children soon followed. The first male child became the third among his family to carry the name of Francis Dundas Ross. Reaching into the Ross clan's ancestry for another patronymic name, his fourth child was named Ronald Munro Ross.

Over the next decade, Francis D. Ross built a record of public service he hoped would provide security for his wife and children. For four years he worked in the Kansas City treasurer's office. Briefly he was diverted into working for a building and loan association, but soon Ross returned to a job in the city controller's office. He quickly grabbed an opening as cashier in the Jackson County controller's office. By 1906, he was its chief deputy, now well positioned to run for elective public office.

On January 1, 1907, Francis D. Ross proudly assumed his newly elected position of county recorder. Ross devoted himself completely to public service. He avoided commercial enterprise, while increasing his political visibility and cultivating social respect. He became well known to civic organizations. Ross also was a Captain in Company D of the Third Regiment of the Missouri National Guard, later promoted to Colonel, a rank he sported as proudly as any royal title of inheritance. Col. Ross purchased a new residence at 3301 Morrell Avenue, in a developing part of the city,

>NO ONE IN OUR FAMILY BACKS DOWN | 283ment>

about a dozen city blocks west from the home of Jesse James Jr. While Col. Ross might have known the philanthropist T. M. James personally through mutual participation in civic organizations, Col. Ross took his family to the Episcopalian church.

Financially, Col. Ross was secure enough to build a summer home for his family at Dodson, ten miles south of Kansas City. A rural environment would provide his children physical advantages. Col. Ross also wanted to distance his children from city temptations that could impact the family's moral integrity.

Though Col. and Mrs. Ross provided the excellent education that made Ronald Munro Ross a promising lawyer with a future, they took no regard of their son's evident psychological shortcomings, which so quickly impacted Jo Frances James when she married him. When Ronald Munro Ross proposed marriage to Jo Frances James, the daughter of Jesse James Jr. and granddaughter of the infamous outlaw, moral integrity still was of high concern to Col. Ross' wife Christine. Jesse Jr.'s wife Stella later wrote, *"Mrs. Ross was not at all happy over this marriage and the thought of mixing good blood with James blood."* [10] Soon after, however, it was Mrs. Ross' son who was headed to prison.

By the time Joie obtained her divorce on August 23, 1930, Ronald Munro Ross was gone. When Ross resurfaced, it was in the harsh limelight his own father feared. Events on October 21st revealed what pressures might have turned Ron Ross into the abusive alcoholic who beat his wife and abandoned his family. A Federal Grand Jury convened in Kansas City to investigate election fraud. Warrants were issued for the arrest of four election judges from the Democratic Party. The four judges were charged with conspiracy to defraud citizens of the right to vote. The named judges were Sam Termini, Pete Constanzo, John Varetta, and Ronald M. Ross. [11]

The career of Ronald M. Ross as a lawyer was eclipsed. His ambitious father, Col. Francis D. Ross, was a reputable public figure no more. The Ross family dispersed in shame. Ron's aunt, Susan Ross, who married a man named Skuthorpe, removed to Australia. His aunt Margaret Ross Campbell removed to Ajo, Arizona, a short distance from the border with Mexico. Ronald M. Ross himself disappeared into historical darkness for nearly a decade. Whether Ross was imprisoned, or not, due to the conspiracy charge brought against him is unclear. What was clear is that Ross no longer was a Kansas City lawyer of any political influence.

In 1938, Ronald M. Ross was in trouble again. He resurfaced in Ajo, Arizona where his aunt had moved. Democrats wanted to elect Sen. Bob Jones as Arizona's new governor. Jones was the working man's candidate. He had served four years as state senator from Pinal County, and another four years representing Maricopa County. Jones had co-authored a minimum wage act for women. When government bureaucracy impeded the prompt payment of pension checks to seniors, Jones ramrodded a bill that provided immediate relief.

Robert Taylor "Bob" Jones was born in Tennessee. His father, who had served the Union in the Civil War, was a peace officer, always involved in his community's development while he also operated a lumber mill. Jones went to work in the West as an engineer and surveyor for railroads. In 1909, work brought Jones to Arizona. Four years later Jones owned a prosperous drug store in Superior, which grew quickly into a chain spanning five cities. Before becoming a senator, Jones was a member of the Superior School Board.[12]

Gov. Robert Taylor Jones
1884 - 1958

News broke on the eve of the election that a sensational affidavit made by the 39 year old election board worker, Ronald M. Ross, stated he attempted to "steal" the Democratic gubernatorial primary for Jones. The affidavit was brought to light by James H. Kirby, the former Secretary of State and native of Randolph County, Missouri, who contested Jones' nomination.

Ross was charged with altering ballots and arranging for "30 Kansas City men and women" to change their votes in a plot to elect Jones. After three days of questioning by Sheriff's officers and the Arizona Attorney General, Ross recanted his previous affidavit, stating he has been "misled" into signing it. On election eve, Ross issued another affidavit "in the interest of justice." His new affidavit stated Ross had not talked directly or indirectly with Jones, nor had he altered any primary ballots.[13]

Jones was elected Governor of Arizona. Nonetheless, Ross was charged with criminal libel against Robert T. Jones the following January. A preliminary motion to dismiss the case failed. Fifty jurors were summoned for interviews.[14] Three days later that included a Sunday recess, Ross stood convicted. The jury deliberated less than an hour. In the trial, it was noted Ross was a "former Kansas City attorney." Ross testified also he was a former election worker for the faction of Tom Pendergast in Kansas City. Sentencing was scheduled for February 13. Ross faced a year in prison, and a maximum fine of $5,000.[15]

On February 13, Ronald M. Ross was given the maximum sentence of one year in state prison by Judge M. T. Phelps of Superior, Jones' hometown.[16] When the Arizona Department of Corrections received Ross on February 16, they issued him number 011325.[17] Ross spent most of his time in confinement, attempting to have his conviction overturned through the Court of Appeal and the Arizona Supreme Court. For all his effort, his conviction remained upheld.[18] In his first year in office, Gov. Jones lowered the cost of operating the penitentiary and its services, further inflicting Ross with unnoticed petty punishments.[19]

Upon release, Ross returned to Missouri, taking up residence in St. Louis. He'd grown pudgy in prison. His five foot, nine inch frame carried 216 pounds, as stated in his enlistment form for the U.S. Army on August 19, 1942. His application stated Ross had four years of college education, but made no mention of his law degree. For an occupation, Ross listed his skills as automotive electrician, automotive mechanic, auto body repairman, motorcycle mechanic, and radiator repairman – the skills he employed in prison. He was identified as divorced without any dependents. Ross enlisted as a private for the duration of World War II. No record is found of Ronald M. Ross following his discharge.

Bob Jones served only a single term as governor, and returned to his drug store business. Jones died in Phoenix, Arizona, on June 1, 1958. Ironically in that same year, the family of Jesse James Jr. learned of the death of Ronald Munro Ross.[20] Young Jim Ross was informed his father was dead. Jim Ross accepted the news with the same fatalism as did his great grandfather when shot.

THE ONLY COUSINS JUDGE ROSS KNEW WERE THE OTHER GREAT GRANDSONS OF JESSE JAMES. They, like Jim, were the progeny of the daughters of Jesse James Jr., Lucille Martha, Josephine Frances, and Jessie Estell James. A fourth daughter Ethel Rose James bore no children.

James Curtis Lewis was born to Lucille Martha James. She was known among the family as Cy. Not living with Jesse Jr. like Jim Ross, Jim Lewis never heard the stories Jim heard. Not until he graduated high school did Jim Lewis learn his great grandfather was Jesse James. His mother Cy advised Jim never to make the fact public. On the rare occasion when he did, mostly while he served in the U.S. Navy, Jim Lewis was disbelieved. As if he grossly exaggerated himself to impress people, Jim was made the butt of jokes.[21] Cy's advice has held him in good stead since. Living in anonymity, and not voicing his relationship to the outlaw Jesse James, has protected Jim Lewis from any of the slings and arrows of the kind aimed at his cousin, Jim Ross.

William S. Hart, Hollywood film star
On a date with Jo Frances James
Chaperoned by Stella Frances McGowan-James

The ancestry which Donald James Baumel inherited through his mother Jessie Estell James from America's iconic outlaw Jesse James and also from Kentucky's famed explorer Daniel Boone determined how Don lived and died. Central to his life was what Don valued most – his privacy.

"If all I did was to walk around saying that I'm a descendant of Daniel Boone and a descendant of Jesse James, I wouldn't have a life of my own." [22]

When Don Baumel died, family members delayed announcing his death, considering whether to announce it at all. If Don had his way, he would have probably preferred to slip away into history unnoticed totally, with no recognition either of his life or of his death by anyone.

Don was last seen among his family at the James Gang & Family Reunion, held in Paso Robles, California in 2002. Months of coaxing by his cousin Jim Ross finally nudged Don to show up. Among two hundred family and friends attending the reunion, Don went virtually unnoticed among them as he circulated freely through all the events. No one had seen Don in years. No one recognized him. He talked with few people.

Donald James Baumel, Judge James R. Ross, & James Curtis Lewis

Great grandsons of Jesse Woodson James

At a break in the events, Jim and Don went to lunch. Don ordered a sandwich, but picked at it sparingly. Then Jim took Don shopping for a western outfit, so Don could be dressed in western style like the rest of family. But in every store, Don resisted. Nothing was purchased. That night at the banquet, however, Don appeared at the family banquet in a western outfit that had more worn authenticity than anyone else in the room. He looked like he just stepped out of the California West when Frank and Jesse last visited Paso Robles. The clothes were Don's own.

Don was born a twin. His twin sister Diane survives him. In high school in Los Angeles, Don and Diane Baumel both were considered "joiners." If a group existed, they joined. Years later in 2007, Barbara Clemens, a classmate from their high school class, confirmed the fact. Diane and Don were elected by their classmates and by school faculty to the Ephebian Society, "on the basis of outstanding character, leadership ability, demonstrated service, and high scholastic achievement." Don was Vice-President of the student body. Diane was class President.

About this time, Don learned he was a direct descendant of the notorious outlaw Jesse James. Like most others among the James family who stumbled upon the family secret, Don was advised not to advertise the fact, but not to deny it either, if questioned. Don chose to avoid the question altogether.

When he joined the U. S. Army, Don's life began to change. He was assigned to a security group, and stationed at a radio squadron in Mobile, Alabama. Don learned tools of the secrecy trade that he employed for his personal benefit later. Exiting the Army, Don enrolled at UCLA in California. He no longer was the socially and politically active student that he once was in high school. Don had changed.

Don knew little of his family history, unlike his cousin Jim who had grown up in the household of Jesse Jr. Don seemed to fear the family past, though. His life became directionless. When his father Mervyn Baumel died in 1964, Don was left a trust fund instead of an outright inheritance. Unlike his cousins descended from the Kansas City millionaire merchant, Thomas Martin James, Don didn't need to worry about maintaining a career, and the possible exposure threatening it.

Most of his life, Don lived in San Francisco. Like a couple of his less recognized cousins, Rev. William Henry James who maintained a mission for the poor and homeless of Kansas City, and Luther Tillman James who founded the Kansas City Provident Association to financially support programs for the poor and homeless, Don developed an affinity for the disenfranchised of San Francisco. Among the faceless on Market Street, Don lived and worked as he pleased, both comfortably and anonymously. Money meant little, if nothing, to Don. Anything he had, he was happy to share, or give away. Like Rev. William Henry James, like his ancestral Mimms cousins, and like his third great grand Uncle Drury Woodson James, Don lived in a hotel.

A heart attack took the life of Donald James Baumel in May of 2011, as one did his cousin Jim Ross in March of 2007, and also Jim's mother Jo Frances James in March of 1964.

Family of James R. Ross
(R-L) Rosemary Ross, son-in-law Jim Barnes, David Ross, Randy Ross, Bonnie Ross-Barnes, & Liza Ross

NO MYTHOLOGY ATTACHED TO JUDGE JAMES R. ROSS, nor to his close cousins. In his own right, Jim's life did not provide grist sufficient to mill into legend. Despite the fact that Jim Ross celebrated his direct descent from America's most notorious outlaw with an assured and sometimes imposing bravura, the fact remained that few beyond his immediate family cared. Only those who appreciated Jim as a living relic of America's past sought his attachment. Others, less honorable, seized upon Jim's natural born relationship to denigrate and attack him. Some, with no substantive argument or actual cause, denied him his ancestry altogether. Even among Jim's extended family of cousins, Jim Ross occasionally could be viewed as an annoyance, drawing unwanted attention upon all those in the family who were unreceptive to the recognition.

Regardless of all, whenever James R. Ross entered a room, he proudly expected to be recognized in his own birthright, as a unique and unusual individual, who just happened to be a direct descendant and living embodiment of a true American historical icon.

Judge James R. Ross 1926 – 2007

In his office before a painting of the Northfield Raid by the James Gang

Chapter Twelve

Destiny on the Run

Herein lays the paradox for the family of Jesse James. Un-reconciled is why America celebrates the outlaw, yet stigmatizes the outlaw's family. The James live lives that are ordinary. The abundance of their accomplishments and social contributions is more than sufficient to mitigate any stigma. Yet, as America amplifies the celebrity of Jesse James for each new generation, the James family feels equally compelled to recede more deeply into self-imposed silence and protective anonymity. With the original cause and necessity for doing so long since gone, the James should be able to live free of the past. Why be compelled to stay the course?

Fifty years after the end of the Civil War, America sought to cleanse her psyche and coalesce the nation in a reassessment of its self-image. The *New York Times* published a feature on November 7, 1915, highlighting what America considered to be its ideals and its shortcomings. Whatever divided the nation before was history.

Topping the weaknesses the *Times* cited was the growing deference to the dominance of money, material success, and the inequality of wealth among the classes in the nation. Next, the *Times* cited the perception of danger in the nation's growing diversity, as well as its ignorance of things foreign that was considered to weaken some imagined national purity. Self-indulgence, superficiality, and complacency were highlighted as further weaknesses destroying the national fabric. The *Times* highlighted a lack of responsible provision for public education and security for children. Evasion of the law ranked highly among America's weaknesses. Intemperance was another. Those prone to hubris and exaggeration were additionally weakened. The *New York Times* concluded that any single weakness, or combination thereof, found in either an individual, an institution, or in the nation as a whole, led to the greatest weakness of all…the depletion of liberty and independence.

FRANK AND JESSE JAMES WERE CONVICTED ALREADY IN THE PUBLIC MIND. Frank James died nine months before the article was published. Jesse James was dead for thirty-three years. In their record of history, the James brothers also stood convicted of every weakness the *Times* cited as a cause for eroding freedom.

America still inclines to miss-characterize the pair as Robin Hood types who redistributed wealth. The folklore was never forged by fact. In reality, neither of the boys was a Robin Hood. They clearly perceived the inequality of wealth in business institutions and sought its redistribution. Squandering what they stole, their selfish pursuit as turf men of the racing track convicted them further of the materialism the *Times* eschewed.

The nation's advancing social diversity and mixture of cultures were perceived as a danger. As war and post-war partisans, the brothers always remained focused narrowly by their Southern consciousness. They sought no understanding of society's change or progress. They lacked the education for comprehension beyond xenophobia

However critical their mission, their persistence beyond the term and scope of the war convicted them as self-indulgent and outlaw. The extension of wartime activity by the James brothers amounted to a reckless self-indulgence and disregard for their community, and especially for their family. The James brothers, however, viewed their mission as acutely as existence itself. For them, complacency was no option.

Hubris caused them to believe a life of warfare could prevail over lives at peace. The James brothers consciously elected to live lives of extremity outside the law. For Jesse James, his addiction to laudanum only served to complicate and advance the insanity of such vain and willful pride. Each was deprived of the freedom of their own futures.

Contrary to mythology, Frank and Jesse James did not live free. The freedoms attributed to them in both historical and contemporary media are false witnesses. In reality, decisions always were forced upon them by circumstance. In the verdict of their actions, they produced no liberty, neither for themselves, their children, their family, or their community. This lacking sensibility became their failure.

The *New York Times* took no note specifically of the James brothers. Like the Civil War, Frank and Jesse James were history. However, the moment was a missed opportunity for the James family to cleanse its own psyche, and elevate its own image in a similar reassessment of self. Whether the James family discussed the published list of shortcomings is improbable. The record is clear, though. Younger generations of the James family turned from blaming the society that afflicted them. As the James brothers did instead, the newer generations of James assessed the outlaws, their family, and themselves as individuals. Reclaiming their independence required investigation, comprehension, and understanding. The younger generation begged the question of their family identity, and their individual identity. They also begged the forfeit of their freedom.

THE *TIMES'* MENU OF AMERICAN IDEALS LONG SINCE HAS RECEDED. In any reconsideration of what produces and defines American liberty, however, those muted ideals remain steadfast and as relevant today as the ideals of 1776 which they mirrored.

As the *Times* noted, foundational to those ideals is the search for truth, human knowledge, and intellectual achievement. America was conceived in the Age of Enlightenment. Since the War of the Revolution, America has remained a beacon of enlightenment, though the nation might experience periods of dimness, if not darkness, in becoming so. When Joseph McJames relocated to Danville, Kentucky his "Athens of the West," he consciously elected to occupy a place of progressive thinking. The idea was not lost on Thomas Martin James either, as he labored to build the prairie metropolis of Kansas City into his own "Athens of the West."

The challenge to the Jesse James family is the same challenge facing the nation every day – to remain each day as a seeker of insight and wisdom, another ideal the *Times* listed. The critical thinking practiced by Daniel Lewis James Jr., who was all for the underdog, became his saving grace when he was subverted as an underdog himself by the falsification and miss-characterization of fact that his own government and friends unjustly showered upon him. Within the James family's critical thinking and self-education evolved into structures that provided the "highest mental culture" as a personal defense against deconstructive forces. In its list of American ideals the *Times* noted, the continuum of enlightenment serves to insure confidence, stability, and perpetuity in democracy and its institutions – the very same goals pursued by the James family.

Also fundamental to America and equally to the James family are the ideals of honesty, fairness, and integrity, without which no person, family, or nation will survive. John James of Alvarado, Texas recognized the unfairness of imposing tenets of his personal faith upon the Choctaw culture, a people who demonstrated a valuable spiritual integrity of their own. To insure honesty, fairness, and integrity, John James respected beliefs not necessarily his own. For his ideal in defending personal freedom, he paid an expense that was dear.

In service to the ideals of nationhood are the ideals of person-hood. These are the common ideals of home, family, faith, business, and community. In this regard, the James family in their non-criminal, conventional lives appeared to have excelled.

The ideal of promoting self-reliance and efficiency arises from the ideal to provide for the education of children. The mapping of enlightenment for the future of a child begins by promoting beauty of art, literature, and life, and the creation of a love for it. Many would discount such enlightenment as unnecessary, even superfluous, or economically inefficient, and altogether irrelevant. Not so the James. Be it home instruction, a curriculum, a school, or a library; or devising a "Camp Creative," the James proved themselves dedicated to providing the foundations required for a child's future success in the broadest spectrum possible.

Outside the home, the exercise of ambition is directed to fuel the attainment of reputation and high professional standards, not necessarily to accumulate wealth to the exclusion of all other values. Money never was its goal among the James. Instead, high income flowed as a natural benefit of having high standards in professional goals. No better example thrived in challenging and advancing the professional standards of community than did Vassie James, who laid siege to the bastions of male dominated business, social, and political barriers altogether.

In America, community ideals more often than not are rooted in spiritual or religious experience. The sheer number of churches founded by the James demonstrates how integral faith is to their community and individual life. From their earliest days as religious rebels, when faced with a critical choice, the James elected to include rather than exclude their enslaved in their church congregations and devotions after which they sought to embrace all comers of whatever belief or circumstance. The James understood that tolerance in all matters religious, social, or personal, generates greater individual freedoms, weaving a more strongly integrated community, society, and nation at liberty.

The highest community ideal cited in the *Times* story requires the greatest discipline and sacrifice of self - to protect the weak and to educate the masses. Lessons like these were not lost to Joseph McJames when he freed his enslaved and devoted himself and his resources to their economic success. Nor was it to Rev. William Henry James in his dedication to serving the poor, or to Luther Tillman James in his founding of the Kansas City Provident Association that became the Kansas City Board of Public Works, or to John Crawford James whose large soul patiently heeded with good grace the complaints of poor parents of low income and disadvantaged students who occupied his expanding school system, ever burdening its resources.

In their individual ways, each among the James has demonstrated service in developing a republic of virtue. Their standard ideal is founded in the core value of individual person-hood. If the persistence of genetic memory lives within each James family member, as well as within the family as a whole, that same genetic memory surely must apply equally in some way to the James family's outlaws.

Undeniable is the fact that Frank and Jesse James are cut from a family whose members did not behave in any way like them. If society stands so ready and willing to stigmatize the James family, absent all evidence of criminality or guilt on their part, should society not equally credit Frank and Jesse James with the same motivational character that is demonstrated by their family? In that reassessment, might there not lay the unexplained reasons why the outlaws behaved as they did? Might there not also lay an explanation of why so many in America identify with Frank and Jesse James?

WHAT IS BAD AND GOOD, AND ALL OF THE SAME? The conundrum perplexed numerous members of the James family, as they tried to reconcile their family's goodness with the stigma of their outlaws.

None among the James ever resolved the conundrum satisfactorily, with the exception perhaps of William Heberd James Jr. Any assessment of the James family and its outlaws must look past their individual acts to consider the panoramic themes of their lives, in the same way Barbara James spoke of her father Dan James who studied classical Greek. "Think BIG." When Heberd chronically quoted passages from Sir Walter Scott's book *Ivanhoe*, William Heberd James unconsciously was thinking big. Heberd came closer than any one of his family to grasping how the soul of the James family and its outlaws lives.

Critics of *Ivanhoe* call its tale a "disarray of conflicting passions" and contradictions, a reflection not too unlike the James family itself. The period is a time of conquest, displacement, and dispossession. Heroism and compassion contend with the glorification of selfish chaotic restlessness. The traditions of human actions are complicated further by surrounding political chaos. The challenge demands order. Hatred smolders. The average person is discontented and oppressed. Civil unrest becomes widespread. The forests are infested by robbers and outlaws. Stability hangs in the balance. Honor is not forgotten, nor is the need for tolerance. An age of personal heroism conflicts with an age of reason. Yet, throughout all, the noble quest for human decency regardless of class, religion, politics, or ancestry, is respected and still desired. Ultimately, the nobility of selflessness and passivity prevails over conflict and war.

Evolutionary psychologists point to the human sense for justice and to its simultaneous natural sense for homicide. Each individual is endowed with an innate sense of justice, abided by a sense for personal revenge. Cultures throughout history consistently reaffirm the paradigm. It is praise worthy for one who has been wronged to avenge the wrong-doing personally. Prior to the establishment of the state and the rule of law, conflict resolution took the form of a blood-feud, much like that exercised by the Scottish clan Ross, the paternal ancestors of Judge James R. Ross,

Jesse James' great grandson, or even those who populated his royal ancestry on his James side.

Sir Walter Scott's *Ivanhoe* celebrates personal revenge as action both honorable and heroic. Scott criminalizes the hero for surrendering to personal passion. He also condemns him for creating social anarchy. Scott draws a distinction between a hero who is a proper hero, and a hero who is dubious and morally dark. Condemned publicly as a dark hero, Daniel Lewis James Jr. wanted to draw the same distinction himself before HUAC, upholding his father's edition of Voltaire's *Candide*, as he also did in writing the screenplays of his B-movies, like *Gorgo*.

If Scott's dark hero affirms the order of personal justice, the proper hero affirms the order of justice that is impersonal, as represented by the social community, its state, or its code of law. Backed by these powerful legal institutions, the proper hero replaces the personal justice of the dark hero by dispatching justice dispassionately. Wrong-doing is more than an offense against one harmed individual; it becomes a broader offense against the community at large. The paradigm renders personal justice as unlawful and illegal. Sole responsibility for revenge or justice rests with the state. The individual's innate sense for revenge is muted and tamed. In its place, manageability creates order and societal benefit universally.

Imposing managed order does not redesign the natural order. A tranquilized society that is starved of action daydreams of violence. As Dan James Jr. learned, classical heroes fall flat in the public imagination, replaced by dark heroes who are bloodthirsty, reckless, and destructive. Any modern menu of books, movies, or entertainment formats, attests to the fact. The civilized society craves the imaginary charismatic leader who will lead the way through blood and gore.

Homicidal fantasy is surfeit in America. Such fantasy suits the hero narrative the nation prefers. Setting aside the legal code, the modern dark hero is free to kill. From Jamestown pilgrims, to the nation's revolutionaries, to its frontier settlers, to the two Civil War factions, to epic tamers of the West, to James Bond, Luke Skywalker, and Indiana Jones, the dark hero continually emerges from the nation's unbridled passions. Not submissive to prudence and reason, the dark hero kills.

In the American fantasy, the dark hero is excused for killing. Though sinful, wrong, and adhering to no law, the dark hero is not considered a villain. Because the dark hero acts with conviction and from deep feeling, his intentions are considered admirable and good. American culture memorializes the dark hero as the noble outlaw, one who is unambiguously criminal, but in his convolution is equal to the state in the dispensation of social revenge and justice.

Walter Scott's dark hero in *Ivanhoe* is Robin Hood. Opposed to official authority deemed corrupt, Robin Hood is not wrong to act out of natural law. Merrily, he eats. Merrily, he drinks. Merrily, he fulfills his appetite for personal revenge and justice. His morality comes intuitively, sufficiently to excuse killing any personal offender. Robin Hood possesses superhuman strength naturally, sufficient to kill any giant. This makes him charismatic among men.

But Scott did not title his book *Robin Hood*. He titled it *Ivanhoe*. Scott did not endorse his dark hero Robin Hood. Scott distrusted the dark hero and his acts. Yet Scott marginalized his title character Ivanhoe to the sidelines, allowing Ivanhoe to progress to a happy-ever-after ending. In the end, Scott disavowed the homicidal personal justice of his dark hero as fantasy, to maintain a cultural order based on impersonal justice.

No wonder Heberd James quoted *Ivanhoe* so often to his children. His father, Luther Tillman, and Uncle John Crawford James, had learned at Brown to disavow factionalism as a pathological impediment to a progressive society. Heberd was resigned to his family's mantle of stigma. But the proper hero in him could not resist reconciling Jesse James ever so elegantly as a hero of mythology, dubious and dark as Robin Hood.

THE SOUL OF THE JAMES FAMILY'S PERSONAL VIRTUE AND THAT OF ITS OUTLAWS IS DISCERNIBLE. At its core, the James family demonstrates a devotion to freedom, faith, and justice as the balance between the eternal power of God and the temporal power of mankind. The James perceives this attainment through one's ownership of self. In the equation of who one is and what one will become lays the destiny of each James family member. Foundational to their self-hood is literacy. One must possess the ability to think, to learn, to act, and to lead. In the end, it is public virtue which must be served. Freedom and liberty of one's family, one's self, and one's community, arises only from personal sacrifice for the greater benefit of all. Within the James family, this is the liberty of soul that composes the true destiny of the James, a destiny that never need run.

This canon of personal virtue and ideals never has been memorialized in any documentary form by the Jesse James family. It simply has appeared and re-appeared in custom, policy, and practice throughout their individual lives, in generation after generation, as being endemic to them as if by genetic instinct. In their sense of nationhood, no synonym defines the word American other than liberty. If anything defines the American identity and character of the James with which so much of their fellow citizenry craves to be identified, it is the James family's dedication to developing, building, and defending this republic of virtue, forged in individual person-hood that forms the soul of a nation.

If this is who the James are, beyond the artificial boundary of Frank and Jesse James still lingers the mystery of how the James became so, the history of the James, and whom the James once were. Leaving the outlaw careers of Frank and Jesse James for future historians to reassess, further definition of the James family identity and character is achievable now, through a deeper investigation into the family's much overlooked patriarch John M. James. And so this history continues to another volume.

Having come this far with their destiny always on the run, no one among the James needs back down now from the family's past, or try to evade its history, as once the James family so notably did in 1896, when the James family elected not to celebrate its formidable heritage, but instead publicly to entomb it. In doing so, they voluntarily sacrificed their family identity.

Joan Beamis

Afterward

Unto the Third Generation

Joan Beamis never wrote her book. Illness overtook her. As a substitute, Joan left an essay that summarized her findings, gleaned from all her years of research. Her genealogy book "Background of a Bandit" and her essay "Unto the Third Generation" became Joan's legacy to the family she never knew, and to future generations of the James family time would not permit her to know.

In her essay, Joan intended to put Frank and Jesse James into perspective for the understanding of the James family. As part of the third generation herself, Joan did not consider her interest in defining and comprehending her James family relationship as the celebration of outlaw behavior that so distressed those who acted with prejudice against her. Joan offered no apology. Joan hoped her essay would allow the James family to live free of its historical impairment.

In effect, Joan had adopted a posture of ministry. She offered objective analysis in the hope, desire, and expectation for resolution, understanding, and relief. Joan grasped how the James family was wounded and diminished by only a few of its own who turned out to be so different among all the others. Joan understood the effect of outlaw notoriety upon the family. Joan grappled further with the assault upon the family, by so many who lionized the outlaws by claiming to be part of the James family, when in fact they weren't. As if offering herself as example, Joan coolly and unemotionally detached herself as the outsider of the James family she sensed she was. She referred to herself in the third person as "the writer."

Unto the Third Generation

By Joan Beamis

To quote my good friends and esteemed co-author, William E. Pullen of Hollywood, Florida: The difference between a murder and an assassination is the prominence of the victim. The victim has to share his place in history with his assassin, and there is a measure of equity in his having to do so, as frequently it has been the case he is remembered mostly for the manner of his "taking off." Four of our presidents have achieved special prominence in this fashion and there is no doubt that Jesse James would have been only a minor footnote in the annals of Missouri had it not been for Robert (Bob) Ford. As we approach the ninetieth anniversary of the death of Jesse James, it is rather interesting to note that interest in him and curiosity about his "real" life continues unabated. In April of this year [1971], the town of Kearney, Clay County, Missouri, near where the James boys grew up, held a month long Jesse and Frank James celebration. Previous to this time, local citizens have been non-committal about the pair, but the passing of the years have dulled the sensitivities of the people of the area as the James boys have long since passed from notorious criminals into folklore and a Robin Hood type of personality and reputation.

But the intervening years have not laid the ghosts to rest amongst the living descendants of Jesse and Frank James. Unto the third generation, nearly all of the family remains reticent and even antagonistic concerning any inquiries about their famous kin.[1] And without a doubt there is ample justification for this attitude.

Since April 3, 1882, people have avidly hounded the family for any and all information they could lay their hands on - and, with rare exceptions, the family has resisted stubbornly any efforts to obtain an "inside" story - if there is one. And there are still a great many people who firmly believe that the "true" story has yet to be told.

No other American criminal has had the distinction of becoming a legend even during his lifetime. No other outlaw has been denied the obscurity of death - at least three characters have come forward since April 3, 1882, claiming to be the "real" Jesse James. With all the evidence in, there is no doubt that Jesse Woodson James was assassinated at St. Joseph's, Missouri on April 3, 1882. But even before he was laid to rest, the whispers started, the rumors grew, the stories told - the victim was not the "real" Jesse James. Even his own family was accused of rigging the murder In order to collect the ransom money. Some of the imposters even took the matter to court - unsatisfactorily. As recently as 1970, the Missouri courts awarded Mrs. Jesse Edwards James, daughter-in-law of Jesse, against a man claiming to be the real Jesse James.

Invasion of privacy was, and still is, considered an insult to most members of the James family. This feeling exists even within the clan itself - from family to family. For ten years, the writer has been engaged in compiling a genealogy of Jesse James with Mr. W. E. Pullen of Hollywood, Florida. As a great granddaughter of Drury Woodson James, uncle to Frank and Jesse James, the writer hopefully thought that the compilation of facts and the collection of anecdotes and family traditions would be a comparatively easy task - but such was not so. It was against the family policy to speak of the boys.[1]

The writer first ran into this wall of silence with her grandmother who was told by her mother never to deny that Frank and Jesse were kin, but never to brag about it or talk about it, and unto the third generation the Jameses do not brag about the connection. Since the publication of the genealogy of the ancestry of Jesse James, sponsored and distributed by The Kentucky Historical Society (with all proceeds going to the Society, since the authors waived all rights to any royalties), some members of the younger generations consider the connection something to be proud of.

Perhaps the passage of time renders their reactions more realistic and justifiable. The James family has much to be proud of - in spite of the criminal career of four of its members. Robert Woodson Hite, known as "Wood," and also murdered by Bob Ford (1881) and his brother Clarence, known as "Jeff," sons of the George and Nancy (James) Hite of Adairsville, Logan County, Kentucky, first cousins of Frank and Jesse James, were members of the robber band.

Through their grandmother Mary (Polly Poor) James, the present family can in one instance trace its ancestry back eleven generations to Dr. John Woodson of Flowerdieu Hundred, Virginia. In 1604 a graduate of Oxford

University, Dr. Woodson and his wife, Sarah Winston, settled in Virginia in 1619. All of the known families in the ancestry of the James family - the Poors, Mosleys, Gardeners, Mims (Mimms), Weldys, Woodsons, Ferrises, Pryors, are traced through this maternal side of the family. Her descendants are eligible, if invited, for membership in a number of historical societies, amongst them The Sons or Daughters of the American Revolution, The Daughters of the American Colonists, The Daughters of the Colonial Wars, and The Jamestown Society.

Not much is known of the paternal side of the family save that Jesse and Frank's great grandfather, according to one family tradition, an emigrant from England, was William James. Why this dearth of information? Two reasons. William James, at the time of his marriage to Mary Hines, 15 July 1774, was a resident of Hanover County and one, possibly two, of his children were born there. They moved to Goochland County, Virginia where the rest of the families were born. Due to the destruction of practically all of the early Hanover County records, nothing is known of the family there. It is known, however, that there were other James and Hines families in Hanover. Some families have come forward with strong traditions of a family relationship with the family of Jesse James, (for example: the family of Senator Ollie James of Virginia - the Thruston-James family of Hanover),[2] that it leads one to believe that the grandfather, William James, must have had brothers, sisters, and perhaps even parents in Hanover County. For this reason the authors of the genealogy of Jesse James have even questioned the fact that William James was the emigrant.

But not to stray from the point: the second reason for the dearth of information on the James or paternal side of the family can be laid to the careers of the James boys. Edna Pearl (West) Preuss, granddaughter of Elizabeth (James) West, another aunt of the James boys, writing in the late 1930s, stated that when the brothers embarked on their life of crime, their names were never mentioned again by the family, that the family's surname was a difficult one to bear and that the family, particularly the men, "had to take it on the chin." She did not elaborate on this remark but it has been said that one or some members of the family were refused employment because of the family connection. Mrs. Preuss' mother, Ann Penelope Bryant, had long and illustrious ancestry and Edna joined a number of historical societies through her mother's family.

But in the twilight of her life, she wished that she knew more concerning her James connections. Her grandmother, Elizabeth (James) West, was considered the family "historian" and was known to be the owner of the original

James Bible which she willed to Edna, and which, like so many others, was destroyed by fire. Aunt West, was undoubtedly a veritable storehouse of James family stories and anecdotes with enough background in fact that would make them verifiable today. Mrs. Preuss remarked that perhaps the reason so little was known concerning the Jameses was because of the notoriety of her cousins that branch of the family was not discussed - even amongst themselves. The relatives by marriage were particularly adamant concerning any mention of the James connection. A biographical sketch of Drury Woodson James in an early history of San Luis Obispo County, California states that his grandfather, "Martin" James fought all through the Revolutionary War "on the staff of a General" - so far a family tradition and unfortunately to date, an unverifiable one.[3] But one must remember that D.W. James was left an orphan at the age of one and any information he may have had about his family came from his brothers and sisters, hence the error of his grandfather's first name, which very well could have been a middle name. The family may have known many such pieces of information, but as has been stated, even the surname was not mentioned.

But by no means does this mean that Jesse and Frank were disowned. They were a source of shame true, to all but their mother, the indomitable Zerelda Cole Samuel. History has not been kind to this strong-minded, self-willed woman. Some of the stories have been downright libelous with no basis in fact - another reason why even the children and grandchildren of her third marriage did not and do not advertise their kinship with their half-brothers. Zerelda Samuel was fanatically loyal - even beyond the grave - she would not let the matter rest. She "ruled the roost" but she had to! Rev. Robert James and Dr. Reuben Samuel, a veterinarian, were gentle, kindly, easy going men - an old-fashioned word such as "courtly" comes to mind in trying to describe them. The mundane decisions of everyday life in the discipline and rearing of a family simply passed them by.

Jesse and Frank were also a source of embarrassment and disapproval to the rest of the family but, with one or possibly two known exceptions, the doors were never totally barred to them. Lodgings, food, horses, if available, were always ready if needed. Uncle George Hite provided shelter and protection for them on many occasions - even after the death of Aunt Nancy. Uncle Drury Woodson James, already a wealthy California pioneer, sent both of them fare to come to California for a visit. He thought the hot sulfur springs at Paso Robles would cure Jesse's lung wound, which it did. And he paid their way home, driving all the way to San Francisco to put them on a boat.

And so they were never apprehended. - And there were no pictures available to help the authorities identify either Jesse or Frank. It is traditional that the only true likenesses of the James brothers were on a breast pin which was worn by their mother - to the day she died. She was fanatical about that pin - one day Jesse's likeness showed, the next day, Frank's. After the loss of her arm in the Pinkerton bombing incident, she never learned to dress herself without help and woe betide the dresser if she did not remember whose turn it was when it came time to put the pin on. Inquiries have failed to reveal the whereabouts of that pin, so it is not known if it is still in the possession of the family. Friends, neighbors, acquaintances - even strangers all maintained a conspiracy of silence when queried about the Jameses. The violent and inhuman treatment of Zerelda Samuel and her family by the Union militia and guerrillas during the Civil War and the harassment of the Pinkerton detectives afterwards resulted in nothing but sympathy for the family amongst the people of the surrounding country. It is not to be denied that they were thieves and murderers - the only excuse that can be made for them is that once started, they could not stop or surrender because they could not be assured of a fair hearing or a just retribution.

Descendants of Susan James and Allen Palmer (this is the spelling his family preferred to the better known "Parmer.") Jesse's sister and brother-in-law who moved to Texas after their marriage state that both of the boys spent at least one winter with them there. During that particular visit, they were reported to have taken part in crimes in the mid-Western area. During their stay in California, D. W. James went into the county seat at San Luis Obispo to swear before a notary that his nephews were guests at his ranch at LaPanza, leaving it only to take the baths in Paso Robles, at the time they were reported taking part in hold-ups in the Kansas-Missouri area. D. W. James' loyalty to his family was such that he never told his young bride, Louisa Dunn James, that she was hostess to a supposed pair of infamous outlaws. All Grandma James knew was that they were nephews of her husband's, destitute and sick after the Civil War and in need of care and help. After their departure she learned of their reputation - and it evidently made no impression on her for Frank returned twice more for extended stays in Paso Robles after D. W. and his partner had sold the LaPanza ranch.

The Younger brothers rode with the James brothers but they have passed into comparative obscurity. Their family was even more intensely persecuted by troops from Kansas who made off with forty saddle horses and their father Henry W. Younger was murdered by Federal troops. Dr. Samuel was strung up four times by Union militia searching for information. When he was finally cut down, his vocal cords were so damaged that never again was he able to speak above a horse's whisper. But the Younger brothers are noted solely for their association with the James brothers. Their lives are almost carbon copies yet only one of the families has become part of American folklore.

And so Jesse James, and to a lesser extent, Frank James, cast a long shadow. Drury Woodson James' daughter [Nanna] would turn in her grave if she could hear her great grandchildren brag of their now illustrious cousin. Her grandchildren knew nothing of the relationship until they were in their twenties and then it came about through an inadvertent slip of their father's tongue - the relationship comes through the maternal side of the family. That gallant old lady, true daughter of her father, refused - absolutely - with her own grandchildren - to do anything more than say: "Yes, I am!" when asked if it was true she was a first cousin of Jesse James. A peculiar look would come over her face - almost of resentment - as if to say "one doesn't ask personal questions!" and she would abruptly change the subject. It is doubtful she even discussed it with her own son and daughter. Most of the information came from Grandma James, Drury Woodson's wife (Mary Louisa Dunn-James). It was the latter who told her grandson-in-law in 1929 that Frank James, under the alias of Scott or "Scotty" once joined a posse of Pinkerton detectives hunting for him. The Jameses had a sense of humor too. Actually the grandson-in-law knew or rather remembered more anecdotes about the James family than his wife did.

An excellent book, with a superb bibliography and index, "Jesse James Was His Name" by Dr. William A. Settle Jr., was published by the University of Missouri Press, 1965. In this writer's mind, it is probably the best and fairest that has been done to date. Also, to this writer's knowledge, Dr. Settle is the only biographer who ever got any information out of Robert James, the only son of Frank James who was pursued relentlessly as long as he lived for information about his father and uncle. One cannot help but suppose that Dr. Settle's obviously sincere and studious approach to the subject matter convinced Robert that he was no ordinary scandal seeker.

An almost unusual sense of family closeness pervades this whole James family in at least two generations prior to Jesse and Frank and as is evident, in the generation that followed. There was a "clannishness" that seemed to bind them together. This was especially evident in the relationship between Jesse's father and his brothers and sisters. With the exception of Nancy Hite and Dr. John James, they all evidently settled in the environs of Kansas City and Drury Woodson in California. Perhaps the fact that they were orphaned at an early age accounts in part for this strong feeling among them. Drury Woodson returned to Missouri twice to visit his kin and carried with him a large sum of money in gold presumably to share with the less fortunately situated members of his family who had reared and loved the boy for twenty years prior to his enlistment in the Mexican War. He returned to stay with his family until he left for California. In 1903, Aunt West (Elizabeth James), at the age of 87 made a trip to California in the company of her great-niece Lucy Mimms, to visit, in her own words: "her baby brother" - who was then a young 77! They hadn't seen each other for over twenty years.

So diversity and trouble could not drive a wedge through this family. It seems to have banded together against outsiders. They do not welcome questions from anyone, sometimes from even one of their own. That Jesse and Frank were outlaws cannot and is not denied but the details of their family life remain inviolate.

In the end, Jesse was stopped by a bullet in the back and Frank surrendered his gun personally to the Governor of Missouri. Frank, tried by a jury of his peers, was acquitted on all charges and died of natural causes in 19___.[4] In the years remaining to him and Annie, he never spoke of his past life and any effort to get him talking was met with reticence and silence. The world may suspect a conspiracy of silence - there must *be a family secret! - but unto the third - and fourth and perhaps more generations to come, the legend of Jesse James will remain what it had become - a part of American folklore. And - as is true of folklore of any people - each bard, each minstrel, each teller of tales will have their own detail to add; the legend will continue to grow - and the family of Jesse James will remain silent - shadowed and silenced by a man whose life of crime spanned no more than fifteen years but left a permanent imprint in the annals of American history and a lasting contribution to American folklore.*

~~~~

Robert Newton "Bob" Ford & his wife Dot Evans

Zerelda Elizabeth Cole-James-Simms-Samuels 1825 – 1911

In her alpaca dress & the broach with images of her sons

Unto the Third Generation clearly was intended to be circulated within the James family, and, when accepted, probably subsequently publicly published. For whatever reason, though, the manuscript never saw its way into publication. Nor was it circulated among the family. No copy of the essay, other than Joan's own copy, is known to exist among all of the James family lines. Joan stowed the essay in her research files.

As the fourth, fifth, and now sixth generations were born, the essay remained a silent sentinel to Joan's experience alone. The testament substituted for a pantheon of personal family history, stories Joan might have collected, and the meaningful experiences that might have been told, shared, and enjoyed among the James family, from which lessons could be drawn for all. The sequestered essay solely sustained the esteem of one family member alone, Joan herself. The James family remained reduced in its antagonism and lack of esteem, by people and events they never reconciled in memory, time, or personal understanding. *Unto the Third Generation* was left cold and alone as a tombstone - an epitaph of mourning for lost family, lost stories and lessons left unlearned.

More than a decade after Joan Beamis died in 1990, her son J. Mark Beamis entrusted her research to The James Preservation Trust. At a moment when America was gripped with issues of identity and personal privacy, Joan's manuscript stated a revelation about the James family that never appeared in her book. Joan identified those within the family whom she believed responsible for its destructive silence. Joan named the aunts and uncles of Frank and Jesse James, and indirectly the outlaw's grandparents John M. James and Mary "Polly" Poor, for establishing the clannishness that enabled the family silence. Joan also revealed she had come to understand her experience as one of the third generation herself, and found acceptance in why the James family had turned its back on her.

MOST EVERYONE WHO STUDIES FAMILY HISTORY with any degree of seriousness comes to understand, as did Joan Beamis, what's at the root of the pursuit. The objective first might appear to assemble solely a database of facts. The names, dates, and places of individuals - their births, marriages, and deaths from one generation to another - and hence the

J. Mark Beamis

Son of Joan Beamis

compilation of a genealogy. Joan learned that the compulsion that drives genealogical research soon turns 180 degrees away from the genealogy, to squarely confront the researcher one-on-one, alone. The researcher, and not the family of ancestors, becomes the true target of genealogical study. Face to face, the study reveals to the researcher one's own place in family, and one's own place in society. Ultimately, the genealogy imparts to the researcher wisdom of whom and what one is in the world, when having descended from so many others who are alike as family, yet so different as individual people.

By reaching past the genealogy into a narrative history of her family, Joan Beamis achieved further resolution for herself regarding her family's ignominy. Joan found much in her family history of which to be proud. Joan tendered her new found analysis and understanding to all her family. But understanding alone could not release the James family affliction, nor cure its wounds. Decades of silence had buttressed a barrier so formidable that Joan herself was kept from being heard by her own family, despite the irony that Joan was the one who had grown deaf. Shut out, too, was the wisdom Joan had gleaned from her research and was willing to share.

The lessons Joan learned through her research was lost completely upon those intended to hear it. Instead, the James family persisted in its universal moral commandment for silence. Beyond Joan's study of the family genealogy, she had learned one more thing about her relatives. Those within the family core who were most negatively impacted by the acts of Frank and Jesse James suffered in very great pain. But the unnecessary pain was of their choice. All Joan could do any more was to pray for them.

With the demise of Joan Malley Beamis, the James family lost its key researcher, but it acquired countless new questions about the identity and history of the family of Frank and Jesse James. Discovery of their elusive James ancestry beyond Frank and Jesse's grandfather John M. James would have to await another generation or the arrival of another dedicated historian, who could add another volume to the James family's lost ancestry and history.

Still left to discover and resolve is the identity surrounding the James family's patriarch John M. James. If William James indeed is not the great grandfather of Frank and Jesse James, as Joan was left doubting, the question remains, who is?

Also left unresolved is the unexplored clue Gilbert Cam of the New York Historical Society left to Joan, regarding John James of Pulaski County, Kentucky. What evidence did Joan leave ignored?

Why are there so many questions asked about John M. James in the family of Frank and Jesse James that cannot find their answers inside the outlaws' family? Why do so many of those answers only appear to be found in the family of John M. James of Pulaski County, who was the grandfather of Joseph McJames and John James of Alvarado, Texas? Are there two individuals named John M. James, living in the same time frame, associating with the same social communities? Or, are the two John M. James one and the same person?

Wherein will be found the incisive clue to resolve these questions? The research reponds, there are answers to be found. A famous Baptist preacher holds the key.

As any historian or genealogist knows, one answer raises five questions. So does the history of the family of Frank and Jesse James. The telling of their story and the answers to their questions awaits another volume of this historical narrative - a history that must reach far back into the period of the American Revolution to reveal a panorama of answers that defines this James family, their character, and what makes them iconically American to their soul.

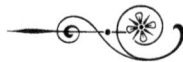

Appendix

Descendants of
John M. James & Mary "Polly" Poor

Family members highlighted in bold are featured in the chapters of Jesse James'
Soul Liberty. Excluded are the 7th and 8th generations. Additional genealogy,
ancestry, descendants, nicknames, dates, and locations of further generations may
be found at: http://jessejamesgenealogy/ericjames.org

1 **John M. James + Mary "Polly" Poor** 1790 - 1826

2 **Mary James 1809 – 1877 + John Wilson "Uncle John" Mimms 1805 - 1870**
... 3 **Robert William Mimms** 1830 – 1893 + Unknown
...   *2nd Wife + **Martha Ann Thomason** 1841 - 1919
...... 4 John Robert Lilburn Mimms 1872 – 1940 + Ann Thomas - 1962
...... 4 Mary Elizabeth Mimms 1874 – 1965 + Walter Andrew Franklin Waers
....   5   Gertrude Waers + S. H. Andrews
....   5   William Waers
....   5   Ruth Ethel Waers 1895 – Unk. + Harold Burton Gibson Sr. 1893 - 1950
....   6   Jeanne Gibson 1919 – Unk. + Ned Bond
....   6   Ellen Gibson 1920 – Unk. + William Layberge
....   6   Harold Burton Gibson Jr. 1923 – Unk.
...... 4 **Lucy Ethel "Lutie" Mimms** 1878 – 1967 + William Edgar Gray Unk. - 1929
...... 4 Ruth Mimms 1882 - 1883
... 3 John Wilson Mimms Jr. 1831 – 1863 + Mary Cordelia Dobbins Unk.- 1864
...... 4 Nancy Mimms 1855 – Unk. + George Shelton
...... 4 John Robert Mimms 1857 – Unk.
... 3 Drury Lilburn Mimms 1833 – Unk.
... 3 David Woodson Mimms 1836 – 1879 + Unknown
... 3 Mary Elizabeth Mimms 1837 – Unk.
... 3 Lucy Frances Mimms 1839 – 1879 + Robert Boling Browder 1838 – Unk.

...... 4 Mamie Browder
...... 4 John Browder 1857 – Unk.
...... 4 Mary Browder 1859 – Unk. + Unknown Smith
.... 5   Unknown Smith
... 3 George Tillman Mimms 1841 – Unk.
... 3 Nancy Catherine Mimms 1843 – Unk. + Charles McBride 1841 – Unk.
...... 4 Gertrude McBride Unk. - 1961
...... 4 Charles McBride 1867 – Unk.
...... 4 Xenia McBride 1871 - 1961
...... 4 Thomas William McBride 1873 – Unk. + Gertrude Unknown
... 3 **Zerelda Amanda Mimms 1845 – 1900 + Jesse Woodson "Jesse" James 1847 – 1882**
...... 4 **Jesse Edwards James Jr. 1875 – 1951 + Estella Frances McGowan 1882 - 1971**
.... 5   Lucille Martha James 1900 – 1988 + Frank Lewis
.... 6   **James Curtis Lewis 1935 -** + Angelica Gloria Alvarado
.... 5   **Josephine Frances James 1902 – 1964 + Ronald M. Ross 1904 - 1958**
.... 6   **James Randall Ross 1926 – 2007** + Rosemary Henderson
.... 5   Jessie Estell James 1906 – 1991 + Mervyn Baumel 1907 - 1961
.... 6   **Donald James Baumel 1933 - 2011**
.... 6   Diane June Baumel 1933 - + James Fairchild
.... 5   Ethel Rose James 1908 – 1991 + Calvin Tilden Owens 1906 - 1975
...... 4 Gould James 1878 - 1878
...... 4 Montgomery James 1878 - 1878
...... 4 **Mary Susan James 1879 – 1935 + Henry Lafayette Barr 1867 - 1935**
.... 5   **Lawrence Henry Barr 1902 – 1984 + Thelma Duncan 1906 - 1998**
.... 6   **Elizabeth Ann "Betty" Barr 1937 -**
.... 5   **Forster Ray Barr 1904 – 1977** + Gertie Marie Essary 1914 - 2001
.... 6   Carl Frederick Barr 1927 -
.... 5   Chester Arthur Barr 1907 – 1984 + Beatrice M. Holloway 1900 – Unk.
.... 6   Frederick Arthur Barr 1937 - + Unknown
.... 5   Henrietta Marie Barr 1913 - 1913
...... 4 Unknown James 1882 - 1882
... 3 Thomas Martin Mimms 1846 – Unk. + Mary Giberson
...... 4 Irene Mimms 1870 – Unk. + William Purnell
...... 4 Thomas James Mimms 1872 – Unk.
... 3 Sarah Ann Mimms 1849 – Unk. + William S. Sullivan 1849 – Unk.
...... 4 John Sullivan 1871 – Unk.
...... 4 Conn Sullivan 1874 –Unk. + Mary Grimm
.... 5   Nannie Sullivan + Herbert Finley
.... 6   Unknown Finley
.... 5   George Robertson Sullivan
......   *2nd Wife of Conn Sullivan: + Tessie Dyer
.... 5   George Robertson Sullivan Sr. + Unknown
.... 6   George /Jr./ Sullivan
...... 4 Fay Sullivan 1876 – Unk. + Andrew Gootee
...   *2nd Husband of Sarah Ann Mimms + James Nicholson Groom
... 3 Henry Clay Mimms 1857 – Unk.

2 **William Henry James Sr. 1811 – 1895 + Mary Barber**
    *2nd Wife of **William Henry James Sr.:** + **Mary Ann Varble 1815 - 1860**

... 3 Julia James 1844 - 1847

... 3 Thomas W. James 1846 – Unk.

... 3 Gustavas James 1847 – Unk.

... 3 William /Jr./ James 1848 – Unk.

... 3 **Mary Ann James 1848 – Unk. + George Kirkpatrick**

...... 4 Mary Kirkpatrick

... 3 Laura James 1851 – Unk. + Charles E. Dixon

... 3 George R. James 1853 – Unk.

... 3 Sarah Alice James 1855 – Unk. + Unknown Eisenhower

      *2nd Husband of Sarah Alice James: + Luther R. Chapman

...... 4 Grace Chapman

...... 4 Ethel Chapman

...... 4 Alvin Chapman

... 3 Luther W. James 1857 – Unk.

2 John R. James 1815 – 1887 + Amanda E. Williams 1817 - 1871

... 3 Robert Woodson James 1838 – 1922 + Mary Elizabeth Deal 1845 - 1923

...... 4 Unknown James

...... 4 Edna Lorena James   1870 – 1951 + W. M. Smith Unk. - 1951

....   5   Juanita Smith 1902 – 1944 + J. Fred Baugh

....   6   Robert J. Baugh

....   6   Margaret E. Baugh

...... 4 Robert Franklin James 1872 – Unk. + Mae Klocke

...... 4 Howard Preston James 1875 – 1955 + Maud Gertrude Easley 1879 - 1953

....   5   Laura Elizabeth James 1901 – Unk. + James Aris Roby Sr. 1891 - 1944

....   6   Carolyn Roby 1927 – Unk. + Jimmie J. John 1930 – Unk.

....   6   James Aris Roby Jr. 1930 – Unk. + Barbara J. Smith 1930 –

....   5   Edwin Easley James 1902 – Unk. + Beulah Chapman

....   6   Howard Chapman James 1925 – Unk. + Helen Lee Shoenfeld

....   5   Eleanor Irene James 1903 – 1962 + Francis Eugene Godfrey Jr.1904 - 1972

...... 4 Alpha O. James 1876 – 1960 + James F. Patterson 1854 - 1946

...... 4 Beulah Irene James 1880 – 1966   + Walter Samuel Douglas Sr. 1871 - 1937

....   5   Alpha Henrietta Douglas 1902 – Unk. + Samuel Neeley 1898 - 1941

....   6   Dorothy Helen Neeley 1922 – Unk. + William H. McClelland

....   *2nd Husband of Dorothy Helen Neeley: + Elmer Zack

....   6   Sammie Jo Neeley 1924 – Unk. + Robert Boone Salsbury

....   6   Barbara Jane Neeley 1927 – Unk. + Raymond Earl Wharton

....   *2nd Husband of Barbara Jane Neeley: + Joseph H. Rudd

....   5   Robert Woodson Douglas 1904 – Unk.

....   5   Doris Nadine Douglas 1906 – Unk. John Aubrey Cutbirth 1905 - 1958

....   6   Purna L. Cutbirth 1927 – Unk. William B. Dixon Sr. 1921-2007

....   6   Patsy Ruth Cutbirth 1929 – Unk. +Donald Lewis MacDonald

....   5   Howard Eugene Douglas 1914 – Unk. + Dara Louise Ridley 1918 - 1976

....   5   Mary Elizabeth Douglas 1916 – 2009 + Roy Lee Rooker Sr. 1918 - 2008

....   6   Roy Lee Rooker Jr. + Joan Unknown

....   5   Walter Samuel Douglas Jr. 1918 - 1918

... 3 Susan Prudence James 1845 – 1919 + John Wesley Smith 1843 - 1916

...... 4 James Henry Smith 1868 – 1930 + Pearl Nichols 1882 - 1964

....   5   Carl Eugene Smith 1915 – Unk. Thelma Elizabeth Brooks 1915 – Unk.

....	6	Stuart B. Smith 1941 – Unk. + Frankie Williams 1941 – Unk.
....	6	Sharon K. Smith 1943 – Unk. + William L. Butler 1943 - Unk.
....	6	Sylvia Ann Smith 1948 – Unk. + Patrick E. Bryant 1948 – Unk.
....	6	Stacy R. Smith 1952 – Unk. + Saundra Brown 1952 – Unk.
....	5	Ralph Donald Smith 1918 – Unk. + Betty Marie Wright 1920 – Unk.
....	6	Stephen W. Smith 1945-Unk. + Marianne F. Rogers 1945-Unk.
....	6	Dianna Jeanne Smith 1950 - + Craig E. Brennecke 1945 – Unk.
......	4	John Richard "J. R." /I/ Smith 1869 – 1958 + Carrie E. Freeman 1873 - 1963
....	5	Howard Kenneth Smith 1902 – 1948 + Maryan D. Lambert 1903 -1977
....	6	Phillip Kenneth Smith1927 – 2010 + Marta Holman
....	6	John R. Smith II 1933 – Unk. + Marilyn M. Combs 1937 - 2009
....	6	Susann E. Smith 1938-Unk. + Edward D. McElvain 1938-Unk.
....	5	Helen Lucille Smith
......	4	Jesse Edward Smith 1872 – 1964 + Sally Livesay Arnold 1873 - 1961
....	5	Edwin Arnold Smith 1903 – Unk. + Melba Deets 1916 – Unk.
....	6	Jesse Deets Smith 1940 – Unk. + Mary J. Brown 1940 – Unk.
....	5	Agnes Prudence Smith 1909 – Unk. + Frank Eugene Cox 1902 – Unk.
......	4	Lula Amanda Smith 1874 – 1966 + Jacob Andrew Carey 1878 - 1955
....	5	Clifford Andrew Carey 1904 – 1949 + Mary D. O'Roarke 1907 - 1986
....	6	Patricia Anne Carey 1931 – 2001 + Unknown Jones
....		*2nd Husband of Paricia Anne Carey: + Unknown Robinson
....	6	Unknown Carey
....	6	Clifford John Carey 1934 - 1990
....	5	Lorene Eldine Carey 1911 – 1997 + Charles Homer Russell 1909 - 1998
....	6	Eugene Russell 1931 - 1947
....	6	Shirley Jane Russell 1933 – Unk.
....	6	Sandra Lou Russell 1938 – Unk. + Marvin Kassen
....		*2nd Husband of Sandra Lou Russell: + George L. Bickel
......	4	George Robert Smith 1877 – 1963 + Annie Laura Bumpass 1881 - 1934
......	4	Anna Myrtle Smith 1879 – 1973 + Charles Wesley Knipple 1872 - 1936
....	5	Ray Wesley Knipple 1921 – Unk. + Margaret Shaw Moss 1919 – Unk.
....	6	Kevin Wesley Knipple 1957 – Unk.
....	5	Betty Maxine Knipple 1924 – Unk. + William Spencer Turner 1918 – Unk.
....	6	Richard S. Turner 1947-Unk. + Jeanne M. Lindstadt 1947- Unk.
....	6	David R. Turner 1948 – Unk. + Beverly D. Crewse 1949 – Unk.
....	6	William Alan Turner 1953 – Unk. + Linda Joyce Marino 1955 – Unk.
....	6	Gregg Michael Turner1958 – Unk.
...	3	John Franklin James 1849 – Unk. + Sarah Elizabeth Bradley 1836 - 1926
...	3	Thomas Martin James II 1852 – Unk + Emily Bradley 1852 – Unk.

*2nd Wife of John R. James: + Emily Bradley Unk. - 1884

2 Elizabeth James 1816 – 1904 + Tilman Howard West 1810 - 1884
... 3 Luther Virgil West 1834 – Unk.
... 3 Mary Mourning West 1834 – Unk.
... 3 Nancy Woodson West 1838 - 1865
... 3 Amelia Putnam West 1840 - 1862
... 3 Oscar Dunreath West 1840 – Unk.
... 3 Richard James West 1843 – 1886 + Ann Penelope Bryan 1847 - 1941
...... 4 Maud West

...... 4 Edward West 1870 – Unk.

...... 4 Ethel West   1872 – Unk.

...... 4 Myrtle West 1875 – Unk.

...... 4 Edna Pearl West 1876 – Unk. + Otto Charles Preuss 1875 – Unk.

.... 5   Hermine Preuss 1903 - 1910

.... 5   Roma Doris Preuss 1913 – Unk.

...... 4 Oscar Dunreath West Sr. 1878 – Unk. + Della Merritt

.... 5   Edna Pearl West 1910 – Unk.

......   *2nd Wife of Oscar Dunreath /Sr./ West: + Helen Field

.... 5   Oscar Dunreath West Jr. 1905 – Unk.

... 3 Henry Clay West 1847 – Unk.

... 3 William Newton West 1847 – 1900 + Laura Emma Bryan 1854 – Unk.

...... 4 Tilman West

...... 4 Serena Lucille West 1884 – Unk. + Richard Schofield

.... 5   Unknown Schofield

.... 5   Unknown Schofield

.... 5   Unknown Schofield

.... 5   Unknown Schofield

...... 4 William Holmes West   1885 – 1974 + Unknown

...... 4 Mary Elizabeth West   1887 – Unk.

2 Robert Sallee James 1818 – 1850 + Zerelda Elizabeth Cole 1825 - 1911

... 3 Alexander Franklin "Frank" James 1843 – 1915 + Anna Ralston 1853 - 1944

...... 4 **Robert Franklin James 1877 – 1959** + Mae A. Sanboth 1881 - 1974

...... 4 Unknown James 1885 - 1885

... 3 Robert B. James 1845 - 1845

... 3 Jesse Woodson "Jesse" James 1847 – 1882 + [2] Zerelda Amanda Mimms 1845 - 1900

... 3 Susan Lavenia James 1849 – 1889 + Allen H. Parmer Sr. 1848 - 1927

...... 4 Unknown Parmer

...... 4 Unknown Parmer

...... 4 Robert Archie Parmer   1872 - 1883

...... 4 Flora Parmer 1877 – 1926 + William Blunt Benson 1876 - 1958

.... 5   Feta Louise Benson

.... 5   Sue Laura Benson 1907 – Unk. + Ray O. Hale 1898 - 1982

.... 5   Allen James Benson 1909 - 1967 + Electra Mae Nichols 1916 – Unk.

.... 6   Robert William Benson 1945 - 1968

.... 6   James Allen Benson 1949 – Unk.

.... 6   Stephen C. Benson 1953 – Unk. + Paula Jo Darling 1954 – Unk.

.... 6   Sue Ella Benson 1955 – Unk. + Paul W. Tanner 1955 - 1987

....   *2nd Husband of Sue Ella Benson: + William Wayne Emanuel

...... 4 Zelma Parmer 1879 – 1972 + George Reynolds Edwards 1877 – Unk.

.... 5   Parmer Wiley Edwards 1905 – 1993 + Ann M. Carreras

....   *2nd Wife of Parmer Wiley Edwards: + Nancy W. Sheldon 1909 – Unk.

.... 6   Nancy Jean W. Edwards 1930 – Unk. + Claxton Walker

....   *2nd Husband of Nancy Jean W. Edwards: + Deane Maury

.... 6   Bruce Parmer Edwards 1931 – Unk. + Maureen Hyland

...... 4 Allen H. Parmer Jr. 1885 - 1887

...... 4 Susan Kate Parmer 1886 - 1903

...... 4 Feta Ann Parmer 1888 – 1978 + David Bert A. Rose Sr. 1883 - 1960

.... 5   Allen Parmer Rose 1913 - 1977
.... 5   Dorothy Ann" Rose 1914 – 1987 +William Allen Jackson 1909 - 1975
.... 6   Sarah Anne Jackson 1933 – + Roy Nikkel
.... 6   Robert Allen Jackson 1934 - + Janice M. Melburn 1935 –
....   *2nd Husband of Dorothy Ann Rose: + Robert Milton Higbie 1911 - 1980
.... 5   Martha Louise Rose   1923 - 1927
...... 4 Infant Parmer 1889 - 1889

2 Nancy Gardner James 1821 – 1875 + George Burns Hite 1825 - 1891
... 3 Mary Elizabeth Hite 1842 – 1880 + Rufus S. Tully 1840 - 1900
...... 4 Phillip Tully + Eva Y. Unknown
...... 4 John Robert Tully + Ruth Simmons
.... 5   Unknown Tully
.... 5   Unknown Tully
.... 5   Unknown Tully
.... 5   Unknown Tully
.... 5   Unknown Tully
...... 4 Irene B. Tully 1870 – Unk.
... 3 Olive Hite 1846 - 1860
... 3 Amanda Cornelia Hite 1846 - 1860
... 3 John William Hite 1846 – Unk. + Mildred B. Moore
... 3 Irene Hite 1848 – Unk.
... 3 Lucy Hite 1849 – Unk.
... 3 Robert Woodson "Wood" Hite 1850 - 1881
... 3 Clarence Jeff "Tuck" Hite 1852 – 1883 + Cornelia Unknown 1854 - 1886
... 3 George Thomas Hite 1852 – 1936 + Mary Deborah Rogers 1865 - 1902
...... 4 Unknown Hite
...... 4 Unknown Hite
...... 4 George Rogers Hite 1897 – Unk.
...... 4 Quincy Hite 1898 – Unk.
      *2nd Wife of George Thomas Hite: + Nanni Jane Unknown
... 3 Nancy Cornelia Hite 1853 – Unk.
... 3 Henry Clay Hite 1855 – Unk.
... 3 Luther V. Hite 1856 – Unk.
... 3 Cornelia Hite 1857 – Unk.
... 3 Juella F. Hite 1858 – Unk.
... 3 Lucy A. Hite 1859 – Unk.
... 3 Jefferson Davis Hite 1860 – Unk.

2 **Thomas Martin "T. M." James 1823 – 1901 + Susan Ann S. Woodward 1827 - 1916**
... 3 **John W. Crawford "J. C." James 1848 – 1933 + Fannie Shouse 1853 - 1933**
...... 4 **Vassie James 1875 – 1953 + Hugh Campbell Ward Sr. 1863 - 1909**
.... 5   **Hugh Campbell Ward Jr. 1899 – 1976** + Holly Ann Reddick
.... 6   Virginia Bulkley Ward
.... 6   Hugh Campbell Ward III
.... 6   Mary Louise Ward
.... 6   Ellen James Ward
.... 6   Teter Ward
.... 6   Natalie Wayne Ward + Joel Shorey Harris

....		6	Seth Crawford Ward + Anne Pendleton. Bowers
....	5		**James Crawford Ward Sr. 1901 – 1972** + Grace Moulton
....		6	Ann Ward 1930 – Unk. + Hugh J. Morgan Jr. 1930 – Unk.
....		6	James Crawford Ward Jr. 1933 – 2000 + Unknown
....			*2nd Wife of James Crawford Ward Jr.: + Unknown
....			*3rd Wife of James Crawford Ward Jr.: + Caroline Hilton
....		6	Grace Moulton Ward 1935 – + Richard R. Hall Sr. 1927-2001
....		6	William Moulton Ward 1936 – Unk.
....		6	Stephen Watkins Ward 1943 – Unk.
....		6	Irene Watkins Ward 1946 – Unk.
....	5		**Frances Ward 1903 – 2001** + **George T. Olmsted Jr. 1903 - 1976**
....		6	Virgina Olmsted 1927 - 1970
....		6	Joan Olmsted 1930 – Unk. + James F. Oates III Unk. – 2005
....		6	George T. Olmsted III 1933 – Unk. + Unknown
....	5		**John Harris Ward 1908 – Unk.** + **Mary Van Etten Unk. - 2002**
....		6	David Harris Ward 1937 – Unk. + Mrs. Henry F. Field
....		6	Tony Ward
....		6	John Ward Unk. - 2002
......			*2nd Husband of **Vassie James:** + **Albert Ross Hill 1869 - 1943**
....	5		Unknown Hill 1920 – Unk.
......	4		Thomas Martin James III 1876 – 1955 + Gertrude Jones 1879 - 1955
....	5		**Barbara James 1905 – 1996** + **Milton M. McGreevy 1903 - 1981**
....		6	**Joan "Jean" McGreevy 1930 – Unk.** + Moulton Green Jr.
....	6		**Thomas James McGreevy 1932 – 1991** + **Susan Colby**
....			*2nd Wife of **Thos James McGreevy: Mary "Molly" Paine**
....		6	Barbara Ann McGreevy 1937 – Unk. + Joseph C. McNay
....			*2nd Husband of Barbara Ann McGreevy: + Unknown Heller
....		6	**Gail McGreevy 1941 – Unk.** + John Watson Harmon
......	4		**Daniel Lewis James Sr. 1880 – 1944** + **Lillian Snider 1883 – Unk.**
....	5		**Daniel Lewis James Jr. 1911 – 1988** + Rosalie Guinott
....			*2nd Wife of **Daniel Lewis James Jr.:** + **Lilith Stanward Unk.- 1999**.
....		6	**Barbara E. James 1937-** + Joseph P. Laurence 1934-Unk.
....			*2nd Husband of Barbara Ellen James: + Daniel E. Willard
....		6	Catherine Vassie James 1945 – Unk. + James McWilliams
....			*2nd Husband of Catherine Vassie James: + Jimmie Yell
......	4		Fannie James 1882 – 1970 + Louis Henry Egan 1881 - 1950
....	5		Elizabeth Egan 1914 – 1980 + Gene B. Starkloff 1915 - 1994
....		6	Rebecca Starkloff 1941 - + Sam Busselle
....		6	Kathleen Von Starkloff
....	5		Alice Egan 1915 – 1992 + Richard John Dolan 1918 - 1993
....		6	Diana Dolan
....		6	Patrick Egan Dolan 1951 - 1969
....	5		Patricia Egan 1918 - 2005
......	4		Helen James 1887 – 1969 + Ike Bourne Dunlap
....	5		Aileen March Dunlap + Harold Kenneth Taylor 1902 - 1962
...	3		**Luther Tillman James 1850 – 1916** + **Mary A. Heberd 1856 - 1914**
......	4		**William Heberd James Sr. 1880 – 1964** + **Aileen Stevens 1886 - 1936**
....	5		**Virginia Aileen James 1904 -** + **Horton Jacques**
....		6	**Virginia Jacques 1931 -** + **Arthur Burdette Church Jr.**

....   *2nd Husband of Virginia Aileen James: + John J. Snyder 1893 – Unk.

.... 5   Eleanor James 1911 – Unk. + Charles Melton McCrea 1905 - 1965

.... 6   Aileen McCrea 1931 – Unk. + Frank Stewart 1923 – Unk.

....   *2nd Husband of Eleanor James: + John Sumners Jr.

.... 5   **William Heberd James Jr. 1916 – + Burleigh Wolferman 1917 - 2004**

.... 6   Judith Gregg James 1944 – Unk.

.... 6   Joanne James 1948 - 1953

.... 6   Thomas Mason James 1950 - + Unknown 1964 -

....   *2nd Wife of Thomas Mason James: + Martha Cronk 1950 -

.... 6   Christopher Matthew James 1956 - + Unknown

...... 4 Crawford Martin James 1885 – 1959 + Kathleen Miller

...... 4 Woodward Shelton James 1889 - 1925

...... 4 Marjorie James 1895 - 1983

... 3 Lykins James 1859 - 1859

... 3 Marion James 1861 – 1862

2 **Drury Woodson James 1824 – 1910 + Mary Louisa Dunn 1844 - 1930**

... 3 Helen James 1866 – 1930 + Edward F. Bennett

...... 4 Herbert Bennett

... 3 **Mary Louisa "Nanna" James 1868 – 1950 + Edward Frederick Burns 1863 - 1918**

...... 4 **Marguerite Hazel Burns 1890 – 1983 + James Francis Malley 1889 - 1974**

.... 5   **James Burns Malley 1921 -**

.... 5   **John Crohan Malley 1925 - + Irene Mailhot 1926 -**

.... 6   Robert Crohan Malley 1958 - + Rebecca Appleton 1952 -

.... 6   Ann Malley 1952 - + Unk.

.... 5   **Mary Joan Malley 1924 – 1990 + John Francis Beamis 1911 -1977**

.... 6   Mary Ellen Beamis 1953 - + Gerald McAtavey

.... 6   **J. Mark Beamis 1955** - + Gabrielle Sullivan 1957 -

....   *2nd Husband of Mary Joan "Joan Beamis" Malley: + Unknown Donovan

.... 5   M. Ivan Malley 1925 – Unk.

.... 5   **Janice Ann Malley 1928 -** + Edward Francis Hawkins Unk.- 1970

.... 6   Gerald L. Hawkins 1954 -

.... 6   Janice A. Hawkins 1955 -

.... 6   Christopher P. Hawkins 1957 - + Suzanne Legere

.... 6   Edward F. Hawkins 1959 - + Diane Monterose 1959 -

....   *2nd Husband of Janice Ann Malley: Robert Donovan

...... 4 **Walter Irvin Burns 1894 – 1978** + Lillian Fairbanks Unl. - 1975

... 3 William Alfred James 1869 - 1930

... 3 Ellen James 1871 - 1941

... 3 Carolina F. James 1872 – 1966 + Otto Shackleford 1869 – Unk.

    *2nd Husband of Carolina F. James: + Thomas Maxwell Unk. - 1943

... 3 Charles James 1872 - 1930

... 3 Edward James 1874 – 1930 + Myrtle Fuller

2 Mary Elizabeth James 1826 – 1845 + John Richard Cohorn Sr. 1804 - 1850

... 3 Mary Jane Cohorn 1845 – 1931 + Henry James Newton 1837 - 1917

...... 4 Willis Newton

...... 4 Elizabeth Newton 1868 – Unk. + Thomas Horsley Sr.

.... 5   Charlie Horsley

.... 5   Richard Horsley

.... 5   Thomas Horsley Jr.

.... 5   Elizabeth Horsley

...... 4 William Denton Newton 1869 – 1946 + Mattie Tomlinson

.... 5   Henry Thomas Newton

.... 5   Roger Newton

...... 4 Laura Bell Newton 1873 – Unk.

...... 4 Emma Jane Newton 1873 – 1960 + Joseph Lewis Sames 1862 - 1922

.... 5   Charles Sames 1889 - 1896

.... 5   Lula Bell Sames 1890 – 1992 + Al Wise

....   *2nd Husband of Lula Bell Sames: + Ward Perkins

.... 5   James Walter Sames Sr. 1893 – 1985 + Hallie May Wise 1902 - 1970

.... 6   James Walter Sames III 1921 - 2005

.... 6   William Lewis Sames 1923 – 2000 + Margaret Sharp

....   *2nd Wife of William Lewis Sames: + Alice Harping

.... 6   Paul Clay Sames 1925 – 1973 + Doris Creek 1927 - 1994

.... 6   Raymond Lee Sames Sr. 1927 – 1998 + Lavern Wright

....   *2nd Wife of Raymond Lee Sames Sr.: + Frances Drury

...   . 6   Dorothy Elizabeth Sames 1929 - + William N. Mulligan Sr.

.... 6   Charles Edward Sames 1931 – 1984 + Joan Coreman

....   *2nd Wife of Charles Edward Sames: + Nancy Stiles 1941 -

.... 6   Joseph Donald Sames 1936 - + Shirley Baldwin 1937 -

.... 6   Betty Ann Sames 1945 - + Robert Glenn Allison Sr.

.... 5   Annie Sames 1895 - 1896

.... 5   Mary Sames 1900 – Unk. +Clarence Moore

.... 6   Elizabeth Moore

.... 6   Richard Moore

...... 4 James E. Newton 1876 – Unk.

...... 4 Alice Newton 1876 – Unk.

...... 4 Quincy Newton 1877 – Unk.

...... 4 Anna Belle Newton 1881 – 1960   +Joe Tindall 1874 - 1928

.... 5   Stella Tindall 1898 - 1973

.... 5   Beatrice Tindall 1900 - 1978

.... 5   Mattie Tindall 1903 – Unk. + Walter Albrough 1899 - 1977

.... 6   Ralph Albrough 1923 -

.... 6   Joan Albrough 1934 -

.... 5   Herman Tindall 1904 - 1975

.... 5   Beulah Tindall 1906 – Unk.

.... 5   Idra Tindall 1908 – 1978

Acknowledgements

When J. D. Kysela S.J., a Jesuit brother, plucked me out of my junior year at St. Ignatius College Prep in Chicago, and installed me in the faculty library for an experiment in teaching and learning American history, Mr. Kysela never learned afterward the effect his experiment had on this student. The techniques I learned for historical research, critical analysis, composition, reporting, and use, I've employed successfully since in many fields outside of history. Most teachers never hear the appreciation which seasons in their students across time. Gratefulness matures too late in years. Writing this history for others now becomes my spiritual expression of gratitude to Mr. Kysela, since the physical act can no longer be expressed. There are others also to whom I am equally indebted.

Back in 1999, Jesse James' great grandson, Judge James R. Ross, sentenced me to ten years of hard labor. He said, "Why don't you write a book about the James family? Everyone writes about Frank & Jesse James. No one ever writes about our family."

The problem was - except for a tightly knit circle - few in the Jesse James family knew who their family was. Worse yet, except for the publicized record of Frank & Jesse, the James family knew very little of its own history.

When Jim and I met, I already had spent two years intensely researching my own heritage. Like most, I came to my study only after suffering intense loss and pain. My mother died within nine months of my father. They had separated legally when I was very young. Living apart and rarely seeing each other except at the occasional family wedding or funeral, my parents never divorced. Catholic tenets deny divorce. When my mother died so abruptly and soon after my father, the joke was she died only to make sure that James boy didn't get past St. Peter's pearly gates. Only at that point did I grasp that some unknown heritage had been lost to me. Putting Mr. Kysela's teaching to use, I went in search of my unknown family history with a passion. The act has since redirected my life. With the help of the following named and countless unnamed, the family that was never provided to me before has been recaptured. For this, I am eternally grateful.

I once heard that my Uncle Dick had done some research about our James family. I knew Uncle Dick to be a quiet man, a very private man. I also knew that he and my father never spoke to each other all their lives, since they fought with each other in their mid-teens over the use of a bicycle. Uncle Dick wrote down the family history he found. I was told this by his sister, my Aunt Deanie. When I asked Uncle Dick, he sent me about a half dozen pages with so much white space; its total content could have been put on a single page or two. But Uncle Dick's report left me plenty of clues, begging to be investigated. I got to work on it.

In the fledgling days of the internet, I encountered two female genealogists. They rapped my keyboard knuckles with the rigor of my grammar school nuns. Family history is not invented, they sternly instructed me. My family history must flow from facts of evidence to evident fact. Their names are as forgotten now, as are most of those nuns. But their instruction and lesson still abides in my gratitude.

Accumulating evidence and documents as instructed also led to fishing for leads. A posting of mine to an internet genealogy bulletin board was answered by Madelyn Teal, a teacher in Texas, also a cousin whom I never knew or met. "You need to talk to Thelma Herrin in Kentucky," she said. "She has all your family history. But do it fast. Thelma's about to turn eighty." I'm grateful for Madelyn's instruction. I followed this teacher's direction, too.

For months afterwards Thelma stuffed my mailbox with packages of information about my family. The stunning material reached back into the Colonial period. I learned Thelma herself was a retired school teacher, too, but she hadn't lost her ability to light a fire where there's evident interest. I couldn't wait to meet her.

When we met, Thelma introduced me to another cousin, who was another teacher. Virgie Herrin-Fuller asked me, "Come to meet your hillbilly cousins?" Cousin Virgie struck me immediately with the humor and self-deprecation that was so rambunctious and recognizable among my aunts and uncles. I found myself unexpectedly comfortable and at home in Kentucky...of all places.

Over the next year and a half I returned to Kentucky as often as I could, photographing all the family sites, meeting countless cousins, and adding more previously unknown family to my genealogy database. Among the new cousins I met was Clel Whitaker, a deacon at the Flat Lick Baptist Church, then about to celebrate its 200th anniversary. Clel and Thelma introduced me to Murrell Stewart who headed a committee which was about to publish a book about the church's history. Murrell promptly asked me, "What's the connection of our church's founder John James from your family to Frank and Jesse James?" He needed to know for the book. The lore had always been part of the church's history, but the connection remained undefined. Gradually, I learned that most everyone in Kentucky knows the families of others going back two hundred years. I disappointed Murrell Stewart with the embarrassment of my ignorance. I, too, wanted to know the answer to Murrell's question.

On January 27, 1999, I was privileged to stand at the same 1799 lectern where formerly stood my fourth great grandfather, John M. James and his son, my third great grandfather, the "talented, but erratic" Joseph Martin James, and other preachers and relatives of my ancestry. I was very moved to address the 1999 congregation of Flat Lick Church. From that moment forward, that privilege has graced me with the sense that my historical sojourn was more meaningful spiritually to more than just myself alone.

At the Kentucky Historical Society, my history mentor became Ron Bryant, the former research librarian for Kentucky's Thomas D. Clarke Center for Kentucky History. Ron provided a dedication to my effort that overflowed my research coffers. After repeated visits to Kentucky, Ron said, "If you just lived here, the flood gates would open for you." On Ron's advice, I moved to Kentucky.

Then indeed, the floodgates of Kentucky did open, but not quite as I expected. Not only did I become awash in information that solved countless historical mysteries, regretfully both Ron and I were rinsed from the Kentucky Historical Society. Sadly, a corrupt Kentucky governor replaced Ron's long tenure of helpful expertise with an election promise of cost efficient government rather than transparent, informative, and effective government. Ron was dismissed and this member of the Kentucky Historical Society found myself an enemy of the State. The Governor's political appointee misdirected the Kentucky Historical Society's Board of Directors to sue me in Franklin County Court (Civil Action No. 06-CI-00365) on the pretext I was creating a "shadow government" by seeking transparent elections of the Society's Board of Directors. Who knew this largely unknown James person, new to Kentucky, possessed so much perceived power as to threaten its very Commonwealth? I already had enough experience with the predecessor of the political appointee to learn that the James were not especially welcome in Kentucky. Previously, I had offered to deposit the Zee James Collection archive with the Kentucky Historical Society. The artifacts had been shipped to Kentucky and sequestered by Jesse's widow and mother at her uncle's farm in Stamping Ground, following the assassination. The artifacts had been in Kentucky for over 120 years. I was told, however, by that previous executive director, "Ship it to Missouri." Ron Bryant's wry humor was a consolation. "It doesn't matter," Ron said to me, "no matter how far back your family's roots may go in Kentucky, if you've just come from California, you're a Yankee!"

I've learned to become grateful to the Society's discriminatory executive director for the punishing lessons politicians provide. Ever since these and other similar regrettable experiences in Missouri, I sincerely question if government sponsored agencies are the appropriate repositories for history and its artifacts at all. To place history at the disposition of fickle politicians, with such feckless senses for history, risks historical preservation and the welfare of history itself. Witness how many records have disappeared from court houses over the years, or the numerous court houses that were burned by fires of suspicious origin to eradicate public records. Politicians are a hazard to history. Just watching them create it should be fair enough warning.

A far different experience awaited me at the Filson Historical Society in Louisville, Kentucky. My research there found all its needed support and helpfulness, performed with the highest degree of professional courtesy, knowledge, efficiency, and understanding. I found the same devotion in numerous other institutions where I conducted my study: The Pulaski County Historical Society in Kentucky; The California Historical Society, the Missouri Historical Society, the Chicago History Museum Research Center, and the Special Collections Research Center of the University of Chicago. I also would add individuals who were particularly helpful: Phil Stewart, former research historian at James Farm & Museum in Kearney, Missouri, who also was fired by a political appointee for answering the history questions of museum patrons; Russ Hatter of the Capital City Museum of Frankfort, Kentucky; Deborah Barker, Director of the Franklin County Historical Society in Ottawa, Kansas; the Midland Library of Midland, Texas, which thanks to a private philanthropist has one of the most competent genealogy libraries servicing a miniscule population in the middle of a desolate West Texas prairie; Paula Sartain of the Paso Robles Public Library, Paso Robles, California; Bernie Becker of the Historical Society of Frederick County, Maryland; Elaine M. Doak, Special Collections Librarian & Archivist of the Pickler Memorial Library; and David Stansbury, formerly President of the Dickson County Historical Society in Tennessee, who lovingly restored at his personal expense one of our James family's historic homes.

College libraries and institutions also proved very helpful and productive for me, in particular Dr. Glen Taul, formerly of Georgetown College in Georgetown, Kentucky; and Angela Stiffler, formerly of the Partee Center for Baptist Studies at William Jewell College in Missouri. Others include Sylvia Kennick Brown of Special Collections at Williams College; Gayle D. Lynch, Senior Library Specialist for Archives at Brown University; Truman State University in Kirksville, Missouri; Ashley Locke, Assistant University Archivist of the Special Collections Research Center at the Estelle & Melvin Gelman Library of the George Washington University Libraries of Mount Vernon College; and Librarian Emeritus Stanley D. Stevens, archivist for the Hihn-Younger Archive, University of California at Santa Cruz. Ian Kennedy of the Nelson-Atkins Museum of Art in Kansas City and Ken Burns of Florentine Films added valuable contributions of their own, as did Neil Chetnick of the Carnegie Center for Literacy & Learning in Lexington, Kentucky with his editorial recommendations.

Special thanks is owed to Nancy B. Samuelson, author of *The Dalton Gang Story*, and John J. Koblas, author of several Jesse James books, including *Faithful unto Death, the James-Younger Gang Raid on the First National Bank*, for their manuscript review and recommendations.

My research did not escape the oversight of Jim Ross. The judge that he was always inquired, "What evidence do you have?" With all the help I had received, there always was ample evidence to show him. But when it came to writing the story of the James family as a narrative history, it was the James family itself who came forward unexpectedly and surprisingly to break five generations of self-imposed silence and self-inflicted anonymity to finally reveal themselves and their James family's history.

Our family web site *Stray Leaves* lists more than 175 other contributors who helped to construct the foundational genealogy from where this historical narrative begins. Their efforts with me consumed more than a decade. Its publication has withstood a dozen years of transparent peer review. Please recognize them, too: www.ericjames.org/contributors.html

As my journey of discovery crisscrossed the country to scour court houses and libraries, I visited the graves of many deceased, and was entertained countless times by those still living. In Texas, Ruby Tidwell-Johnson, the wife of Cousin Dennis Johnson, was most generous in providing me with her years of accumulated research on their individual family line of John James of Alvarado. At the same time I met the late Billie Shirley "Cricket" Mills, and was welcomed into her home as graciously as I was among so many other cousins whom I was just getting to know, and who all were becoming thrilled by the prospect of our family pulling together again.

In particular I am grateful to those whose interviews provided valuable substance for this history: Vern Reuben James, Raymond James, James R. Malley S.J., John Malley, James Walter Sames III, Virginia Jacques-Church, Barbara James daughter of Daniel Lewis James Jr., Dr. T. Robert Hopkins, and, of course, to Judge James R. Ross.

So many of those I met now are gone. Just as this book was about to be published the sister of Joan Beamis, Janice Malley, died, too. Many, like Thelma Herrin, Virgie Fuller, and Vern Reuben James, were in in their eighties when I first met them. Most all, especially my late Uncle Dick and the late Jim Ross, told me they were looking forward to this book and its publication. They acquired their eternal knowledge of this book before its publication. The constant regret of anyone who studies family history is that we come to the pursuit of family history and the telling of it too late in life. How often you hear the refrain, "I wish I had asked the questions," or "I wished we had talked about it while they were alive." It must be recognized that such loss is self-inflicted unnecessarily, if only some time is spent doing so. Today I try whenever possible to enlist and educate our youngest family's members about their wonderful history.

I am especially indebted to J. Mark Beamis. Without solicitation, Mark contributed the research archive of his mother Joan Beamis, which became the foundation for this initial volume. Other contributions, like Mark's, will appear in successive volumes.

Lastly, recognition must be given to a group of patrons and supporters who made this physical publication possible. The patrons are: Charles Broomfield and Steven Leonard of the James Preservation Trust, Nancy B. Samuelson, James Houston, Phillip Cole, J. Mark Beamis, John Malley, Jennifer Sepaniak, Mary Huey Alvarez, and William & Leslie Penn.

I am proud to have had their association and support. With their assistance, the story of our James family history now is told. The journey has been a spiritual one for me. The spirit now moves forward for countless others to enjoy the benefits of discovery.

Rev. Robert Sallee James 1818 - 1850, *Father of Frank & Jesse James* (L)
Author Eric F. James 1943 - (R)
Both pictured about age 28

The Author

Eric F. James is a co-founder of The James Preservation Trust, with the late great grandson of Jesse James, Judge James R. Ross. Eric also is archivist of the Joan Beamis Research Archive which produced the first published genealogy of the Jesse James family, *Background of a Bandit*. In recent years, Eric exhumed Jesse's twin children in Waverly, Tennessee, re-interring with their parents in Kearney, Missouri.

Since 1997, Eric has written and published the official web site for the Jesse James family. *Stray Leaves, a James Family in America since 1650* at www. ericjames.org contains photos, stories, editorial content, a blog, videos, plus an extensive interactive genealogy database. Eric is a regular contributor to the *James-Younger Gang Journal*. He also maintains a social presence on *Facebook* and *YouTube*.

Formerly, Eric's weekly newspaper column appeared in the publications of *California's Daily "Law" Journal*. He also was a contributing editor for *California Real Estate* magazine.

In his earliest career in the entertainment industry, Eric was a successful actor, appearing in the national daytime TV series *Bright Promise*, numerous television series such as *Columbo, Ironsides*, and *Name of the Game*, three Broadway productions including *Boys in the Band* in which he played the lead role of Michael, and in fifty theatrical productions in local and regional theatre across the nation. As an equally successful business executive, Eric pioneered the field of international real estate brokerage, as president of R.E.A.L. International and several Asian-American companies. For a decade, Eric devoted himself to public service as a city commissioner for Dana Point, California.

Illustrations

Abbreviations:

JPT-James Preservation Trust, JBA- Joan Beamis Archive, PD-Public Domain

Chapter 2 - Talented, but Erratoc

- Flat Lick Baptist Church – JPT, courtesy of Flat Lick Baptist Church
- Gen. Joseph Martin - PD
- Rev. Jeremiah Vardeman – PD, courtesy Partee Center for Baptist Studies, William Jewell College
- Georgetown College, Giddings Hall - PD
- Rhoda May – JPT, courtesy of Gwen Smith-Gershwin, 5th great granddaughter of the subject
- Earnest Smythe & Raymond Edward James - JPT
- Samuel Chaudoin & Sarah "Sallie" James - JPT
- Rev. Joseph Martin Shadowen – JPT, courtesy of Bro. Wendell Butte
- Rev. Martin Nall James Family – JPT, courtesy of Jimmy Dean Fitzpatrick Jr. second great grandson of the subject
- Mary Harriet & Susan Harriet James - JPT
- Edward Perry James Family - JPT
- Judge John Thomas James - JPT
- Rev. Joseph Martin James Home - JPT

Chapter 3 - Goodland

- Joseph McAlister James, aka Joseph McJames - JPT
- Danville, Main & Third Street - PD
- James Hall, Danville – Sanborn Maps
- St. James Hotel, Danville – JPT, courtesy of Boyle County Library
- Weisiger Park, Danville - JPT
- Oakland Church Cemetery, Harrodsburg - JPT
- Springhill Cemetery, Harrodsburg - JPT
- Francis Marion James Sr. - JPT
- Goodland, 1910 - PD
- Maple Grove, Coffeyville – JPT Richard Donald James Archive
- Condon Bank, Coffeyville - PD
- Dead Daltons, Coffeyville - PD

Chapter 4 - An Independent Free Man

- John James, of Alvarado – JPT Dennis & Ruby Tidwell Johnson Archive
- William Henry James – JPT J.W. McDaniel Archive
- Andrew Jackson James – JPT J.W. McDaniel Archive
- Harvey James – JPT J.W. McDaniel Archive

ILLUSTRATION | 341

- ⹌ Sarah Ellen James-Grubbs – JPT David & Linda Farabee Archive
- ⹌ Choctaw Village, Indian Territory, Oklahoma - PD
- ⹌ John James in new clothes – PD, *"My Experience with Indians"*
- ⹌ Choctaw Academy of Richard Mentor Johnson - JPT
- ⹌ Nicholas Henry "Nick" Dawson - PD
- ⹌ Myra Maebelle Shirley - PD
- ⹌ Emma Wren Shirley & Family – JPT, Billie "Crickett" Mills Archive
- ⹌ Enoch Elbert "Elo" James – JPT, Billie "Crickett" Mills Archive
- ⹌ Will Aylette Shirley Home - JPT, Billie "Crickett" Mills Archive
- ⹌ Stella, Florence, Ella Shirley - JPT, Billie "Crickett" Mills Archive
- ⹌ Stockbridge Academy – Chuck Hudson, www.mychoctawfamily.com
- ⹌ Elliston E.Dyer - PD, *"My Experience with Indians"*
- ⹌ Flodelle Dyer - PD, *"My Experience with Indians"*
- ⹌ Willard Dyer - PD, *"My Experience with Indians"*
- ⹌ Winona Dyer - PD, *"My Experience with Indians"*
- ⹌ Lillian Dyer - PD, *"My Experience with Indians"*
- ⹌ Elliston Dyer James - JPT, Billie "Crickett" Mills Archive
- ⹌ Mountainview - JPT, Billie "Crickett" Mills Archive
- ⹌ Frank James & Rev. Joe Mack James – PD & image from the grave of Rev. Joe Mack James.
- ⹌ William Wythe James - PD
- ⹌ Jackson Waite James Family - JPT Dennis & Ruby Tidwell Johnson Archive
- ⹌ Frank James & Jackson Waite James – FJ image, James Farm & Museum; JWJ, JPT, Billie "Crickett" Mills Archive
- ⹌ Mary Ellen James-Saunders - JPT

Chapter 5 - *The Highest Mental Culture*

- ⹌ Thomas Martin "T. M." James – JPT, Virginia Jacques-Church Archive
- ⹌ Col. John "Jack" Harris - PD
- ⹌ Seth Edmund Ward - PD
- ⹌ Rev. William Hickman - PD
- ⹌ Samuel Hughes Woodson Esq. - PD
- ⹌ Thomas Hoyle Mastin - PD
- ⹌ Rev. Isaac McCoy - PD
- ⹌ Rev. Johnston Lykins - PD
- ⹌ John Calvin McCoy - PD
- ⹌ Louis Wayland Shouse - PD
- ⹌ Joyce Clyde "J. C." Hall - PD

- ❧ Rev. Robert Stewart "R. S." Thomas PD
- ❧ Rev. Joseph Cowgill Maple - PD
- ❧ Calvary Baptist Church, Kansas City - PD
- ❧ John Bristow Wornall - PD
- ❧ Oliver Perry Moss - PD

Chapter 6 - Only a Large Soul Can Do This

- ❧ James Elementary School, Kansas City - PD
- ❧ T.M. James & Co. & Commerce Bank – Missouri Valley Special Collections, Kansas City Library
- ❧ Phoebe Routt Ess – Elmwood Cemetery Society, Kansas City, Missouri
- ❧ J. Van Clief "J.V.C." Karnes - PD
- ❧ Joseph S. Chick - PD
- ❧ Robert N. "R. N. Snyder - PD
- ❧ Jefferson Davis - PD
- ❧ 909-911 Walnut, Kansas City - PD
- ❧ R. A. Long Building, Kansas City - PD
- ❧ Luther Tillman James – JPT, Virginia Jacques-Church Archive
- ❧ Rev. William Henry James – Zee James Collection
- ❧ Charles J. Schmelzer - PD
- ❧ William Heberd James Jr. – JPT, Virginia Jacques-Church Archive
- ❧ Aileen Stevens-James – JPT, Virginia Jacques-Church Archive
- ❧ Eleanor "Ellie" James-McCrae – JPT, Virginia Jacques-Church Archive
- ❧ Virginia Aileen-Jacques – JPT, Virginia Jacques-Church Archive
- ❧ Graduation Virginia Aileen James & Eleanor Pendleton Chinn - Special Collections Research Center at the Estelle & Melvin Gelman Library of the George Washington University Libraries of Mount Vernon College.
- ❧ Arthur Burdette & Virginia James-Church with Horton & Virginia Aileen James-Jacques – JPT, Virginia Jacques-Church Archive
- ❧ Jacqueline Aileen Church-Symonds – courtesy of the subject
- ❧ T. M. James & Sons Building, 1896 - JPT, Virginia Jacques-Church Archive

Chapter 7 - Breaking Barriers

- ❧ Vassie James - PD
- ❧ Hugh Campbell Ward - PD
- ❧ William Miles Chick - PD
- ❧ Frank James - JPT, Sara Jane Race Duke Archive
- ❧ Gov. Lawrence "Lon" Vest Stevens - PD

ILLUSTRATION | **343**

- Herbert Spencer Hadley - PD
- Alice Lee Hadley - PD
- William Stone "W. S." Woods - PD
- William Thompson Kemper Sr. - PD
- Gov. Thomas Theodore Crittenden Jr. - PD
- Hugh Campbell & Vassie James Ward Home - PD
- Albert Ross Hill - PD
- Pembroke Hill School – Missouri Valley Special Collections, Kansas City Public Library
- Jacob & Ella Loose - PD
- Hill Hall, College of Education, University of Missouri – College of Education, University of Missouri
- Vassie James-Ward-Hill - PD

Chapter 8 - Underrated Men & Unleashed Feminists

- *Vase of Flowers* Painting by Jan Van Huysum – Courtesy Nelson-Atkins Museum of Art
- *Warren's Old Style* Papers - PD
- Williams College Summer Science Camp – Williams College, http://science.williams.edu/summer-science-camp/
- Robert Franklin "Bob" James - JPT, Sara Jane Race Duke Archive
- George Hebert Walker & Lucretia Wear - PD
- James Crawford "Jay" Ward – Unidentified newspaper clipping
- Genevieve Underhill Ward & Edwin Barnes Tucker – Courtesy of the subjects.
- John Harris Ward Mosaic - PD
- Women of the Suffragette Movement - PD
- Margaret Sanger - PD
- Mary Godwin Van Etten-Ward - PD
- *John in the Wilderness* Painting by Caravaggio – Courtesy Nelson-Atkins Museum of Art
- Barbara James-McGreevy & children Barbara Ann McGreevy-McNay, Gail McGreevy-Harmon, Thomas James McGreevy, & Joan "Jean" McGreevy – JPT, Virginia Jacques-Church Archive, Unidentified newspaper clipping
- Gale McGreevy-Harmon Esq. – Courtesy of the subject's business web site
- Joan "Jean" McGreevy-Green - PD
- Rev. Mollie Paine McGreevy - PD
- Pamela McGreevy - PD
- Susan Colby Brown-McGreevy - PD
- T. M. James & Sons China Company Advertisement - PD

Chapter 9 - All For The Underdog

- ❧ Daniel Lewis & Lilith Snyder James - PD
- ❧ Barbara James
- ❧ Seaward – Courtesy of the Huntington Hartford Library
- ❧ Charlie Chaplin - PD
- ❧ Charlie Chaplin in *The Great Dictator* - PD
- ❧ Albert Maltz - PD
- ❧ Norma Barzman - PD
- ❧ *Bloomer Girl*, Playbill – Courtesy of the New York City Library
- ❧ Yip Harburg - PD
- ❧ House Un-American Activities Committee (HUAC) - PD
- ❧ Dorothy Comingore - PD
- ❧ *Candide* by Voltaire - PD
- ❧ Lester Cole - PD
- ❧ *Gorgo* Movie Poster - PD
- ❧ *The Giant Behemoth,* Poster for U.K. & U.S.A. - PD
- ❧ *Famous All Over Town*, Book - PD
- ❧ "kangaroo court of intellectuals" - PD
- ❧ Thomas Hart Benton, Artist - PD
- ❧ Sen. Thomas Hart Benton - PD
- ❧ Col. Maecenas Eason Benton - PD
- ❧ Benton's Indian Murals - PD
- ❧ Benton's Jesse James Painting - PD
- ❧ James R. Ross Figure at Hearst Castle - JPT

Chapter 10 - Useful to the Lord

- ❧ James Malley Burn, Esq. – JPY, JBA, courtesy of the subject
- ❧ Rev. James Malley, S. J. – JPT, JBA, courtesy of the subject

Chapter 11 - No One in Our Family Breaks Down

- ❧ Judge James Randall Ross - JPT
- ❧ Jesse Edwards James Jr. - PD
- ❧ Andrew Exler, aka Crusader – Courtesy of the subject
- ❧ Gov. Robert Taylor Jones - PD
- ❧ William S. Hart, Jo Frances James, & Stella McGowan-James - JPT
- ❧ Donald James Baumel, James R. Ross, James Curtis Lewis - JPT

ILLUSTRATION | **345**

- Family of James R. Ross – JPT, courtesy of Liza Ross-Suwczinsky
- Judge James R. Ross & *Northfield Raid* Painting – Courtesy of the Orange County Register

Afterward - Unto the Thrid Generation

- Joan Beamis - JPT, JBA, courtesy of J. Mark Beamis
- Robert Newton "Bob" Ford & Dot Evans – JPT, JBA
- Zerelda Elizabeth Cole-James-Simms-Samuels - JPT, *Sara Jane Race Duke Archive*
- J. Mark Beamis JPT, JBA, courtesy of the subject

Notes

Chapter 1 - Some Kind of Outsider

1. Beamis, Joan. Unpublished, handwritten manuscript. The Joan Beamis Research Archive, The James Preservation Trust. 2002.

2. Ibid.

3. Rousseau, Richard W., S.J., *New England Jesuit Oral History Program, Vol. 42.* "James B. Malley, S.J., Interview with Fr. James B. Malley, S.J.," Weston, Massachusetts, Society of Jesus of New England, 2007. ISBN 1-60067-040-7.

4. *New York Times,* April 19, 1906.

5. "Edward F. Burns Is Called by Death" *San Francisco Chronicle.* Jan 29, 1918.

6. Ibid.

7. Obituary of James Francis Malley, unidentified publication, provided to the James Preservation Trust by his son, John Crohan "Jack" Malley, 2007.

8. Correspondence with the author, July 25, 2008.

9. Ibid.

10. Letter from Joan Beamis to Gilbert A. Cam, New York City Library, May 14, 1954. Joan Beamis Research Archive. The James Preservation Trust, 2002.

11. Letter from Othor L. MacLean to Mrs. Joan F. Beamis, dated October 27, 1963 and February 24, 1964. Joan Beamis Research Archive, The James Preservation Trust.

12. Beamis, Joan, *A History of Drury Woodson James, as Told by his Daughter* .Joan Beamis Research Archive, The James Preservation Trust, 2002. The document consists of only two typewritten pages.

13. The sword was inherited by Elliston Dyer James, son of John James of Alvarado. When Elliston died on June 8, 1972, all of his possessions were seized by Elliston's son, Jerry James. Barring his other siblings from access, Jerry sold the sword at a yard sale for a few dollars. In 2009, Welty Eugene Whitaker, known in Somerset, Pulaski County, Kentucky as Gene Whitaker, stated to the author he had met Elliston Dyer James. Elliston had shown Gene the Quantrill sword. Gene described the sword as not being a full length saber, but rather a utility sword of shorter length, commonly issued to Union soldiers in Kentucky during the Civil War. Elliston stated further to Gene that William Wythe James had informed John James of Alvarado that the sword had been seized from a Union soldier when Quantrill raided Danville, Kentucky. Gene Whitaker is a third great grandson of John M. James of Pulaski County. Gene further

stated that the husband of his grandaunt, Thomas Jerome Graves husband of Louisa DeBord, had attended Frank James trial. Gene stated that Rome, as he was called, was a wagoner and possessed a unique ability for backing up wagons hitched to a full horse team. Rome was hired to back up wagons to blockade the court house where Frank James was being tried. Rome was instructed to sit inside the courtroom. Unable to get inside, Rome sat on an open window ledge, from where he observed the entire trial. His uncle described Frank James as being a "stammerer" in his testimony. He also described Jesse James' son, the boy Jesse Edwards James Jr., as being precise, quick to respond, and energetic when put on the stand.

14. Photocopy of the original letter on record with The James Preservation Trust. The letter was obtained from Billy Shirley-Mills, great granddaughter of John James of Alvarado. A corresponding photocopy of the letter also was found on record with the Pulaski County Historical Society in Kentucky, deposited there by Thelma Hays-Herrin, whose spouse Lem Garland Herrin is a second great grandson of John M. James of Pulaski County, and a first great grandson of the "talented, but erratic" Rev. Joseph Martin James. The paternal great grandfather of Billie "Cricket" Shirley-Mills is James Tolbert Shirley, born in Adair County, Kentucky. Shirley died in Venus, Texas. This Shirley family's lore states it is related to Myra Maebelle Shirley, aka Belle Starr. Family photos evidence a strong physical alikeness, but the specific point of relationship remains unproven by documentary evidence.

15. Writing in numerous letters, Joan attempted to identify Johnny James, who appeared to be the only other unidentified James living in San Luis Obispo County, California and working as a ranch hand on the La Panza Ranch of Drury Woodson James. Joan never was able to identify him. Johnny James appears to have been John Franklin James, born in Logan County, Kentucky in 1849 to Dr. John R. James, a brother of Drury Woodson James. Having gone to California, Drury's nephew Johnny James never returned home to Logan County.

16. A few typed chapters from Stella's book *In the Shadow of Jesse James* appear in Joan's research archive, indicating Stella kept her promise. Stella McGowan James died on April 1, 1971. Her book was not published in her lifetime. Later in 1989, Stella's book was published by arrangement of Judge James R. Ross, the son of Jo Frances James and great grandson of Jesse James. A year earlier, Ross published his own book *I, Jesse James*. Dragon Publishing Corporation published both books.

17. Included in Stella's letter were photos from the Christmas party at the home of Jim Ross, and a newspaper clipping dated July 17, 1954 from the *Independence Examiner* in Missouri, titled "For Daughter-in-law of Jesse James - Visit with President Truman Highlight." The article highlighted Stella's visit to Missouri, her meeting with Harry Truman, and her visitations with local James relatives.

Chapter 2 - Talented, but Erratic

1. Spencer, J. H. History of the Kentucky Baptists, Vol. I, Cincinnati, Ohio: J.R. Baumes, 1886, p. 417. See also: *The Payroll of James Gilmore's Company of Virginia Militia While on Duty under the Command of Brigadier General Morgan While in South Carolina 1780.* Virginia State Library, Archives Division. Auditor of Public Accounts. Militia Lists 1779-1782.

2. Pension claim of Joseph McAlister, #S31241. Executed September 13, 1832, at

which time he was aged 78 and living in Pulaski County, Kentucky. Pension application # S10294 of Col. Anthony Crockett 1754-1838, who served with Joseph McAlister, describes their service in detail. *"...I enlisted for two years in Capt. Thomas Posey's company of the 7th Virginia Regiment commanded by Lt. Col. Alexander McClanahan at that time my company marched down to opposite Gwinn's Island at which place and (old) Point Comfort we were stationed as a guard, where we remained until after the Battle of Princeton when my company marched to Philadelphia, where Col. Morgan raised his rifle regiment by selecting men and officers from the army. Capt. Posey and many of his men including myself joined Col. Morgan's Regiment and we were stationed in the vicinity of Philadelphia but were almost continually in motion, during the spring and summer of 1777, we marched several times into New Jersey and had several skirmishes with the British at Bunbrook and Sommerset and Piscatawa and in the month of August 1777 we were ordered to the north to aid our Army in opposing Burgoyne, we marched from near Philadelphia across through New Jersey and struck the North River at Peakskill when we went on board sail boats and sailed up to Albany and from there joined the American army near Still Water, and were actively engaged in the skirmishes and battles which eventuated in the Capture of Burgoyne's army the 17th October 1777 -- Soon after which event we marched back and joined Genl. Washington at White Marsh where we had a skirmish with the British who then occupied Philadelphia and afterwards we attacked some Hessians at a place in New Jersey called Hatternfield about five miles from Philadelphia, we killed some of them and drove the balance to their boats in the Delaware near Philadelphia we then returned to White Marsh where I remained until my time expired and I was honorably discharged ..."*

3. Marriage Bonds, Rockbridge County, Virginia, 1778-1801. Bondsman David Hay. Witnesses Robert Robinson and James Sterling.

4. *Pulaski County Marriage Records Book, Vol. I, 1799-1850,* Pulaski County, Kentucky, Historical Society, p. 80.

5. Tibbals, Alma Owens. *History of Pulaski County*, Bagdad, Kentucky: Grace Owens Moore, 1952, pp. 10-11.

6. *DAR Patriot Index*, National Society of the Daughters of the American Revolution, Washington D.C., 1966, p. 365.

7. Spencer, History of Kentucky Baptists, I: p. 416.

8. Pusey, Dr. William Allen, "General Joseph Martin of Virginia, An Unsung Hero of the Virginia Frontier," Read before the Filson Club, February 3, 1936, The Filson Club History Quarterly, Vol. 10, No 2. April 1936, Louisville, Kentucky.

9. Aronhine, Gordon, "General Joseph Martin a Forgotten Pioneer, 1740-1898," Historical Sketches of Southwest Virginia, Publication 21966.

10. Pusey.

11. Spencer, I: p. 416.

12. Taylor, John, *Baptists on the American Frontier: A History of the Ten Baptist Churches of Which the Author Has Alternately Been a Member*, Annotated 3rd ed., ed. Chester Raymond Young, Macon, Georgia; Mercer University Press, 1995, p. 98.

13. Lamkin, Jr., Adrian, *Jeremiah Vardeman, Pioneer Preacher*, Liberty, Missouri; William E. Partee Center for Baptist Studies, William Jewell College. The primary source is an article by John Mason Peck in the August 1854 issue of *The Christian Repository*.

"One of the young visitors to the 1834 meeting at Providence Church reported on Vardeman's weight. 'After we had gone some distance in my father's carriage I was put into old Brother Jeremiah Vardeman's fine cushioned carriage and given the front seat - he being very fat had the back seat all to himself. His son, Jerry, sat outside and drove. I remember how exceedingly easy the old gentleman was and how fearful he was of being shaken up, and how he kept putting his head out the window, calling to Jerry not to drive over the gopher holes and buffalo wallows which abounded on every side'."

14. Snyder, Robert, *A History of Georgetown College*, p. 7.

15. Perkins, J.H. & Peck, John Mason, "Rev. Jeremiah Vardeman," *Annals of the West*, Pittsburg, Pennsylvania, W.S. Haven, 1856, p. 354.

16. Lamkin.

17. Spencer, I, p. 238.

18. Ibid., I, p. 416.

19. The History Committee: Oscar Davidson, Mildred Ellis, Lewis W. Shepherd, Chairman, Assisted by Eldred M. Taylor & Jacqueline Taylor. *History of the First Baptist Church, Somerset, Kentucky, 1799-1974*. One Hundred Seventy-fifth ed. Wolfe City, Texas; Southern Baptist Press, 1974, p. 8.

20. Ibid., p. 19. The namesake of Robert Sallee James, the father of Frank and Jesse James, derives from this Sallee family. Rev. John M. Sallee was the son of Joel W. Sallee, a clerk and deacon of the First Baptist Church of Somerset for more than forty years. After leaving the First Baptist Church, John M. Sallee preached in Casey and Lincoln counties, finally moving to Nelson County in 1879 to become pastor of the Cox's Creek Baptist Church. Between 1890 and 1899 he pastored in Henderson County, Kentucky before moving to Texas where he died. From Virginia, the Sallee family first migrated to Mercer County in Kentucky, settling between Harrodsburg and Danville. William Sallee operated the livery in Danville and was certainly known to Joseph McAlister James. William Johnson Sallee 1775-1830 served in the Mounted Volunteer Militia under Battalion Commander Rennick. He served in the War of 1812 under Thomas Dollarhide of Somerset, and returned to his duty as Postmaster for Pulaski County. He died in 1830 and was buried in Sinking Creek Church Cemetery in Somerset, Kentucky.

21. Stewart, Murrell P. *Flat Lick Baptist Church, Its Place in History, 1799-1999*, Bicentennial Edition, Somerset, Kentucky; Flat Lick Baptist Church, 1999, pp. 49-59.

22. Pusey.

23. Elby, Jerrilyn, *They Called Stafford Home*, Heritage Books Inc., 1997, pp. 45-47.

24. Ibid.

25. Spencer. I: p. 87 Craig's brothers Lewis and Joseph were ministers. Lewis was the most accomplished in preaching, number of baptisms, and the founding of churches. Among the brothers of Rev. Joseph Martin James, Revs. John James and Daniel Field James were more methodical, dutiful, and organizational in their approach.

26. Ibid., p. 87.

27. Ibid., p. 237.

28. Ibid., p. 88.

29. Ibid., p. 87.

30. Ibid., p. 89.

31. Ibid., p. 89.

32. Perrin, William Henry. *History of Bourbon, Scott, Harrison and Nicholas Counties, Kentucky,* 1882. The school year called for a month long vacation in the spring and fall. Payment for room and board was 3 pounds in cash or 500 pounds of pork upon entrance, plus 3 pounds cash at the start of the 3rd quarter. Students were to provide their own beds. Beds for eight or ten boys were available at 35 shillings per year.

33. Snyder.

34. Ibid., p. 10. Rev. Josiah Pitts also maintained an active trade between Frankfort and New Orleans, shipping tobacco, wheat, hemp, flour, bacon, and whiskey by river boat, then returning via the Natchez Trace to Georgetown and Lexington with letters of credit upon eastern businesses. He remained a minister as well as a teacher at Georgetown College.

35. *Marriage Records, Laurel County, Kentucky. Book AA,* p. 18. The marriage record identifies the groom as Joseph M. James and the bride as Permelia Waddle. Permelia had provided her mother's maiden name of Waddle, leading to speculation Permelia herself may have been an illegitimate child. No witnesses to the marriage are identified. The parties are identified as "of age." Officiating was George Brock. The marriage took place thirty days following the birth of the couple's first son, John Thomas James.

36. *Pulaski County Marriage Records, 1799-1850, Vol. I,* Somerset, Kentucky; Pulaski County Historical Society, p. 8. Marriage record of Joseph Martin James and Rhoda May. July 21, 1830. Witness: Randolph Bobbitt.

37. Pusey.

38. James family lore also attributes the bastard child Tempy Spratt to Rev. Joseph Martin James. The child is mentioned in the will of his father, John M. James, who provided a choice of his slaves of Rachel or Jenny for *"Tempy McAlister supposed to be a grandchild of mine."* The child was raised in the household of Rev. Robert McAlister. The mother was Esther Spratt. Eventually the child married John William McAlister, the brother of Martha Betsy McAlister, Rev. Joe's first wife. If the child is indeed the daughter of Rev. Joe, the conception would have occurred when Rev. Joe was age eleven.

39 Spencer. I, p. 416.

40. History Committee. pp. 72-73.

41. Spencer, I, pp. 417-418.

42. Battle, Perrin, & Griffin, *Kentucky, A History of the State*, ed. 8-B, Pulaski County. See biography of James T. [Terrell] May, who is a nephew of Rhoda May.

43. *Lincoln County, Kentucky*. Paducah, Ky. Turner Publishing Company. 2002, p. 227. In early Pennsylvania the term "Black Dutch" was used derogatorily, similar to the slur "Black Irish." The term was commonly applied as a political slur. Dutch is the English pronunciation of Deutsch in German. Historically, Schwarze Deutsche, Black Germans, or Black Dutch lived along the Danube River in the Black Forest of Austria and Germany. During the Roman period, the occupying Roman army was composed of mercenaries who guarded the border of Germany. Black Africans, the Garamante or Tubu, from central Sahara guarded the Danube. These African mercenaries left

German progeny who have dark black hair and dark eyes.

44. Goodspeed, Weston A., Leroy C. Goodspeed, Charles L. May. *History of Lawrence, Orange and Washington Counties, Indiana From the Earliest Time to the Present; Together with Interesting Biographical Sketches, Reminiscences, Notes, Etc.* Chicago, Goodspeed Bros. & Co., Publishers, 1884. See biography of James G. May, a first cousin of Rhoda May.

45. Squire is not a title. Squire William Lee is his actual name. Another Squire Lee is found on the 1860 census of nearby Vermillion County.

46. Cunningham, J. O. *History of Champaign County*, 1905. Reprint: Urbana, Illinois; Champaign County Historical Archives, Urbana Free Library, p. 1009.

47. James, John. *Stray Leaves From My Diary*. Unpublished manuscript diary widely distributed among the James families of John James (1852-1927), identified herein as John James of Alvarado. *"My little and only sister Mary Martha when 2 years old got choked to death on a grain of corn. While Father was a prisoner of war at Marietta, Ga. 1000 miles away but in a vision the night and hour she died he saw her come to his pallet dressed in white and was the most beautiful, Father woked [sic] up his bedfellow and told him of his strange vision and looked at his watch and noted the time."*

48. Unidentified 1936 newspaper, "Grandmother Owens at 92 does own work, gardening." Found in the files of Thelma Jane Hayes-Herrin, spouse of Lem Garland Herrin, grandson of Joseph Allen and Susan Harriett James Herrin. Shopville, Kentucky. 1997. According to Virgie Lucille Herrin-Fuller a grandniece of Mary Harriett, shortly after the publication of this newspaper article, Mary Harriet took her first ride in an airplane at age 92. Upon landing she was reported to be singing at the top of her voice, "Nearer My God to Thee."

49. Joseph Allen Herrin maintained a diary during his Civil War service. In it he recorded the shooting of Andrew James. The diary presently is owned by Nelva Ann Herrin, a daughter of Thelma Jane Hayes-Herrin and Lem Garland Herrin, a great grandson of Rev. Joseph Martin James and Rhoda May. The Herrin family still resides on John M. James' original settlement land in Shopville, Kentucky. Thelma Hayes-Herrin died on January 16, 2006.

50. Research leaves it unclear which of the remaining two sons fought in the Civil War, according to the statement of Rhoda May-James that she had two sons fighting on each side. Family lore states Edward Perry James fought for the South.

51. Spencer. I, pp. 417-418.

Chapter 3 - Goodland

1. *House Journal 1807-1808,* p. 97. See also p. 105: request for inquiry implicating the conduct and integrity of Harry Innes as judge of the Court of the United States for Kentucky. See also p. 159: resolution with respect to Harry Innes recognizing charges brought by Benjamin Sebastian, judge of the Kentucky Court of Appeals, 1792-1806. Sebastian stood accused of being a paid agent of Spain. The charge was investigated by the Kentucky legislature, and Sebastian resigned in disgrace. John M. James voted NAY in opposition to Sebastian's charges.

2. The ancestral line of Harry Innes Todd (1880-1905) is as follows. Parents:

Admiral Chapman Coleman Todd (1848-1929) & Anna Eliza James (1849-1925). Grandparents: Rep. Harry Innes Todd (1818-1891) & Jane Ballinger Davidson (1820-1901). Great grandparents: Justice John Harris Todd (1795-1824) & Maria Knox "Mary" Innes (1796-1851). 2nd Great grandparents: Chief Justice Harry Innes (1751-1816) & Ann Harris (1760-1851).

3. John Bradford, Editor and Publisher, *Biographical Encyclopedia of Kentucky*, 1868, J. M. Armstrong & Co. p. 415.

4. *Catalogue of Officers and Students, Year Ending June 30, 1853,* Centre College, Danville, Kentucky.

5. Spencer, I, p. 484.

6. Meece, O'Leary *Condensed Minutes of the Pulaski County Court, Order Book Number One, 1799-1803*, p. 88. Courthouse, Somerset, August 28, 1809. Agenda Item 10. *"Ordered that Pulaski County be laid off into five districts for the purpose of appointing patrollers. Henry James appointed in the East End. John Griffin to be appointed in the South part of the county."* The historical pronunciation of the word "patroller" is pata-roller. See also: Goodell, William, *The American Slave Code in Theory and Practice: Its Distinctive Features Shown by Its Statutes, Judicial Decisions, and Illustrative Facts.* New York: American Foreign Anti-Slavery Society, 1853.

7. The 1810 census for Pulaski County, Kentucky identifies John M. James as owning 22 slaves. At the time of his death, the number of identifiable enslaved had dropped to 12. They were then distributed among the James family. Wilson (1) went to Molly James and her husband Sen. Jack Griffin. Gill (2) went to Capt. John Henry "Harry" James. Slave Joe (3) and his wife Fan (4) plus their two small children Jefferson (5) and Mary (6) went to Elizabeth "Betsy" James and her spouse Rev. Jeremiah Vardeman. Nancy James received the slave Dick (7). Rev. Joseph Martin James received Jenny (8). Rev. Daniel Field James received Gillard (9) and his wife Milly (10). On January 13, 1823 prior to John's passing, John McAlister took possession of an unidentified slave girl (11), having previously received the slave Rachel (12).

8. In the 1988 novel *Beloved,* by Toni Morrison, a character describes Pulaski County as *"...the meanest place for Negroes he had ever seen..."* The book won the 1988 Pulitzer Prize for fiction. Morrison, Tony, *Beloved,* New York, Alfred A. Knopf Inc., 1987.

9. Of Richard Mentor Johnson's two daughters by his wife, the former slave Julia Chinn, one daughter Imogene Chinn, a mulatto, was born in 1812 and married Daniel B. Pence. Their daughter Mary Jane Pence, born in 1825, married her cousin Josiah "Joe" Pence, born 1827, an older brother of Bud and Donnie Pence of the Quantrill's Guerillas and the James Gang. Daniel B. Pence and Imogene Pence had slaves of their own - John & Leanna Samuel. Their descendants migrated out of Kentucky in 1877 to found the town of Nicodemus, the first black settlement on the Kansas frontier and the only one to survive to present day. Nicodemus resident and Samuels descendant, Angela Bates-Tomkins, founder of the Nicodemus Historical Society and an historian with a former history as a military weapons and training analyst in Washington D.C., testified to the author at the Johnson Family Reunion, held at Ward Hall, Georgetown, Kentucky, on July 22-24, 2005, cosponsored by the Georgetown & Scott County Museum, Scott County Genealogical Society, and the Scott County Historical Society.

10. At about this time Kentucky was finding itself with an enslaved population in excess of its agricultural needs. Slave markets emerged in Louisville and Lexington to

sell the excess slaves *"down the river"* to Mississippi and New Orleans.

11. While no documentary records exist for real property transactions between Joseph McJames and enslaved people in Boyle County prior to the Civil War, records are found after the war. On March 20, 1867, Joseph McJames is identified as selling land Mack formerly had purchased from John Tompkins, an executor, to the purchaser John Corwan *"a man of color,"* for cash and notes in the amount of $5,500. The records show the note was paid by Corwan, January 16, 1868. Boyle County Deed Book 9, p. 620.

12. In 1860 there were 3,279 enslaved persons in Boyle County and 503 holders of enslaved persons. There also were 5,590 whites and 435 free blacks. Brown, Richard C. *A History of Danville & Boyle County, Kentucky 1774-1992,* Danville. Bicentennial Books, 1992, pp. 17-18.

13. Sanborn Fire Insurance Maps for Danville, Kentucky, Heritage Center, Harrodsburg, Kentucky, 2004.

14. In Danville, William Sallee operated the local livery stable on Fourth and Walnut Streets, today a parking lot adjacent to the Methodist Church. Sallee resided one block north of James Hall at 238 N. Third St. in Danville.

15. Deed Records, Boyle County, Kentucky; McJames to Hutchinson, Bk. 10, p. 395.

16. Fackler, Calvin Morgan. *Early Days in Danville,* Louisville, The Standard Printing Co. 1941, 4th reprinting 2002, Boyle County Genealogical Society, pp. 108, 237. See also Note 22. Relatives of President George Washington lived in Boyle County. As early as the 1780s Washington had lands surveyed for him. Washington acquired land in adjacent Lincoln and Garrard Counties, as well as in nearby Pulaski County. On December 14, 1853, Mack James sold 238 acres to Robert W. Washington and his wife Sarah for $9,524, with a one-third down payment and three annual installment payments, due between 1855 and 1857. The property was surveyed by James McKee and adjoined lands owned of Sheltons and Kempers. Deed Records, Boyle County, Kentucky, Book 5, p. 294. Robert W. Washington is also identified as a great nephew of the President and also as an incorporator of The Merchant's Deposit Bank of Danville.

17. Richard W. Griffin, P.H.D. *Newspaper Story of a Town, a History of Danville, Kentucky.* Hundredth Anniversary Edition of the Kentucky Advocate, Danville, Kentucky: Danville-Advocate Messenger, 1965, pp. 22-23.

18. Griffin, pp. 95-96.

19. Griffin, pp. 75-78, 137-138.

20. "Recollections: An Oral History of Boyle County," *The Kentucky Advocate,* June 23, 1991. James Hall was remembered as recently as 1991. Reed S. Nichols, then 68 years old, recollected his boyhood, *"...there was a theater on Third Street run by John Stout, Stout's Theater. At first it was upstairs, but then they moved it down on Third, right about where the Third Street barbershop is now."*

21. Griffin.

22. Fackler, pp. 29-30. Fackler identifies the name of the tavern as "The Big Black Horse." Jeremiah Clemens (1763-1826) and Mark Twain (1835-1910) shared a common ancestor in Ezekial Clemens, born February 1, 1696 in Virginia and spouse Christina Castell. Ezekial Clemens was Jeremiah's grandfather and Twain's second great grandfather, as evidenced by Twain's pedigree: Parents: John Marshall Clemens

& Jane Casey Lampton. Grandparents: Samuel B. Clemens & Pamela Goggins. First great grandparents: Jeremiah Clemens (1732-1811) & Elizabeth Moore. Second great grandparents: Ezekial Clemens & Christina Castell.

23. Read, Opie, *Mark Twain and I,* Chicago, Reilly and Lee, 1940, p. 11.

24. The Black Horse Inn resembled a Virginia ordinary, with a pub on the first level and sleeping rooms above. Four to six people occupied a single room with a broad single bed, remaining fully dressed during sleep. Linens were changed infrequently. The Inn also functioned as the local stage coach stop in Danville.

25. Griffin, pp. 75, 77.

26. Mack James himself was a Field descendant, as a great grandson of Mary Field and Joseph James, the Elder. When Mack's grandfather entered Kentucky, Daniel Field the family solicitor continued to handle the family's residual business matters in Virginia. Mack's first cousins, Reuben and Abraham Field, who lived in Beargrass before it became better known as Louisville, were part of the Corps of Discovery of the Lewis & Clark Expedition.

27. Griffin, pp. 75-78. Mack clearly intended the St. James Hotel to compete directly against the Gilcher brothers' new hotel. In 1875 Peter and Frank Gilcher purchased the old Henderson building on Danville's Main Street a block away. With extensive renovation the property became an immediate success as Gilcher's European Hotel. In the 1970s, the St. James Hotel was torn down. The Gilcher's hotel later became the Gilcher Department Store. In 2006 the vacant Gilcher building also was taken down, except for its historical Main Street facade. Behind the facade was erected a parking garage and surgical center for the Ephraim McDowell Regional Hospital.

28. "Recollections: An Oral History of Boyle County," *The Kentucky Advocate*, June 23, 1991. In 1991, Hazel Penn Rawlings Roberts, then age 91, recalled *"Malcolm Weisiger was a well-known, rich man of Danville. He enjoyed his picture show on the corner of Fourth and Main Street in Danville for many years. It was called the Colonial Theater. On the first floor of the three story brick building, which was once used on the second and third for the Clemens Hotel years ago."*

29. Fackler, pp. 21-22. On June 18, 1785, Isaac Hite was charged with erecting a court house in Danville. Hite lived in Jefferson County at the time. His occupation as a surveyor followed his service as a Captain under James Harrod. On May 31, 1792, Hite gave a deposition in a lawsuit between Rev. Lewis Craig and John Campbell. In 1782 he had been a store partner with George May in Danville. Hite's court house was not on the site of the present court house. The present Danville court house was erected in 1846 and the land originally was part of the original Clemens Hotel. Isaac Hite is the great granduncle of Maj. George Burns Hite who married Jesse & Frank James' aunt, Nancy Gardner James.

30. Historians have been at odds over the purpose of Quantrill passage through Kentucky in this campaign. Some historians maintain the guerillas were *en route* to assassinate President Lincoln. Three months following the raid on Danville, Lincoln was assassinated on April 15, 1865 by John Wilkes Booth.

31. Sanders, Stuart W. *Quantrill's Last Ride,* www.civilwarhistory.com, retrieved May 20, 2007.

32. Brown, Richard C. *A History of Danville and Boyle County, Kentucky, 1774-1992,* Danville. Bicentennial Books, 1992, p. 41.

33. Sanders.

34. A second great granddaughter of John M. James, Virgie Lucille Herrin-Fuller (1922-2009) of Somerset, Kentucky, stated in a 1997 interview with the author her recall as a child of hearing stories among the family about Frank and Jesse James rolling down the hill before the stone home built by Joseph Martin James.

35. Tuggle, George. *Pulaski Revisited,* The Pulaski County Historical Society. Lexington, Powell Printing, 1982, p. 46.

36. *Counties of Warren, Benton, Jasper, and Newton, Indiana,* Chicago. F. A. Battey & Co., Publishers, 1883, p. 595.

37. The log cabin originally faced Newton Street. As town lots were sold, the cabin was replaced by a newer residence in the 1920s. James family lore stated the original log cabin remained encased within the newly constructed home. The lore was proved untrue in September of 2005. The residence was undergoing restoration then. A visual inspection by the author of the dismantled interior revealed no log cabin inside the home. However plank board siding, 18 inches and wider, used as former exterior wall siding, was identified as being the original exterior siding to the 1920's residence. The plank board used as the home's original exterior siding probably was milled from the logs of the original cabin built by Marion James.

38. *Newton County Enterprise*, September 5, 1901, by William W. Gilman. The newspaper article identified early pioneers of Goodland: Carry Hopkins, William Foster, Andrew J. Ball. Ziba Wood, Thomas Shively, Isaac Atkins, Amos Crider, O.W. Church, and two others not identified. When Marion James married Nancy Angeline Logan on February 4, 1869, she had become the widow of Ziba Wood's brother, Benjamin T. Wood, another founder of Goodland who died in 1868.

39. *"The First Hotel,"* unidentified newspaper article, Goodland Public Library.

40. While identified in the newspaper story as Pittigon, his actual surname may have been Pennigon or Pettigrew, but more likely Pettijohn from the Pettijohn family of Pulaski County or Pennington from Pennington family of Danville in Boyle County, Kentucky. The 1870 Newton County census identifies him as James Penniger. James Pittigon was born in Kentucky in 1836. He also farmed 100 acres of Francis Marion James' 600 acre farm in Goodland. On March 8, 1892, James Pittigan (sic) of Goodland, Indiana, was awarded U. S. Patent No. 470,594 for a Wash Board. When James Pittigan died April 2, 1910 at age 74 in Chicago, Illinois, he was buried in Goodland.

41. McDowell was a pioneer in abdominal surgery, having performed the first hysterectomy in 1809 on patient Jane Todd Crawford without benefit of anesthesia. The operation was performed in his home on 2nd St. South of Main St. in Danville, Kentucky. The home presently is a museum.

42. *History of Coffeyville*, Coffeyville, Kansas; Coffeyville Journal Press, 1969, p. 25.

43. *Coffeyville Star*, Coffeyville, Kansas. July 28, 1881.

44. Ibid. August 18, 1881. The parents of the brothers who made up the Dalton Gang were James Lewis Dalton Jr. and his wife Adelaine Lee Sullivan Younger. Adelaine's half-brother was Henry Washington Younger, an early acquaintance of John M. James in Crab Orchard, Lincoln County, Kentucky, and father of the Younger Gang. Cole, Jim, and Bob Younger were her half-nephews. At the time of this newspaper announcement Adelaine and her husband lived outside Coffeyville. A few years later

they moved to Oklahoma.

45. The unidentified Younger may have been Bruce Younger, an uncle of the Dalton Gang through their mother Adeline Lee Sullivan Younger, who was Bruce's sister. Bruce also was a half uncle to Cole Younger and the Younger Gang. On May 15th of the previous year, Bruce had married Myra Maebelle Shirley, known as Belle Starr. After three months she abandoned him, leaving him at his residence in nearby Chetopa in Labette County, where Joseph McJames also had farms and ranches.

46. *The Star*, Independence, Kansas. August 3, 1883. *"Rev. John R. James, of Kentucky, accompanied by his accomplished bride, is now visiting his estimable parents. Mr. And Mrs. Jos. McJames, of Cherokee township. Mr. James is well known and highly appreciated for his talents and Christian virtues, in this county, having resided here several years. His is cordially welcomed back by troops of admiring friends."* August 10, 1883: *"Rev. John R. James of the Baptist denomination occupied the pulpit of the M.E. Church in this city last Sunday evening, delivering a very able and entertaining sermon to a crowded and appreciative audience - giving promise to a brilliant career of usefulness in the future."* At 5 pm on November 22, 1887, on his way to preach a sermon, Rev. James was thrown from his buggy when his horse was startled and ran off. He died and was buried in Lancaster, Kentucky in the Warren family plot of his wife's family in Garrard County, the place where his great grandfather, John M. James, first arrived in Kentucky with the Traveling Church.

47. Ibid. June 21, 1883.

Chapter 4 - An Independent Free Man

1. James, John. *Stray Leaves From My Diary.* Unpublished manuscript and diary of John James of Alvarado, Texas (1852-1927), widely disseminated among the descendants of Cyrenius Waite James.

2. James, John. *My Experience with Indians,* Austin, Texas, Gammel's Book Store, 1924.

3. James, p. 34.

4. Ibid., pp. 34-35. Also, Thoburn, Joseph Bradfield, *A Standard History of Oklahoma, Vol.*, Chicago and New York, The American Historical Society, p. 1241.

5. James, John, *Stray Leaves From My Diary.*

6. Richard Mentor Johnson (1781-1850) was a third cousin of Elizabeth Lightfoot (1725-1823). She was a great grand aunt of John James, and married Joseph James, the Younger (1743-1783). Johnson's first wife was an enslaved woman from the Lightfoot family. His second wife, Julia Chinn, is presumed to be an enslaved person of the Chinn family.

7. Morton, Jennie C. "Dick Johnson's Indian School at Sulphur, Scott County, Ky." *Register of the Kentucky State Historical Society,* Frankfort, Kentucky.

8. "Col. Dick Johnson's Indian School." *The Register of the Kentucky Historical Society,* Louisville, Kentucky; Geo. G. Fetter Company, 1905, pp. 33-35.

9. Wade, Houston. *The Dawson Men of Fayette County,* Houston, Texas, 1932.

10. Cates, Cliff Donohue. *Pioneer History of Wise County: from Red Men to Railroads.* Wise County Old Settlers' Association, p. 178.

11. James, p. 38.

12. Ibid., pp. 38-40.

13. Ibid., p. 137.

14. Ibid., pp. 142-146.

15. Correspondence of Tiajuana Chochnauer and the author, 1999. James Preservation Trust. See also: "The Choctaw Family of Elliston E. Dyer. *Stray Leaves, A James Family in America since 1650,* ww.ericjames.org/Dyer_Family.html

17. James, *My Experience with Indians,* pp. 138-140.

18. Interview with Billie Shirley-Mills (1924-2000), great granddaughter of John James (1852-1927). Jackson Waite James Family Reunion; Cleburne, Texas; June, 1998.

19. Photo image taken from cemetery tombstone of Rev. Joseph Mack "Joe" James (1857-1929), Weldon Cemetery; Weldon, Texas, 2001.

20. Unidentified newspaper from Charleston, Coles County, Illinois, circa 1917: *"Outlaw Won to the US, After 50 years, William James is again a citizen."* The article highlights many of same international exploits voiced by William Wythe James, as did the article about him that appeared in the *Alvarado Weekly Bulletin.*

21. Interview of Welty Eugene Whitaker, Somerset, Kentucky November 5, 2009.

22. Interview with Billie Shirley-Mills.

23. Interview with Paul Maurice James, a great grandson of John James (1852-1927). Jackson Waite James Family Reunion; Cleburne, Texas; June, 1998.

Chapter 5 - The Highest Mental Culture

1. Obituary: "Uncle of the James Boys-Dies at Kansas City and Leaves a Million." Appearing in three newspapers. *Daily Review,* Decatur, Illinois, December 26, 1901; *St. Louis Republican,* St. Louis, Missouri, December 26, 1901; *Kansas City Star,* Kansas City, Missouri, December 26, 1901. *"T.M. James, uncle of Frank and Jesse James, died here yesterday at the age of 79 years. His estate is estimated at $1,000,000."*

2. Among Baptists in the early 1830s, a split occurred between those supporting missionary churches and those defined as anti-missionary. In 1835 there were 8,723 Baptists in Missouri, among 150 churches and 77 ministers. Of the anti-missionary Baptists there were 3,366 members, among 80 churches and 49 ministers. Within a decade, the missionary Baptists had increased 9,964 and the anti-missionaries 970. See: *Foreign Missions in Missouri During One Hundred Years,* speech by Rev. R. L. Davidson, to the Missouri Baptist General Association, 1906.

3. *History of Todd County, Kentucky,* ed. J. H. Battle, 1884, F. A. Battey Publishing Co., 1884, pp. 340-341.

4. Mimms, Robert William. *Autobiography and Travels, Remarks, etc.* Kansas City, Mo. Jan. 1869-70. pp. 1-2. Joan Beamis Archive. The James Preservation Trust. Mimms expected to publish his manuscripts, the cover of which he inscribed as, *"A book, containing a biographical sketch of the leading features in the life of Robert William Mimms, together with some of his lectures and writings in manuscript."*

5. *History of Jackson County, Missouri.* Union Historical Company, Birdsall, Williams & Co. Kansas City, Mo. 1881, p. 380.

6. *Friends of the Youngers Research*, Margarette Berry Hutchins, Complied by Wilma Carroll Hillman, Friends of the Youngers, Inc. June, 2000, pp. 16, 26. Col. Charles Lee Younger initially fathered two children by a slave named Fanny, and two additional children by his first wife Nancy Toney, before Younger married Sarah Sullivan Purcell in Crab Orchard, Kentucky. Between 1808 and 1817, Younger fathered six more children by Sarah Purcell in Kentucky, including Henry Washington Younger the future father of the Younger Gang brothers. Relocated to Missouri, Younger kept a mistress, Permellia Dorcus Wilson, on the west bank of the Missouri River across from his home with Sarah Purcell. Younger fathered nine more children with Wilson. No evidence establishes whether or not Younger ever married Permellia Dorcus Wilson.

7. A survey of deeds and land purchases reveals that much of today's Kansas City International Airport is built upon lands once owned by Tilman Howard West.

8. Letter from Thelma Duncan-Barr to James Walter Sames III, 1980. James Preservation Trust, Joan Beamis Archive. See also "Residence," *Kansas City Times*, July 29, 1972.

9. *History of Jackson County, Missouri,* p. 353.

10. Pence, Samuel Anderson, *I Knew Frank...I Wish I had Known Jesse*, Two Trails Publishing, Independence, Missouri, 2007, p. 124.

11. *Experiment Station of the Kansas State Agricultural School*, Bulletin No. 51, June 1895, pp. 5658. Today the farm is called Airdrie Stud, and is home to former Kentucky Gov. Brereton C. Jones, a cousin of Jesse and Frank James, and his wife Libby Lloyd, a second great granddaughter of R. A. Alexander. In the Civil War, William Clarke Quantrill and the James brothers stole thoroughbred horses from this farm and Stonewall Farm nearby.

12. Hatter, R., Hughes, N., Burch, G., *Frankfort Cemetery, the Westminster Abbey of Kentucky*, Frankfort Heritage Press, Frankfort, Ky. 2007, p.203.

13. Spencer, J. H., *History of Kentucky Baptists*, Vol. I, pp. 152-162.

14. *History of Jackson County, Missouri,* p. 179.

15. Ibid., p. 105.

16. *Register of the Kentucky State Historical Society*, Vol 14 #42, p. 14.

17. Holcombe, R. I., Ed, *History of Greene County, Missouri*, 1883, Chapter 3.

18. Ibid., Chapter 4.

19. "Jotham Meeker's Journal," Vol. 3, 18531854, Kansas City Historical Society, Index 220. Meeker was a Baptist associate of Rev. Isaac McCoy, involved in the Indian missions. See also: Letter from D. D. Mitchell to G. W. Manypenny, Commander of Indian Affairs, Washington, dated April, 29, 1853. Volume: 9 Page: 444 (Microfilm reel MS96) Transmits the official bond of B. A. (Burton Allen) James as Indian Agent for the Sac & Fox Agency.

20. "Rev. Isaac McCoy, Early Baptist Indian Missionary," *The Baptist Encyclopedia*, 1881.

21. Little, James A., *Kirtland to Salt Lake City,* Salt Lake City, Utah, self-published, 1890, pp. 224-225.

22. *History of Boone County, Missouri*, St. Louis, Western Historical Company, 1882, p. 361. Hickman's Ferry was operated by David H. Hickman, son of David McClanahan Hickman of Paris, Bourbon County, Kentucky. They came to Missouri

about 1821. Their cousins from Frankfort, Rev. William Hickman and sons Ezra and Edward Alfred Hickman, did not arrive in Westport until 1829. David McClanahan Hickman, established the town of Columbia, Missouri. He organized the Bonne Femme Academy, with Warren Woodson as teacher. He served in the Missouri state legislature, representing Boone County, and started a bank with income earned in the Far West. His son, David Henry Hickman put the Hickman family's western riches to work, establishing the Jefferson City Railroad Co., the Columbia Fire Insurance Co., and the Columbia, Rocheport and Arrow Rock Railroad Co. He served as a William Jewell College trustee in Liberty; and presided over the Missouri Baptist Association. The *Missouri Statesman* reported on August 16, 1850 of the seasonal return to Boone County of the Hickman family from their enterprise in the Far West. *"The Ferry Company of D.H. Hickman reached home in good health on Sunday last...Aug. 11, 1850...Their location on the Platte River was about 130 miles west of Fort Laramie and 730 miles from St. Joseph, Missouri. They left the ferry location for home on the 8th of July. Previous to their leaving the great body of the emigration had passed. Yet on their homeward trip, they met about 500 wagons before reaching Fort Laramie and nearly 600 more between the later place and Fort Kearney. Of this number about 700 were Mormons en route for the Great Salt Lake."*

23. Stone, L. B. *West Family Register*. Chapter XII, p. 265.

24. *History of Jackson County, Missouri*, p. 438.

25. *"Jotham Meeker's Journal."* Meeker was a printer from Cincinnati. Following the federal government's decision to move eastern Indians west of the Missouri River, Meeker was sent to Kansas by the Board of Baptist Missions. Assigned to the Shawnee tribe as a printer-missionary, Meeker published *The Shawnee Sun* newspaper, and Indian language primers employing phonetics.

26. Cutler, William G., *History of the State of Kansas,* A. T. Andreas, Chicago, Illinois, 1883. Franklin County, Part 10, "Centropolis."

27. *Missouri Baptist Biography*, Vol. I, Western Baptist Publishing Company, Kansas City, 1914, p. 210.

28. *History of Jackson County, Missouri,* p. 843.

29. T. M. James was a cousin of Meriwether Lewis, too, as a 9th cousin, twice removed. The relationship was so distant, T. M. never would have known or recognized it, the fact being he was an orphan who knew little about his James family ancestry.

30. *The Kansas City Star*, article about Daniel Lewis Shouse, 1950.

31. Creel, George & John Slavens, *Men Who Are Making Kansas City,* Hudson-Kimberly Publishing Company, Kansas City, Missouri, 1902.

32. Creel & Slavens.

33. T. M. James sold his interest to S. D. Pitkin. *Kansas City Genealogist*, Vol. 34, #2, "T.M. James, Merchant," p. 82.

34. Thomas A. Smart speculated in local land sales. Smart opened his mercantile store in Westport about 1838. On May 26, 1868, Smart purchased block 55, lots 13 and 14 of Union Cemetery, with other investors Thomas Martin James, Daniel Lewis Shouse, and Burton Allen James. Building a sizeable estate, Smart went into banking, and later became a judge. See also, Note # 38.

35. *Missouri Baptist Biography*, p. 309.

36. Letter from Lutie Mimms Gray to Joan Beamis, dated February 10, 1962.

"T. M. James hired my father's young brother (his namesake). T. M. Mimms was a shipping clerk in his extensive queens ware business in K. C. Mo. And Uncle Tom Mimms worked for his uncle T. M. James in that capacity for <u>more</u> than fifty years, I believe." Joan Beamis Research Archive, James Preservation Trust, 2002. See also, Kansas City Directory, 1877.

37. *History of Jackson County, Missouri*, pp. 445-446. Col. E. M. Samuels also was an incorporator with Dr. Johnston Lykins of the New Orleans, Shreveport, Kansas City Railroad Company, approved by the Louisiana Legislature. See also, *Jewell is Her Name*, p. 17. Col. Samuels, born in Henry County, Kentucky, arrived in Missouri in 1832 with his son George Warren Samuel. He purchased land in Clinton County and formed the town of Plattsburg. His business was opened in July, 1834. *History of Clinton County, Missouri*, 1881, National Historical Company, St. Joseph, Missouri, pp. 92, 93, 95.

38. Union Cemetery Association, Jackson County, Missouri. *"Purchased block 30, lot 3, with Burton Allen James (Aug 8, 1861 block 1, lot 7) and Daniel Lewis Shouse (block 1, lot 18), and on Jan 30, 1865, Thomas [Martin] James, block 7, lot 6 1/2",* and *"May 26, 1868 Thos. A. Smart, block 55, lots 13 and 14."* See also, Note # 34.

39. History of Jackson County, Missouri, p. 492.

40. *Kansas City, An Illustrated Review of Its Progress and Importance*, 1886.

41. Obituary. *St. Louis Republican,* December 26, 1901.

42. Personal correspondence, Thelma Duncan-Barr to Joan Beamis, July 24, 1971. Joan Beamis Archive. James Preservation Trust, 2002.

43. Ibid.

44. 1880 Census, Jackson County, Missouri, 5th Ward.

45. *Missouri Baptist Biography*, p. 308.

46. "T.M. James, Merchant" *Kansas City Historical Society*, Vol. 34, #2, p. 83.

47. *Missouri Baptist Biography*, Vol. I, Western Baptist Publishing Company, Kansas City, 1914, pp. 308-310.

48. *Jewell is Her Name*, pp. 27-29.

49. The Thomas' daughter, Eliza, married the artist George Caleb Bingham, who proclaimed he possessed "an unchristian fondness for women." When married, Bingham's peripatetic life rattled young Liza, who was forced to recover among her Thomas family in Louisiana. Eliza eventually found solace for her marriage by aiding orphans. In 1876 Eliza died in the Missouri State Lunatic Asylum. After which, Mattie Livingston-Lykins, the widow of Dr. Johnston Lykins who died in 1876, married Bingham.

50. *Missouri Baptist Biography*, p. 213.

51. Ibid. Also, *1878 United States Biographical Dictionary and portrait gallery of eminent and selfmade men: Missouri volume.* U.S. Biographical Publishing Co. Los Angeles Public Library book R977.8 U61; FHL film 1,425,620, item 1.

52. *History of Jackson County, Missouri*, p. 593.

53. Obituary. *Daily Review*, Decatur, Illinois. December 26, 1901. Also: St. *Louis Republican*, December 26, 1901.

54. *Missouri Baptist Biography*, p. 312.

55. Obituary from an unidentified publication, contained in the family bible of Jesse Edward Smith, grandson of Dr. John R. James. Sandra Lou Russell Kassen Archive,

James Preservation Trust.

56. Ibid., p. 313.

57. Ibid., pp. 308-309.

58. *The United States Biographical Dictionary and Portrait Gallery of Eminent and Selfmade Men*, United States Biographical Publishing Co., New York, New York. 1878, pp. 772-774.

59. *County of Christian, Kentucky. Historical and Biographical*. Edited by William Henry Perrin. F. A. Battey Publishing Co., 1884, pp. 404-405.

60. Meacham, Charles, *History of Christian County, Kentucky,* 1930.

61. *Index of the Circular Letters of the Bethel Baptist Association 1825-1884.*

62. Spencer, I, p. 727.

63. Hester, Hubert Inman. *Jewell Is Her Name, A History of William Jewell College,* Liberty, Missouri. William Jewell College, 1967, p. 240.

64. Ibid. pp. 56-57, 240-241.

Chapter 6 - Only a Large Soul Can Do This

1. "The Colleges - How Class-Day was Celebrated at Brown University," *New York Times,* June 27, 1871.

2. Greenwood, J. M., *The Service of J. Crawford James as a Member and Officer of the Board of Education*. Transcript, ed. 1912. G1/5:12. Special Collections, Pickler Memorial Library, Truman State University. Greenwood was superintendent of the Kansas City schools, elected in 1874, when the town had only forty-nine teachers.

3. "Henry and Phoebe Routt Ess, Attorney/Clubwoman and Reformer," *Biography*. Missouri Valley Special Collections, Kansas City Public Library.

4. James, J. Crawford, *To the Members of the Board of Education, Kansas City, Missouri*. The letter of resignation of John Crawford James. G1/5:12. Special Collections, Pickler Memorial Library, Truman State University. See also, "J. Crawford James Dies," Obituary dated January 21, 1933, unidentified newspaper. Brown University, Alumni Archives.

5. Greenwood, J. M.

6. James, J. Crawford.

7. "J. Crawford James Dies."

8. *Kansas City: Its Resources and Their Development, a Souvenir of The Kansas City Times,* 1890, pp. 19-20. Also: Conrad, Howard Lewis, *Encyclopedia of the History of Missouri*, New York & Louisville, The Southern History Company, Conrad & Company, 1901, p. 122.

9. Robert M. Snyder was born in Columbus, Ohio on March 10, 1852, the son of John Snyder of Kentucky and Sarah Pence of Tennessee. The father of Sarah Pence is Jacob Pence, born in Virginia. The relationship to the Pence brothers of the James Gang is certain, although the specific identity of the relationship is not, due to multiple Pence family members bearing the name Jacob. Robert M. Snyder was educated in Louisville, Kentucky. In St. Louis, he became a merchandise broker. In Kansas City he operated the firm of Perrin & Snyder, a wholesale upscale grocery business. As a cattle

rancher he accumulated $50,000 with which he capitalized the Mechanic's Bank. He was president of the City National Bank, and later a director of the National Bank of Commerce in Kansas City. In February of 1902, the reformer Joe Folk indicted Snyder for bribery of a City Councilman to pass a bill permitting the St. Louis Transit Company to consolidate of the street railway companies, save one. Snyder was convicted and sentenced to three years in the penitentiary. The indictment was part of reformer Folk's "bootle scandals" that deposed political boss, Col. Ed Butler, whose blacksmith shop was farrier to the city railway horses.

10. "The Greatest Thing in All Kansas City - What the Commercial Club has Accomplished There," *New York Times,* February 12, 1903.

11. *Alumni Monthly,* Brown University, March, 1933.

12. David, Billingham and Jackson, Donald C. *Big Dams of the New Deal Era, A Confluence of Engineering and Politics.* University of Oklahoma Press, 2006, pp. 202-203.

13. "Rites for J. C. James," *Kansas City Star,* January 22, 1933.

14. Greene, George E. *History of Old Vincennes & Knox County, Indiana.* Chicago, S. J. Clarke Publishing Company, 1911, p.478. See also the individual biography of William Heberd.

15. Beamis, Joan. *Rev. William James.* Unpublished manuscript, Joan Beamis Archive, The James Preservation Trust.

16. *Liberty Tribune,* Clay County delinquent tax lists: October 6, 1865, p. 3, col. 1; also, July 20, 1866, p. 4, col. 1.

17. Paxton, William McClung, *Annals of Platte County, Missouri, from its exploration down to June 1, 1897,* Kansas City, Missouri, Hudson-Kimberly Publishing Company, 1897, p. 190

18. Obituaries, *The Kansas City Times,* Saturday, November 16, 1895; "A Veteran Minister Dies," *The Kansas City Star*, Saturday, November 15, 1895, p. 2, col. 2; "A Pioneer's Funeral," *The Kansas City Star*, Saturday, November 16, 1895; and *Kansas City Journal*, Saturday, November 16, 1895.

19. Beamis. *Rev. William James.* See also: Kansas City Directory, 1882, 1884, 1886-87, 1887-88.

20. *Encyclopedia of the History of Missouri,* Howard Louis Conrad, p. 499.

21. *The Charity Organization Movement in the United States, A Study in American Philanthropy.* Frank Dekker Watson. 1922. pp. 328-329.

22. *Missouri Historical Review.* Francis Asbury Sampson, State Historical Society of Missouri, Vol. XV, Ed. Floyd Calvin Shoemaker, Columbia, Missouri, 1921, pp. 212-213.

23. Stevens, Walter Barlow, *Centennial History of Missouri,* p. 362.

24. "The Schmelzer Arms Company," *Kansas City Times,* October 18, 1975.

25. *Kansas City Times,* July 29, 1972. Unidentified article regarding the Stevens-James residence, and the Herman Schmeltzer residence.

26. "Class of 1902," A *History of the Class of 1903, Yale College*, Yale University. See biographical data of William Heberd James Sr. Also, "Class of 1903," *History of the Class of 1903, Yale College,* Yale University, p. 159.

27. Interview of Virginia Jacques Church with the author, 2011

28. Virginia Aileen James graduated George Washington University's Mount Vernon Campus in 1923. Together in her class was Eleanor Pendleton Chinn, the granddaughter of John Pendleton "Black Jack" Chinn, a Quantrill Raider and close friend of Frank James.

Chapter 7 - Breaking Barriers

1. Creel, George, John Slavens, *Men Who Are Making Kansas City, A Biographical Directory*, 1902. Vassie James is identified in the biography of her husband, Rep. Hugh Campbell Ward.

2. Oates, Cynthia G., "Alumni News; Then & Now," *Vassar Alumni Quarterly,* Vol. 98, Issue 1, Winter, 2001.

3. Ibid.

4. *The United States Biographical Dictionary and Portrait Gallery of Eminent and Self-Made Men.* Vol. Missouri. See Seth E. Ward.

5. Chesterfield County Court Order Bk. 1, p. 1, p. 138; Leonard, C.M. *The General Assembly of Virginia,* Virginia State Library, Richmond, 1978.

6. *Harvard College, Class of 1886, Secretary's Report, No. VI,* New York, Dec. 1906, p. 161.

7. "Obituary Hugh Campbell Ward," *American Bar Association, Report of the Thirty-Second Annual Meeting Baltimore,* Lord Baltimore Press, 1909, p. 636.

8. "The Kansas National Suspends - Heavy Withdrawals of Deposits Have Forced It to the Wall," *New York Times,* July 15, 1893. See also: "Suspension of the Bank of Kansas City," *New York Times,* March 19, 1895.

9. *History of Jackson County, Missouri,* p. 552.

10. *Harvard College, Class of 1886, Secretary's Report,* p. 161.

11. *Register of the Society of Colonial Wars in the State of Missouri,* 1904-1906. p. 92; and 1907-1909, p. 147-148. See also Creel & Slavens.

12. "Obituary Hugh Campbell Ward," *American Bar Association, Report of the Thirty-Second Annual Meeting Baltimore,* p. 636.

13. *The Kinnears and Their Kin,* Emma Siggins White, Martha Humphreys Maltby. Tiernan-Dart Printing Company, Kansas City, Missouri, 1916, p. 488.

14. *Report of the Adjutant General of the State of Kentucky, Soldiers of the War of 1812.* Frankfort, KY.; E. Polk Johnson, 1891, p. 636.

15. "Herbert S. Hadley - The Man from Missouri, A Character Sketch of the Young Western Attorney General Who is Conducting His State's Fight Against the Powerful Standard Oil 'Trust'," *New York Times,* January 14, 1906.

16. *Register of the Society of Colonial Wars in the State of Missouri.*

17. Kremer, Gary R., professor of History. "Dr. William Stone Woods Namesake of the University," *Alumni Magazine,* William Woods College, Fall/Winter, 1999.

18. *Biography of William T. Kemper,* Kansas City Library.

19. "Big Bank Suspends, Blame Oil Company," *New York Times,* December 6, 1907. See also: Stevens, Walter Barlow, p. 382.

20. The portrait of Hugh Campbell Ward by George Caleb Bingham was last known to have resided at 28 Beech St. in Cohasset, Massachusetts, its owner listed as

Hugh Campbell Ward, presumed to be Hugh and Vassie's son, who died in Cohasset.

21. *History of Wyandotte County Kansas and its people* ed. Perl W. Morgan. Chicago, Lewis Publishing Company, 1911. Chapter XXVIII, "Kansas City of Today, Street Railway Facilities."

22. "Kansas City Beats 42-Year Franchise," *New York Times,* December 17, 1909. The Metropolitan Railway met defeat at the polls. The mayoral career of Thomas T. Crittenden Jr. ended the following year.

23. Obituary, "Hugh Campbell Ward," *New York Times*, August 17, 1909.

24. "Jesse Clyde Nichols (1880-1950) Memoir," *Planning for Permanence: The Speeches of J. C. Nichols,* Western Historical Manuscript Collection, J.C. Nichols Company Records (KC0106). See also: Stevens, Walter Barlow, *Centennial History of Missouri,* pp. 248-253.

25. *Missouri, Special Limited Supplement,* 1930, p. 29.

26. *An Historical Survey of the Kansas City, Missouri, Parks and Boulevards System, 18931940.* The Kansas City Design Center in cooperation with the Western Historical Manuscript Collection, Kansas City, 1993.

27. Gallagher, John B. *Book of the Republican National Convention, Kansas City, Mo. June 12, 1928*; Kansas City Chamber of Commerce, 1928.

28. "Red Cross Is Sending Officers To Near East - Dr. A. Ross Hill, Vice Chairman, and Admiral McGowan to Sail - Appeal for Clothing," *New York Times,* October 13, 1922.

29. Coleman, Daniel. *Vassie James Ward Hill, School Founder and Educator, 1875-1953.* Kansas City Public Library, Missouri Valley Special Collections.

30. "Little Tammany," *Time* magazine, April 9, 1934.

31. "Missouri Sons of the South," Chapter 35, 1927. *Confederate Trails* magazine, reprint by Two Trails Publishing, p. 907.

Chapter 8 - Underrated Men & Feminists Unleashed

1. Society of Alumni of Williams College, Alumni Records, Updated record of George Olmsted Jr., Class of 1924.

2. "Our Library's History," Warren Memorial Library, Westbrook, Maine. 2008.

3. "Last of the Paternalists," *Portland Main Evening Express,* October 30, 1976. Also, "George Olmsted Jr., Donor of Westbrook Athletic Field, Fine Athlete as a Youth." Unidentified newspaper clipping from the Williams College Alumni archives.

4. *Williams Alumni Review,* Fall, 1977, p. 34.

5. "Last of the Paternalists."

6. *Williams Alumni Review.*

7. Ibid, Fall, 1993; Vol. 86, No. 1, p. 6.

8. *"Kids Get Experiment Experience at Williams Science Camp."* Williams College Public Affairs, July 21, 2008.

9. Works authored by James F. Oates Jr. include, *Business and Social Change, The Contradictions of Leadership, The Religious Condition of Young Men,* "The Corporation

and the Community," published in *The Corporation and the Campus; Corporate Support of Higher Education in the 1970's,* and *Commercial Morality and the Y.M C.A.*

10. Biography of James Franklin Oates, Jr. (1899-1982). Northwestern University Archives, Papers, 1924-1981.

11. Obituary. *Kansas City Star,* November 19, 1959.

12. "Scharff Is Victor In Hard Golf Tilt," *New York Times,* June 25, 1921. Also, "American Golfers Win," *New York Times,* June 28, 1921.

13. Society of Alumni of Williams College, Alumni Records, Affidavit of James C. Ward, May 17, 1961.

14. Mudd Library, Princeton University.

15. Obituary. *Princeton Alumni Weekly,* April 1, 2001.

16. Obituary. *Kansas City Times,* April 5, 1973.

17. Obituary. Williams College Alumni Records, unidentified newspaper and date.

18. "Clarence J. Van Etten," *Grand Rapids and Kent County, Michigan: historical account of their progress from first settlement to the present time,* Ernest B. Fisher, editor. Ann Arbor, Michigan; University of Michigan Library, 2005, p. 390.

19. Smucher, O. M. *Sun Times,* October 25, 1959.

20. Smucher, O.M. "J. Harris Ward's Meteoric Rise at Edison Co. Told," Chicago *Sun-Times,* May 25, 1958. See also: "Executive VP Will Succeed Evers Oct. 31," *American,* October 21, 1959.

21. Ibid.

22. Clark, William. "J. Harris Ward's Task: Pursuit of Excellence." *Tribune,* October 17, 1960.

23. Ibid.

24. Display ads for New York Life Insurance Company: *New York Times,* September 19, 1962, April 1, 1963, March 11, 1968, March 16, 1970, and March 8, 1972.

25. *Daily News,* July 29, 1974.

26. *Eulogy, J. Harris Ward Memorial Service, August 1, 1974.* Edward H. Levi Papers (1894-1998), Special Collections Research Center, University of Chicago Library, Box 303, Folder 6.

27. *Daily News.*

28. Griffith, Shirley & Sarah Long, *Margaret Sanger, 1883-1966: She Led the Fight for Birth Control for Women,* People of America, Voice of America Special English Program. 2007. Transcript of radio broadcast.

29. Ward, Roger. *Durer to Matisee, Master Drawings from The Nelson-Atkins Museum of Art.* Kansas City, Missouri. 1996. pp. 12, 133-134.

30. Robb, Peter. *M., The Man Who Would Become Caravaggio,* Picador, 2001.

31. Equally unnoticed is the fact that a founder of the Nelson-Atkins Museum is related to the Younger brothers of the James Gang. Mary McAfee Atkins, the wife of James Burris Atkins, is a half 7th cousin of the brothers Jim, Bob, and Cole Younger. Born near Harrodsburg in Mercer County, Kentucky, Mary McAfee's family was among the founding pioneers of the Commonwealth of Kentucky. Mary lived within close proximity to the Youngers and James in nearby Lincoln County. Kit Chinn, son of Col. Jack Chinn,

is the husband of her second cousin. Mary also is a distant cousin of Quantrill raider Sidney Washington Creek. A kinship of distance rarely, if ever, is acknowledged, except for curiosity's sake.

32. Among publications authored and co-authored by Gail Harmon are: *Being a Player, a guide to tax regulations governing lobbying by charities; Maximize Your Grassroots Power: Legal Guide to List Enhancement and Citizen Contact; EAdvocacy for Non-profits: the Law of Lobbying and Electionrelated Activity on the Net;* and the *Nonprofit Navigator,* a newsletter formerly titled *Tax Monthly for Exempt Organizations and Tax Monthly for Associations.*

33. Blog, *Peace Works, Kansas City*: http://www.peaceworkskc.org/letter.html. Retrieved: March 17, 2009

34. *Kansas City Star*: http://blogs.kansascity.com/unfettered_letters/ environment/. Retrieved March 17, 2009

35. "Thomas J. McGreevy, Stockbroker, 58," *New York Times*, March 16, 1991

36. Smith Brady, Lois, "Pam McGreevy and Dan Newman," *New York Times*, June 1, 1997.

37. Smith Brady.

38. *Washington Matthews: Studies of Navajo Culture, 18801894,* edited by Katherine Spencer Halpern and Susan Brown McGreevy, University of New Mexico Press, Albuquerque.

39. McGreevy, Susan Brown, *Indian Basketry Artists of the Southwest, Deep Roots, New Growth,* Santa Fe, School of American Research Press, 2001

40. Peerman, Dean, "BareBones Imbroglio: Repatriating Indian Remains and Sacred Artifacts," *Christian Century,* October 17, 1990, pp. 935-937.

41. Letter from Lutie Mimms Gray to Joan Beamis, dated February 10, 1962. Lutie wrote to Joan, responding to Joan's letter requesting information about Joan's relationship to the Jesse James family. *"I do know that T. M. James, or Thomas Martin James, was the brother of Robert* [Sallee] *James and Mary James Mimms, and had two sons Crawford and Luther. Their home was, and is today, Kansas City, Mo. Their mother, Aunt Sarah, wouldn't have anything to do with her husband's relatives. However, as far as I know, their descendants still live in Kansas City, Mo."* Joan Beamis Research Archive, James Preservation Trust, 2002.

42. Interview with Judge James R. Ross.

Chapter 9 - All for the Underdog

1. Association of Yale Alumni.

2. McDowell, Edwin "Daniel Lewis James is Dead at 77; Wrote About Los Angeles Barrio," *New York Times* Obituaries, May 21, 1988, p. 10.

3. An inheritance from her grandfather, Col. Andrew Jackson Snider, made Lillie Snyder wealthier than her husband D. L. James. As an infant, Col. Snider was held by Andrew Jackson, and then given his name. As a boy, A. J. Snider left home to drive cattle across the Alleghenies. At seventeen, he drove a shipment of mules to Singapore and India. Returning to America after a year, A. J. located in Leavenworth, Kansas, but soon departed for the gold rushes at Pike's Peak and Montana. Snider became a government

contractor in Montana Territory then served as a Brigadier General on the staff of Gov. Green Clay Smith of Kentucky. Smith was a Baptist preacher. When Smith retired from Montana, he preached at the First Baptist Church in Somerset, Kentucky, founded by the "talented, but erratic" Rev. Joseph Martin James. Smith was born in Madison County, the former home of the grand parents of Frank James' wife, Annie Ralston. His middle name of Clay came from his mother Elizabeth Lewis Clay, a second cousin of the statesman Henry Clay. In the spring of 1870, A. J. Snider relocated to Kansas City and established a cattle business. His operations extended into Texas and Oklahoma, where he operated a large ranch on the Cherokee Strip in Southern Kansas Indian Territory, selling as many as 30,000 head of cattle per year. On December 8, 1890, the *New York Times* reported Snider had telegraphed A. B. Mayes, Chief of the Cherokee Nation at Telequah, stating, "*I am prepared to offer you $10,000,000 in cash for the 6,500,000 acres of land known as the Cherokee Strip.*" Snider attempted to preempt the Federal Government's acquisition of the land. The purchase money was not entirely his own. A. J. represented a stockmen's association. A. J. already controlled 165,000 acres of the Strip where his own ranch was located. He also sat on the board of the Traders Bank in Kansas City, owned by Col. J. T. Thornton. In 1858, A. J. Snider married Hannah Catherine Beery. Her relatives included the actors Noah Nicholas Beery and his actress wife Marguerite Walker Lindsay, their actor son Noah Lindsay Beery, Wallace Beery the husband of actress Gloria Swanson. Lillie Snider's father Chester Allyn Snider was born of A. J. and Hannah Catherine Beery. Catherine's father was president of the Evans-Snider-Buel Company of St. Louis, Chicago, and Kansas City. Lillie's father was a member of the Kansas City Social Club and the Commercial Club with T. M. and J. C. James. He also was a director of the National Bank of Commerce and the Bank of Commerce, counseled by Vassie James' husband, Hugh Campbell Ward. For many years Chester Allyn Snider directed the Kansas City Livestock Exchange, and was vice president of the Kansas City Symphony Orchestra. When Lillie's mother, Lillie C. Hyatt died, her father married Olivia Olga Oglesby, daughter of Gov. Richard James Oglesby of Illinois. They lived in Illinois. Lillie remained in Missouri, placed in the custody of her pioneer grandfather, until she married D. L. James.

4. Dunne, John Gregory. "The Secret of Danny Santiago," *New York Times Review of Books,* August 16, 1984.

5. Wheeler Dryden, a half-brother of Charlie Chaplin through their mother Hannah, sometimes is credited with co-writing *The Great Dictator*. Dryden in fact was the film's assistant director responsible for the order of cast and crew. Spencer Dryden, the son of Wheeler Dryden, became a drummer with the rock band The Jefferson Airplane and later with New Riders of the Purple Sage. Like Daniel Lewis James Jr., Spencer Dryden maintained privacy about his family background, so he could be known for his music and not as the nephew of the famous and adored, but politically tainted, Charlie Chaplin.

6. Dunne.

7. Ibid.

7. James, Barbara, correspondence with the author.

8. James, Barbara, "HUAC, The Blacklist, and Dan and Lilith," unpublished memoir, 2008, The James Preservation Trust.

9. Ibid. Both Marilyn Monroe and Groucho Marx warned Norma Barzman and her husband Ben Barzman that they were being spied upon. The couple fled to Europe. Ben

Barzman was blacklisted. His best recognized screenplays are: *The Boy with Green Hair*, *El Cid*, and Costa Gravas' *Z*. Though never subpoenaed to appear before HUAC, Joseph Losey was blacklisted. The Loseys fled to England. His collaboration with dramatist Harold Pinter, produced three films: *The Servant, Accident*, and *The Go-Between*. For Norma Barzman, see: *The Red and the Blacklist: A Memoir of a Hollywood Insider*, Norma Barzman, Nation Books, 2003; - also issued as: *The Red and the Blacklist: The Intimate Memoir of a Hollywood Expatriate*, by Norma Barzman, Friction Books. Also: *Tender Comrades: Interviews with Blacklisted Hollywood Reds*, Paul Buhle and Patrick McGilligan, St. Martin's Press, New York, 1997. For Louise and Joseph Losey, see: *Joseph Losey*, Colin Gardner, Manchester University Press, Manchester, England, 2004.

10. Dunne, John Gregory. Ed. Calvin Trillin, *Regards, the Selected Non Fiction of John Gregory Dunne,* Thunder's Mouth Press, 2006.

11. Mantle, Burns, Ed., *The Best Plays of 1942-43,* New York, Dodd, Meade & Co., 1943.

12. Meyerson, Harold & Ernie Harburg, *Who Put the Rainbow in the Wizard of Oz?*, University of Michigan Press, 1993, pp. 185-188.

13. James.

14. Dunne.

15. James, Daniel; Santiago, Danny. "Writing Bloomer Girl," *New York Times Review of Books,* Vol. 31, No.17, November 8, 1984.

16. James.

17. Ibid.

18. Bentley, Eric, *Thirty Years of Treason, Excerpts from Hearings before the House Committee on Un-American Activities 1938-1968.* New York, Thunder Mountain Press/Nation Books 2002, pp. 395, 439. First published by Viking Press, 1971.

19. Navasky, Victor S., *Naming Names,* New York, Hill and Wang, 1991, p.227.

20. Navasky, p. 227.

21. Ibid.

22. Ibid.

23. Dunne.

24. James.

25. Melvin Levy is best known for writing television episodes of *The Lone Ranger, Bonanza*, and *Charlie's Angeles*. The Seattle born author initially wrote novels. One reviewer stated of Levy's novel *The Pioneers* that it "points the moral of communism more convincingly than many avowed 'proletarian' novels." In Hollywood, Levy was blacklisted.

26. Lester Cole is the author of forty-five screenplays, starting with *Charlie Chan's Greatest Case*, and ending with *Born Free*

27. James.

28. Buhle, Paul and Dave Wagner, *Blacklisted, The Film Lover's Guide to the Hollywood Blacklist,* New York, Pargrave MacMillan, 2003, p. 82.

29. Buhle and Wagner, Paul and Dave. *Hide in Plain Sight, The Hollywood Blacklistees in Film and Television, 1950-2002.* New York, Pargrave Macmillan, 2003, p. 53.

30. Abrams, Garry, "The Three Lives of Danny Santiago," *Los Angeles Times,* June 12, 1998.

31. Abrams.

32. Santiago, Danny. *Famous All Over Town*. New York: Simon & Schuster, 1983.

33. Huerta S.J., Fr. Alberto. "Daniel Lewis James (1911-1988): Socrates and Santiago in California," *Californian* magazine, Nov.-Dec., 1988, pp. 48-53.

34. Huerta.

35. Writers Guild of America: Blacklist Corrections. *"Gorgo - Screenplay and Screen Story by Robert L. Richards and Daniel James, 1960. King Bros. and MGM, original credits read 'Screenplay and Screen Story by John Loring and Daniel Hyatt.' Robert L. Richards' pseudonym was John Loring. Hyatt was a pseudonym for James, the Hyatt name coming from Dan's mother-in-law, Lillie C. Hyatt. The Giant Behemoth - Dianmon Pictures/Allied Artists, 1958. Original screenplay credits: Eugene Lourie. Corrected to: Screenplay by Eugene Lourie and Daniel James. Story by Robert Abel and Allen Adler."*

36. Huerta.

37. Limerick, Nelson Patricia, *Something of the Soil, Legacies and Reckonings of the New West*, W. W. Norton & Company, 2001, p. 272.

38. Tom Benton additionally was a cousin to the Scholl brothers, Daniel Boone and George Thomas Scholl, of Quantrill Raiders and the James gang. Benton's ancestral cousin, Elizabeth Bryant of the Daniel Boone family, married Rev. Jeremiah Vardeman, after his first wife Elizabeth James died. Elizabeth's parents were John M. and Clara Nall James. A number of the Nall family who lived in Missouri are cousins to Benton, also.

39. Benton, Thomas Hart, *An Artist in America,* Columbia & Longdon, University of Missouri Press, 1983, pp. 4, 11.

40. Benton, p. 22.

41. Ibid., pp. 253-254.

42. "Ken Burns' America: Thomas Hart Benton." PBS Video. Florentine Films, 1988. Also: Burns, Kenneth Lauren *"Thomas Hart Benton, Final Script"* Florentine Films, 1988, p. 29.

43. Burns, p. 32.

44. Barbara James. Not to be confused with the Caucus Room mural by Benton, the 1936 painting *Jesse James* by Thomas Hart Benton, hangs at the Reynolds House Museum of American Art, at Wake Forest University in Winston-Salem, North Carolina. Reynolda House was the home of R. J. Reynolds, founder of the R. J. Reynolds Tobacco Company, and grandfather of Susan Bagley-Bloom, a former spouse of the author.

45. Hughes, Robert. *American Visions: The Epic History of Art in America*. New York, Alfred A. Knoph, 1997.

46. Burns, p. 16. The same description could be apt of the artist Caravaggio in the Baroque period, whose painting *John, the Baptist,* aka *John in the Wilderness,* was donated by Milton and Barbara James McGreevy to the Nelson-Atkins Museum of Art in Kansas City.

47. *"Benton Hates Museums,"* *Time* magazine, April 14, 1941.

48. Burns, p. 26.

49. Huerta.

Chapter 10 - Useful to the Lord

1. The reference is to that of the family of his great grandfather Drury Woodson James, who founded Paso Robles, California, following the Mexican War.

2. "Man of Cloth" *Dartmouth Alumni Album.* Joan Beamis Archive, The James Preservation Trust.

3. Interviews & correspondence with Rev. James Malley S.J., 2004-2006.

Chapter 11 - No One in Our Family Backs Down

1. Ross, James R., *I Tried My Best,* unpublished memoir, circulated by the author to his immediate family, 2003, p. 1.

2. "Jesse James Kin Granted Divorce," *Abilene Morning Reporter,* Abilene, Texas, August 24, 1930. August 23 - *"Mrs. Jo Frances Ross, a granddaughter of Jesse James, was granted a divorce today from Ronald M. Ross, lawyer, to whom she was married September 2, 1925, custody of their 4 yr. old son, Ronald M. Ross Jr., was awarded the mother."*

3. Ross.

4. Ibid., pp. 45-46.

5. Ibid., pp. 48-49.

6. "State of California, Commission on Judicial Performance, Inquiry Concerning Judge James Randall Ross, No. 141, April 30, 1998," the official record of the Censure of James Ross.

7. Vardon, Susan Gill, "Andrew Exler," *The Orange County Register,* September 16, 2004.

8. Interviews with Judge James R. Ross, Fullerton, California 2002-2005.

9. Whitney, Carrie Westlake, *Kansas City, Missouri, Its History and Its People, 1800-1908,* Vol. II, Chicago, The S. J. Clarke Publishing Co., 1908, p. 679.

10. Stella Frances McGowan, letter to book author Homer Croy, dated Long Beach, California, Jan 6, 1949. Joan Beamis Archive, James Preservation Trust.

11. "Four Indicted in the Kansas City Election Frauds," *Jefferson City Post Tribune,* Jefferson City, Missouri. October 21, 1930.

12. Walker, Gladys. "Robert T. Jones," Superior Historical Society.

13. "Ross Recants on Election Eve – Story is a Hoax," *Yuma Daily Sun,* Yuma, Arizona, November 8, 1938.

14. "Begin Trial of Ronald M. Ross, Criminal Libel," *Yuma Daily Sun,* Yuma, Arizona, January 27, 1939.

15. "Ross Convicted of Libel Count," *Yuma Daily Sun,* Yuma, Arizona, January 31, 1939. See also: "Attorney Convicted of Libel," *Albuquerque Journal,* Albuquerque, New Mexico, January 31, 1939.

16. "Ross Sentenced to Year in Prison," *Yuma Daily Sun,* Yuma, Arizona, February 14, 1939.

17. *Index to Prison Register,* Arizona Department of Corrections.

18. "Conviction Upheld," *Albuquerque Journal*, Albuquerque, New Mexico, November 28, 1939.

19. Walker.

20. Letter from Stella Frances McGowan-James to Henry Hoffman, January 5, 1959. The Joan Beamis Research Archive. The James Preservation Trust.

21. Interview with James Curtis Lewis. Annual Meeting of the James-Younger Gang. San Angelo, Texas. October 4-6, 2001.

22. Interview with Donald Baumel at the James Gang and Family Reunion. Paso Robles Inn, Paso Robles, California. September 12-14, 2002.

Afterward - Unto the Third Generation

1. Preparing this book, the author was informed by the great granddaughter of Jesse James, Elizabeth Ann Barr known as Betty Barr, through Marjorie Earline Highley-Best a mutual friend, "Tell Eric James to mind his own business." Marjorie Best is a granddaughter of Rev. Robert Earl Highley, who wrote *Jesse James, Though Officially Dead Lived On For 65 Years*, published in 1981. Rev. Highly baptized Betty Barr's grandmother Mary Susan James-Barr, the daughter of Jesse James. Rev. Highley also claimed a relationship to the James family through common ancestry in the Poor family. Highley's claim has not been proven.

2. The reference is to Oliver Murray "Ollie" James, 1871-1918. Ollie James served in the U. S. House of Representatives from 1903 to 1913, representing Kentucky and not Virginia, as Joan misstates. Ollie James then was elected to the U. S. Senate, serving from 1913 to 1918, when he died. The family of Ollie James long has denied any connection with the Jesse James family. Receiving a request to be interviewed for this book, a representative of the Ollie James family responded succinctly by stating nothing more than, "Our family comes from Culpeper County, Virginia, and is a different family." While the reference to Culpeper County constitutes no absolute denial nor proof of a non-relationship whatsoever, the belief of the Ollie James family in fact is supported by DNA testing, which has identified a test subject who claimed to be related to their ancestral James line as distinctive and different from numerous other James families, including the family of Jesse James, and to John M. James of Culpeper County in particular.

3. *Thompson & West's History of San Luis Obispo County*, California, Reproduction of 1883 edition, Howell North Books, Berkeley, California, 1966, pp. 275-276. This Thompson & West History misidentifies both the father and grandfather of Drury Woodson James. *"His parents were Jackson James and Polly Poor, both natives of Virginia, in which State they were married prior to their removal to Kentucky. Martin James, the grandfather of D. W., was a soldier of the Revolution, as was also his grandfather Poor, both fighting through the contest for independence..."*

4. In Joan's manuscript this space is left blank, clearly indicating the probable future entry of the year in which Frank James died as that being the year 1915.

Bibliography

Unpublished Primary Sources

Association of Yale Alumni

Boyle County Court, Danville, Kentucky
  Boyle County Deed Book

Brown University
  Alumni Records

Centre College, Danville, Kentucky
  Catalogue of Officers and Students, Year Ending June 30, 1853

Commonwealth of Kentucky
  Report of the Adjutant General of the State of Kentucky, Soldiers of the War of 1812,
Frankfort, KY

Florentine Films, Walpole, New Hampshire
  Burns, Kenneth Lauren, "*Thomas Hart Benton, Final Script,*" 1988

Harvard College, Class of 1886, Secretary's Report

Heritage Center, Harrodsburg, Kentucky
  Sanborn Fire Insurance Maps, Danville, Kentucky,

Kansas City Library, Kansas City, Missouri
  Biography of William T. Kemper
  "Henry and Phoebe Routt Ess, Attorney/Clubwoman and Reformer," Biography

Kansas City Historical Society, Kansas City, Missouri
  "Jotham Meeker's Journal," Vol. 3

Kentucky Historical Society, Special Collections, Frankfort, Kentucky
  "*House Journal,*" 1801, 1803, 1807-1808

Laurel County, Kentucky
  Marriage Records, Laurel County, Book AA

James Preservation Trust, Danville, Kentucky
  Joan Beamis Archive
    Letters

Joan Beamis to Gilbert Cam
Othor L. MacLean to Joan Beamis
Thelma Duncan-Barr to James Walter Sames
Thelma Duncan-Barr to Joan Beamis
Lutie Mimms Gray to Joan Beamis
Carl Briehan to Joan Beamis
Stella McGowan-James to Joan Beamis
Jo Frances James to Mary Louis James-Burns
Manuscripts
    "Unto the Third Generation"
    "Rev. William James"
    "A History of Drury Woodson James, as Told by his Daughter"
    Mimms, Robert William, "Autobiography and Travels, Remarks, etc"
Photos
Author's First Edition of *"Background of a Bandit"*
John James, of Alvarado Archive
Manuscripts
    "Stray Leaves from My Diary"
Letters
    John James to Mary Ann Thompson-Romjue
Newspaper clippings
Malley Family Archive
Correspondence of James Malley S.J.
Correspondence of John Crohan "Jack" Malley
Photos
Daniel Lewis James Archive
Manuscripts, play scripts, transcripts
James, Barbara, "HUAC, The Blacklist, and Dan and Lilith"
Sara Jean Race Duke Archive
Thelma Hayes-Herrin Archive
Sandra Lou Russell Kassem Archive
Judge James Randall Ross
Correspondence
Manuscript
    "I Did My Best"
Photos
State of California Commission on Judicial Performance
    Inquiry Concerning Judge James Randall Ross, No. 141
State of Arizona Department of Corrections
    Prison Record, *Index to Prison Register*
Tiajuana Chochnauer
Correspondence
James Walter Sames III Archive
Photos
Henry James Newton Photos

Virgie Herrin-Fuller Archive
 Photos
 News Copies
 Scrapbook
Virginia Jacques Church Archive
 Photos

Northwestern University Archives, 1924-1981
 Biography of James Franklin Oates, Jr. (1899-1982)

Princeton University, Mudd Library

Rockbridge County, Virginia
 Marriage Bonds, 1778-1801

Society of Alumni of Williams College
 Alumni Records

Truman State University, Pickler Memorial Library, Special Collections
 Transcript
  Greenwood, J. M., *The Service of J. Crawford James as a Member and Officer of the Board of Education.* ed. 1912, G1/5:12.
  James, J. Crawford, *To the Members of the Board of Education, Kansas City Missouri.* The letter of resignation of John Crawford James, G1/5:12.

Mount Vernon College for Women

Northwestern University Archives, Papers, 1824-1981
 Biography of James Frankln Oates Jr.

Union Cemetery Association, Jackson County, Missouri

United States Patent Office, Washington D. C.
 James Pittigan, Goodland, Indiana, U. S. Patent No. 470,594 for a Wash Board

University of Chicago Library, Special Collections
 Edward H. Levi Papers (1894-1998)
  "Eulogy, J. Harris Ward Memorial Service"

Vassar College
 Alumni Records

Virginia State Library, Richmond, Virginia
  Chesterfield County Court Order Bk. 1, p. 1, p. 138; Leonard, C.M. *The General Assembly of Virginia*

Warren Memorial Library, Westbrook, Maine
 "Our Library's History"

Western Historical Manuscript Collection, State Historical Society of Missouri, Columbia, Missouri
 J.C. Nichols Company Records
 The Kansas City Design Center
  "An Historical Survey of the Kansas City, Missouri, Parks and Boulevards System"

Williams College Alumni Records
  Affidavit of James C. Ward, May 17, 1961
  Record of George Olmsted Jr., Class of 1924

Williams College Public Affairs
  Records

Published Primary Sources

Abrams, Garry, "The Three Lives of Danny Santiago," *Los Angeles Times,* June 12, 1998

American Bar Association, *Report of the Thirty-Second Annual Meeting Baltimore*, Lord Baltimore Press, 1909

Burns, Kenneth Lauren, "Ken Burns' America: Thomas Hart Benton." PBS Video. Florentine Films, 1988

Creel, George, John Slavens, *Men Who Are Making Kansas City, A Biographical Directory*, 1902

Experiment Station of the Kansas State Agricultural School, Bulletin No. 51, June 1895

Fisher, Ernest B., Ed., "Clarence J. Van Etten," *Grand Rapids and Kent County, Michigan: historical account of their progress from first settlement to the present time,* Ann Arbor, Michigan; University of Michigan Library, 2005

Gallagher, John B. *Book of the Republican National Convention, Kansas City, Mo. June 12, 1928*; Kansas City Chamber of Commerce, 1928

Griffith, Shirley & Sarah Long, *Margaret Sanger, 1883-1966: She Led the Fight for Birth Control for Women,* People of America, Voice of America Special English Program. 2007. Transcript of radio broadcast.

Harvard College, *Harvard College, Class of 1886, Secretary's Report, No. VI,* New York, Dec. 1906

Hutchins, Margarette Berry, *Friends of the Youngers Research,* Complied by Wilma Carroll Hillman, Friends of the Youngers, Inc. June, 2000

James, Daniel; Santiago, Danny. "Writing Bloomer Girl," *New York Times Review of Books,* Vol. 31, No.17, November 8, 1984

Index of the Circular Letters of the Bethel Baptist Association 1825-1884

James, John. *My Experience with Indians,* Austin, Texas, Gammel's Book Store, 1924

Kansas City Genealogist, Vol. 34, #2

Kansas City Times, Kansas City: Its Resources and Their Development, a Souvenir of The Kansas City Times, 1890

Kentucky Historical Society, "Col. Dick Johnson's Indian School." *The Register of the Kentucky Historical Society,* Louisville, Kentucky; Geo. G. Fetter Company, 1905

Mantle, Burns, Editor. *The Best Plays of 1942-43,* New York, Dodd, Meade & Co., 1943

M.B.R., "Man of Cloth," *Dartmouth Alumni Album.* Joan Beamis Archive, The James Preservation Trust

McGreevy, Susan Brown, *Indian Basketry Artists of the Southwest, Deep Roots, New Growth,* Santa Fe, School of American Research Press, 2001

Meece, O'Leary *Condensed Minutes of the Pulaski County Court, Order Book Number One, 1799-1803*

Meyerson, Harold & Ernie Harburg, *Who Put the Rainbow in the Wizard of Oz?* University of Michigan Press, 1993

Morton, Jennie C. "Dick Johnson's Indian School at Sulphur, Scott County, Ky." *Register of the Kentucky Historical Society,* Frankfort, Kentucky

National Society of the Daughters of the American Revolution, *DAR Patriot Index,* Washington D. C.

Peace Works, Kansas City: http://www.peaceworkskc.org/letter.html, March 17, 2009

Pence, Samuel Anderson, *I Knew Frank...I Wish I had Known Jesse*, Two Trails Publishing, Independence, Missouri, 2007

Princeton University, *Princeton Alumni Weekly*, April 1, 2001

Pusey, Dr. William Allen, "General Joseph Martin of Virginia, An Unsung Hero of the Virginia Frontier," Read before the Filson Club, February 3, 1936, The Filson Club History Quarterly, Vol. 10, No 2., April 1936, Louisville, Kentucky.

Register of the Society of Colonial Wars in the State of Missouri, 1904-1906, p. 92; and 1907-1909

"Rev. Isaac McCoy, Early Baptist Indian Missionary," *Baptist Encyclopedia*, 1881

Shoemaker, Floyd Calvin, Ed., *Missouri Historical Review.* Francis Asbury Sampson, State Historical Society of Missouri, Vol. XV, Columbia, Missouri, 1921

Stone, L. B., *West Family Register*

Vassar College, *Vassar Alumni Quarterly,* Vol. 98, Issue 1, winter, 2001

Ward, Roger. *Durer to Matisse, Master Drawings from The Nelson-Atkins Museum of Art.* Kansas City, Missouri. 1996

White, Emmas Sigging, and Martha Humphreys Maltby, *The Kinnears and Their Kin,* Tiernan-Dart Printing Company, Kansas City, Missouri, 1916

Williams College, *Williams Alumni Review,* Fall, 1977. Also: "*Kids Get Experiment Experience at Williams Science Camp.*" Williams College Public Affairs, July 21, 2008

William Woods College, *Alumni Magazine,* William Woods College, Fall/Winter, 1999

Yale University, *A History of the Class of 1903, Yale College*

Newspapers, Periodicals

Abilene Morning Reporter

Albuquerque Journal

Alvarado Weekly Bulletin

American

Coffeyville Star

Daily Constitution

Daily News

Daily Review

Jefferson City Post Tribune

Kansas City Journal

Kansas City Star

Kansas City Times

Liberty Tribune

Missouri Statesman

New York Times

Newton County Enterprise

Portland Express

San Francisco Chronicle

St. Louis Republican

Sun Times

The Kentucky Advocate

The Orange County Register

The Star

Time

Tribune

Yuma Daily Sun

Secondary Sources: Articles & Dissertations

Alumni Magazine, William Woods College, Fall/Winter, 1999

Coleman, Daniel. *Vassie James Ward Hill, School Founder and Educator, 1875-1953.* Kansas City Public Library, Missouri Valley Special Collections

Davidson, Rev. R.L., *Foreign Missions in Missouri During One Hundred Years,* speech to the Missouri Baptist General Association, 1906

Dunne, John Gregory. "The Secret of Danny Santiago," *New York Times Review of Books,* August 16, 1984

Huerta S.J., Fr. Alberto. "Daniel Lewis James (1911-1988): Socrates and Santiago in

California," *Californian* magazine, Nov.-Dec., 1988

"Missouri Sons of the South," Chapter 35, 1927, *Confederate Trails* magazine, reprint by Two Trails Publishing

Peerman, Dean, "BareBones Imbroglio: Repatriating Indian Remains and Sacred Artifacts," *Christian Century,* October 17, 1990

Rousseau, Richard W., S.J., *New England Jesuit Oral History Program, Vol. 42.* "James B. Malley, S.J., Interview with Fr. James B. Malley, S.J." Weston, Massachusetts, Society of Jesus of New England, 2007, ISBN 1-60067-040-7.

Sanders, Stuart W. *Quantrill's Last Ride,* www.civilwarhistory.com. May 20, 2007

Walker, Gladys. "Robert T. Jones," Superior Historical Society

Watson, Frank Dekker, *The Charity Organization Movement in the United States, A Study in American Philanthropy,* 1922

Secondary Sources: Books

A Standard History of Oklahoma

Aronhine, Gordon, "General Joseph Martin a Forgotten Pioneer, 1740-1898," Historical Sketches of Southwest Virginia, Publication 21966

Barzman, Norma, *The Red and the Blacklist: A Memoir of a Hollywood Insider*, Nation Books, 2003

Barzman, Norma, *The Red and the Blacklist: The Intimate Memoir of a Hollywood Expatriate*, Friction Books.

Battie, J. H. Ed., *History of Todd County, Kentucky*, F. A. Battey Publishing Co., 1884

Battle, Perrin, & Griffin, *Kentucky, A History of the State*, ed. 8-B, Pulaski County

Bentley, Eric, *Thirty Years of Treason, Excerpts from Hearings before the House Committee on Un-American Activities 1938-1968,* New York, Thunder Mountain Press/Nation Books 2002, pp. 395, 439. First published by Viking Press, 1971

Benton, Thomas Hart, *An Artist in America,* Columbia & Longdon, University of Missouri Press, 1983

Bradford, John, Editor and Publisher, *Biographical Encyclopedia of Kentucky*, 1868, J. M. Armstrong & Co.

Brown, Richard C. *A History of Danville and Boyle County, Kentucky, 1774-1992,* Danville. Bicentennial Books, 1992

Buhle, Paul & Dave Wagner, *Blacklisted, The Film Lover's Guide to the Hollywood Blacklist,* New York, Pargrave MacMillan, 2003

Buhle, Paul & Dave Wagner, *Hide in Plain Sight, The Hollywood Blacklistees in Film and*

Television, 1950-2002. New York, Pargrave Macmillan, 2003

Buhle, Paul & Patrick McGillihan, *Tender Comrades: Interviews with Blacklisted Hollywood Reds*, St. Martin's Press, New York, 1997

Cates, Cliff Donohue. *Pioneer History of Wise County: from Red Men to Railroads.* Wise County Old Settlers' Association

Conrad, Howard Lewis, *Encyclopedia of the History of Missouri*, New York & Louisville, The Southern History Company, Conrad & Company, 1901

Counties of Warren, Benton, Jasper, and Newton, Indiana, Chicago, F. A. Battey & Co., Publishers, 1883

Creel, George & John Slavens, *Men Who Are Making Kansas City,* Hudson-Kimberly Publishing Company, Kansas City, Missouri, 1902

Cunningham, J. O. *History of Champaign County*, 1905. Reprint: Urbana, Illinois; Champaign County Historical Archives, Urbana Free Library

Cutler, William G., *History of the State of Kansas*, A. T. Andreas, Chicago, Illinois, 1883

David, Billingham and Jackson, Donald C. *Big Dams of the New Deal Era, A Confluence of Engineering and Politics.* University of Oklahoma Press, 2006

Dunne, John Gregory. Ed. Calvin Trillin, *Regards, the Selected Non Fiction of John Gregory Dunne,* Thunder's Mouth Press, 2006

Elby, Jerrilyn, *They Called Stafford Home,* Heritage Books Inc., 1997

Fackler, Calvin Morgan. *Early Days in Danville,* Louisville, The Standard Printing Co. 1941, 4th reprinting 2002, Boyle County Genealogical Society, Danville, Kentucky

Gardner, Colin, *Joseph Losey*, Manchester University Press, Manchester, England, 2004

Goodell, William, *The American Slave Code in Theory and Practice: Its Distinctive Features Shown by Its Statutes, Judicial Decisions, and Illustrative Facts.* New York: American Foreign Anti-Slavery Society, 1853

Goodspeed, Weston A., Leroy C. Goodspeed, Charles L. May. *History of Lawrence, Orange and Washington Counties, Indiana From the Earliest Time to the Present; Together with Interesting Biographical Sketches, Reminiscences, Notes, Etc.* Chicago, Goodspeed Bros. & Co., Publishers, 1884

Greene, George E. *History of Old Vincennes & Knox County, Indiana.* Chicago, S. J. Clarke Publishing Company, 1911

Griffin, P.H.D., Richard W., *Newspaper Story of a Town, a History of Danville, Kentucky.* Hundredth Anniversary Edition of the Kentucky Advocate, Danville, Kentucky: Danville-Advocate Messenger, 1965

Hatter, R., Hughes, N., Burch, G., *Frankfort Cemetery, the Westminster Abbey of Kentucky*, Frankfort Heritage Press, Frankfort, Ky. 2007

Hester, Hubert Inman. *Jewell Is Her Name, A History of William Jewell College,* Liberty,

Missouri. William Jewell College, 1967

History Committee: Oscar Davidson, Mildred Ellis, Lewis W. Shepherd, Chairman, Assisted by Eldred M. Taylor & Jacqueline Taylor. *History of the First Baptist Church, Somerset, Kentucky, 1799-1974.* One Hundred Seventy-fifth ed. Wolfe City, Texas; Southern Baptist Press, 1974

History of Boone County, Missouri, St. Louis, Western Historical Company, 1882

History of Clinton County, Missouri, National Historical Company, St. Joseph, Mo. 1881

History of Coffeyville, Coffeyville, Kansas; Coffeyville Journal Press, 1969

History of Jackson County, Missouri, Union Historical Company, Birdsall, Williams & Co. Kansas City, Mo. 1881

Holcombe, R. I., Ed, *History of Greene County, Missouri*, 1883

Hughes, Robert. *American Visions: The Epic History of Art in America*. New York, Alfred A. Knoph, 1997

Kansas City, An Illustrated Review of Its Progress and Importance, 1886

Kansas City Directory, 1882, 1884, 1886-87, 1887-88

Kentucky Historical Society, The *Register of the Kentucky State Historical Society*, Vol. 14, #42

Lamkin, Jr., Adrian, *Jeremiah Vardeman, Pioneer Preacher*, Liberty, Missouri; William E. Partee Center for Baptist Studies, William Jewell College.

Limerick, Nelson Patricia, *Something of the Soil, Legacies and Reckonings of the New West,* W. W. Norton & Company, 2001

Little, James A., *Kirtland to Salt Lake City,* Salt Lake City, Utah, self-published, 1890

Mantle, Burns, Ed., *The Best Plays of 1942-43,* New York, Dodd, Meade & Co., 1943.

McGreevy, Susan Brown & Katherine Spencer Halpern, Eds., *Washington Matthews: Studies of Navajo Culture, 18801894*, University of New Mexico Press, Albuquerque

McGreevy, Susan Brown, *Indian Basketry Artists of the Southwest, Deep Roots, New Growth,* Santa Fe, School of American Research Press, 2001

Meacham, Charles, *History of Christian County, Kentucky,* 1930

Missouri Baptist Biography, Vol. I, Western Baptist Publishing Company, Kansas City, 1914

Morgan, Perl W. Ed., *History of Wyandotte County Kansas and its people,* Chicago, Lewis Publishing Company, 1911

Morrison, Tony, *Beloved,* New York, Alfred A. Knopf Inc., 1987

Navasky, Victor S., *Naming Names,* New York, Hill and Wang, 1991

Paxton, William McClung, *Annals of Platte County, Missouri, from its exploration down to June 1, 1897,* Kansas City, Missouri, Hudson-Kimberly Publishing Company, 1897

Perkins, J.H. & Peck, John Mason, "Rev. Jeremiah Vardeman," *Annals of the West*, Pittsburg, Pennsylvania, W.S. Haven, 1856

Perrin, William Henry, Ed., *County of Christian, Kentucky, Historical and Biographical*. F. A. Battey Publishing Co., 1884

Perrin, William Henry. Ed. *History of Bourbon, Scott, Harrison and Nicholas Counties, Kentucky,* 1882

Pulaski County Marriage Records, 1799-1850, Vol. I, Somerset, Kentucky; Pulaski County Historical Society

Read, Opie, *Mark Twain and I,* Chicago, Reilly and Lee, 1940

Robb, Peter. *M., The Man Who Would Become Caravaggio,* Picador, 2001

Spencer, J. H. History of the Kentucky Baptists, Vol. I, Cincinnati, Ohio: J.R. Baumes, 1886

Snyder, Robert, *A History of Georgetown College,* n.p.

Stewart, Murrell P. *Flat Lick Baptist Church, Its Place in History, 1799-1999,* Bicentennial Edition, Somerset, Kentucky; Flat Lick Baptist Church, 1999

Taylor, John, *Baptists on the American Frontier: A History of the Ten Baptist Churches of Which the Author Has Alternately Been a Member*, Annotated 3rd ed., ed. Chester Raymond Young, Macon, Georgia; Mercer University Press, 1995

The Dawson Men of Fayette County, Ohio

The United States Biographical Dictionary and Portrait Gallery of Eminent and Selfmade Men, United States Biographical Publishing Co., New York, New York. 1878

Thoburn, Joseph Bradfield, *A Standard History of Oklahoma, Vol.*, Chicago and New York, The American Historical Society

Thompson & West's History of San Luis Obispo County, California, Reproduction of 1883 edition, Howell North Books, Berkeley, California, 1966

Tibbals, Alma Owens. *History of Pulaski County*, Bagdad, Kentucky: Grace Owens Moore, 1952

Tuggle, George. *Pulaski Revisited,* The Pulaski County Historical Society. Lexington, Powell Printing, 1982

Vassar Alumni Quarterly, Vol. 98, Issue 1, Winter, 2001

Wade, Houston. *The Dawson Men of Fayette County,* Houston, Texas, 1932

Whitney, Carrie Westlake, *Kansas City, Missouri, Its History and Its People, 1800-1908,* Vol. II, Chicago, The S. J. Clarke Publishing Co., 1908.

Index

C

D

H

M

N

P

www.ingramcontent.com/pod-product-compliance
Lightning Source LLC
Chambersburg PA
CBHW070945150426
42812CB00066B/3300/J